ALSO BY DR. EDWIN M. SWENGEL

The Plainston Chronicles: Volume I, Conception, 1919-1935
The Plainston Chronicles: Volume II, Conversion, 1935-1951

ALSO BY JANE SWENGEL CREASON

When the War Came to Hannah
The Heron Stayed

Conspiracy

A SEQUEL
TO THE PLAINSTON CHRONICLES,
VOLUMES I AND II

DR. EDWIN M. SWENGEL
AND
JANE SWENGEL CREASON

Order this book online at www.trafford.com
or email orders@trafford.com

Most Trafford titles are also available at major online book retailers.

Printed in the United States of America.

ISBN: 978-1-4669-7087-8 (sc)
ISBN: 978-1-4669-7088-5 (e)

Trafford rev. 01/31/2013

 www.trafford.com

North America & international
toll-free: 1 888 232 4444 (USA & Canada)
phone: 250 383 6864 ♦ fax: 812 355 4082

Contents

Dedicated to all
teachers, students, parents, administrators, board members,
and others who have ever thought,
There has to be a better way.

Foreword

Whenever I see a book with co-authors, I wonder how two people can write the same book, especially if it's a novel as *Conspiracy* is. I can't speak for other pairs of authors, but I can explain what happened here.

Many years ago, my dad, known to everyone as Mac—his middle initial is for McMunn, his mother's maiden name—wrote *The Plainston Chronicles, 1919-1951, Volumes I and II*. Then in 1990, he wrote *Conspiracy* for the Turner Tomorrow Contest. In that novel, he takes the town of Plainston of *The Plainston Chronicles* into an unspecified future time period. Even though *Conspiracy* is in a sense a sequel to *The Plainston Chronicles,* it is complete within itself.

For years, he tried to find mainstream publishers for *The Plainston Chronicles*. Finally, when he was in his early nineties, he decided to self-publish with Trafford. The manuscript was prepared with lots of typing help from my sister, Marcia Powell, who lived just a couple of hours away in Los Angeles. I, on the other hand, was two thousand miles away in Illinois.

Then Dad dusted off the almost twenty-year-old manuscript for *Conspiracy*. Again, Marcia typed page after page into his computer—fifteen chapters—and Dad began to revise as much as his weakened body allowed. Before he was finished, he died in October of 2010 at the age of ninety-three.

With my sister's blessing, I started to work on the manuscript because this is a book that cries for readers. It is a novel supporting a vision. What I bring to the table is forty years of teaching experience in language arts and English at the grade school, middle school, high school, and college levels. I've also published two novels, *When the War Came to Hannah* and *The Heron Stayed,* and edited four books written by our son/grandson, Todd E. Creason.

I had originally planned only to edit the manuscript, but that plan was soon scrapped. For one thing, because he'd just started to revise, there were some inconsistencies in the timeline and details about people and places. Then the wonderful surprise came when Marcia and I found a loose-leaf binder with a copy of the original 1990 manuscript in a storage unit. There were twenty-four chapters, not the fifteen we'd thought there were. Again, there were all sorts of consistency problems. The most dramatic was a chapter from the computer version that wasn't even in the longer paper version—a chapter that didn't quite fit.

After some discussion with Marcia, I essentially started over—taking on the role of co-author, not just editor. I broke open a packet of 5x8 index cards and began to take notes about the characters, the places, and the events. I made a timeline for all the chapters, making sure that the seasons progressed in order and that the weather fit. I made detailed notes about the six schools—who and what were in each. I moved paragraphs around—leaving out sections that seemed repetitious, adding sections to further develop what Dad had written. Then I worked to make the punctuation, the phrasing, and the word choice sound as if the story were being told by one voice, not two.

After almost two years of working on and off, I'll admit that this has been the most difficult writing I've ever done. It's now up to you readers to judge whether or not my efforts—which have been a true labor of love—have succeeded.

Jane Swengel Creason
January, 2013

Chapter 1

The Assignment

"Well, dammit, Kiki! Will you, or won't you?"

My boss stared at me. He never could tolerate indecision.

"Want me to flip a coin?" he said when I didn't answer.

After a few days of investigating and mulling, I felt that the pros and cons about balanced out. So why not toss the choice to chance?

"Okay, flip! Heads, I go. Tails, I stay."

Max flipped a quarter halfway to the ceiling, deftly caught it, slapped it onto his left wrist, and thrust it still covered under my nose. After pausing a few moments to sustain the tension, he slowly removed his right hand. Heads!

*   *   *

So there I was, two weeks later, a sixty-five-year-old man, a widower of almost two years who hadn't yet adjusted to life alone, tooling along a dreary two-lane state highway in a small bright-red Ford rental in subfreezing weather, heading not toward the Outer Banks where I'd planned to retire but toward a new assignment—all because of a coin toss.

The destination was Plainston, the only walled city in the country—with a moat no less. A century ago, Plainston was an ordinary Midwestern town of about 2,000 souls, but a very gradual change had taken place so that in the 1970s, the citizens there decided to separate themselves physically—the mental and spiritual separateness had already occurred—and the wall was built. Plainstans were always free to come and go, even to leave permanently, but by the 1990s, those from the "outside"—well, that was another story. I was an "outsider" being invited in, with the backing of my employers, the nonprofit Global Betterment Organization, known as the GBO, whose initial curiosity about this unusual community had turned into a deep interest. I was to find out what Plainston was all about.

*   *   *

The offer of the Plainston assignment hadn't interested me when Max had first proposed it, especially since what I wanted to do was retire. Checking out the alleged Utopianism of a place one of my commentator colleagues had dubbed "that loony-boony burg" had near zero appeal. My career as a reporter was centered mainly on big cities, and Plainston, with a population of about 50,000, wasn't even a county seat. That was its larger neighboring city, Prairie Grove, a sprawling newly-named metropolis created when twin cities, Normal and Hartland, had joined in the late 80s.

"But they especially asked for you, Kiki," Max had said. "The lady who called knows you're planning to retire, so you'll have time to stay in Plainston and write an unbiased description of the city. She made several very complimentary remarks about you and your style of reporting."

I wasn't beyond being swayed by flattery, especially when it involved my literary talents. I asked for time to think it over and to get some basic background information.

"That's not a good idea," Max warned. "They want you to learn about Plainston firsthand. Don't go there with a lot of secondhand information or more likely misinformation."

I laughed. "Surely, Max, after all these years, I can separate information from misinformation—the chaff from the wheat, you know—and, at the same time, remained open-minded."

"All right, but I need an answer soon."

* * *

I spent just a few days searching the internet, finding a few facts but mostly opinions about Plainston. The information was sparse and generally superficial.

One breezy article was headlined, "Plainston: No Billboards, No Buses, No Bustle, No Busts." The "No Busts" referred to Plainston's claim to be drug-free and largely crime-free. The reporter summarily described Plainston as "a therapeutic retreat from megalopolitan stress, a mildly novel tourist attraction offering peace and quiet in an orderly, friendly, healthful environment. The food is organically grown, most locally, then tastefully prepared."

One tongue-in-cheek reporter praised Plainston with faint damning in an article entitled "Plainston! America's Most UN-American City!" He reported,

> Plainstans make an awful lot of stuff themselves—and make it good, very good! It lasts and lasts. They don't throw stuff away. It's recycle and repair. That's just not the American way.
>
> And they do all this without any good old American competition. Yet Plainston doesn't appear to be Communist or Socialist. It's probably mostly Democratic or more likely populated with independent ticket-splitters, and that's very un-American!
>
> The spookiest thing is no cars. There are lots of bikes and electric-powered carts for the feeble, but there are no traffic lights, no traffic. Eerie!
>
> And Plainstans don't have to use will power. For example, they don't have to avoid junk food because they don't have any junk food around. They don't need will power to quit smoking or drinking since you can walk two miles and not get a Camel, and there's nothing more alcoholic than wine and beer.
>
> Also, regrettably, Plainstans have no conscience about the plight of the poor and homeless since they don't have any such folks in Plainston to care for. They claim to know how to get rid of poverty and homelessness, not just in Plainston but anywhere in the whole wide world. How's that for arrogance?

Summarizing that article later for Max, I said, "So it seems that to be a good American—I emphasize *good*—you must be a Republican voter. You also need to drive a car that's not electric, eat junk food, smoke and drink, and have the poor and the homeless in your community."

Max, who isn't noted for having a sense of humor, laughed loudly.

Other anti-Plainston articles often carried emotionally-charged headlines: "Something's Rotten—and It's Not in Denmark" and "Plainston: Its Beauty Is Only Skin Deep" and "What the FBI and CIA Are Not Telling Us about Plainston."

When I ran a quick internet check of both FBI and CIA investigations of Plainston, I found nothing suggesting any illegal or immoral goings-on. Suspicion-mongers, however, took the agencies to task for not investigating thoroughly what was behind such questionable activities as, according to one reporter, "inviting foreigners from all around the world to live and work permanently in Plainston."

One thread, often only hinted at, ran quite consistently through these reports about Plainston. That thread was the idea, as one writer stated, "that a special force of some kind drives Plainstans to live differently but apparently successfully and happily." The *apparently* was what intrigued me—the unwillingness of the reporters to see success and happiness without assuming that there must be something else involved—something that is likely sinister.

My working bias has always been a skeptical belief that nothing is as good as reported or as bad—although occasionally things are better or worse in reality than alleged. None of these reports met my criteria for getting at the roots of Plainstans' admittedly non-traditional life style, their different social order. Most of the authors seemed content to ask only Who runs Plainston? or Who inspired its radical development? None of the reporters identified any charismatic figures, living or dead, who fit the role of great leader. However, all observers agreed that unusual and remarkable social and economic developments had taken place over the years and that the developments were continuing, even accelerating. The question that remained unanswered was Were the changes for good or ill?

I found one unusually insightful article in an obscure journal of social psychology. The author discussed the probable long-term social-psychological effects of what appeared to be Plainston's increasing separation from the outside world. It had been a fairly open society until the early 1990s when Plainstans had finished redesigning and rebuilding their city "according to human scale." At that time, the permanent resident limit was set at 40,000 with facilities to house and serve another 10,000 or more visitors and university students.

The writer of this scholarly article predicted a kind of social inbreeding that would lead to increasing intolerance of the majority society, making Plainstans unable to adapt to life outside their walls. She wrote, "That cannot but eventuate in a closed, ingrown society that will inevitably suffer moral, spiritual, intellectual, and possibly even physical degradation." At that point, Plainston's "Golden Age" would end.

In contrast to that scholar's pessimistic emphasis on Plainstans' inwardness, I found several articles reporting their growing involvement in politics at all levels. Plainstans had been among the prime movers who'd organized several special interest splinter groups into a well-integrated and unified third party, the Future Is Now, called the FINs, which was running a string of candidates for seats in both state legislatures and the U.S. House of Representatives in the upcoming mid-term election.

Among the political commentators who were beginning to pay increasing attention to the FINs was the widely-read investigative reporter and syndicated columnist Wilber Bickersley. He claimed to have uncovered the hand-in-glove relationship between Plainstans and the FINs. He warned in one article that "the FINs threaten much more than the stability of our two-party system. More potentially destructive is the fact that the FINs are the political arm of the Plainston conspiracy. Plainstans seek to revolutionize—although they cloak their intentions in the less threatening term *reform*—much more than our political system. They want to change the world a la Plainston. What hubris! What idiocy! What fantasy! What a threat!"

I'd known Wilber Bickersley for years. He'd been a very bright student in my political science classes when I'd started my assistant professorship at the University of Illinois decades ago. Wilber had been a firebrand radical in those days, and he'd continued to find fault with much of American culture—political, social, and moral—when he became a popular columnist and a radio and television panelist. I'd read his stimulating, though often muckraking, commentary off and on for years.

I have to admit that the various opinions I read sparked my curiosity about Plainston, especially since factual material was mostly missing. I found no objective studies of any demographic group, no reports based on statistics related to school performance or the standard of living or crime rates—only lots and lots of opinions. Investigative reporters like facts.

Even so, I was wavering about taking on a long-term assignment versus retiring to warmer climes. That had been my frame of mind when I'd gone to Max's office and turned my life over to the toss of a coin.

*   *   *

After taking care of all the minutiae involved with moving from one place to another, I flew from Washington, D.C., to Indianapolis and then from there to a regional airport in Illinois. After picking up my rental car, I decided to grab a bite to eat at the little café at the airport. When a young black waiter with friendly dark eyes delivered my steak and eggs, he asked where I was headed.

"Plainston," I said.

"Oh, Plainston!" he exclaimed, both his voice and face indicating intense interest. "Unusual place, Plainston. I suppose you have a pass to get in or some kind of pull. That place is getting tighter all the time."

Pretending ignorance, I asked, "Oh? What's the problem?"

"Nobody seems to know for sure. Some people around here think they've got something great that they aren't quite ready to unveil, like a company with a big breakthrough they're keeping secret 'til it's ready to market. But other folks think Plainston is up to something bad, maybe brainwashing that makes everyone seem so happy and satisfied—and keeps them in Plainston or brings them back if they leave for a while."

"Do you think it's something like Huxley's *Brave New World*?" I asked, testing his familiarity with that classic anti-Utopian novel which was often mentioned in the reports I'd read.

He smiled, pleased that I would make such a comparison, and said, "No, I don't think Plainston is an anti-Utopia."

As the café had no other patrons, he sat down at my table, and we continued our talk.

"I really haven't made up my mind about Plainston," he went on. "It has a reputation for genuine integration of all races, and that's still pretty rare. But when you think seemingly good people are hiding something, even if it's something good, doesn't it make you feel at least a little suspicious and uncomfortable?"

I nodded, and he continued.

"I'd like to get into their university, but Plainston kids get almost all the undergraduate slots. The University of Plainston admissions people told me that if I do well here at State and present a research project—something of real significance for society—I have a good chance of being accepted for graduate study."

An elderly woman, who'd been mopping the floor near our table, stopped working and started to say something, but the young waiter held up an open hand.

"Now, Thelma. You know Bob has told you not to air your views about Plainston to our visitors. It's impolite and bad for business."

"It's a free country, Douglas boy," she said through clenched teeth. "I've as much right to speak my mind as you just did. It's my Christian duty to warn folks about those sun-worshiping heathens."

"Now that's enough, Thelma!" Douglas said sternly. "You've said your piece. Now get on with your mopping, or I'll report you to Bob."

Thelma glared at him, then jammed her mop into a bucket, slopping water over the side. When she was out of earshot, Douglas smiled and, in a somewhat confidential tone, explained, "Plainston uses different kinds of solar energy. Thelma calls that 'heathen sun worship.' She belongs to a fundamentalist white supremacy group. You noticed how she called me 'boy.' The boss threatened to fire her if she didn't use my name, so now it's always 'Douglas boy' with lots of emphasis on the *boy* part."

Douglas gave me a wry smile, then added, "Thelma's really harmless, but I'm not so sure about the group she belongs to. There's considerable racism here in Prairie Grove. Thelma's bunch hates the integration in Plainston."

As much as I was intrigued with these unexpected opinions of Plainston, I knew the January sun was getting low, and I had about forty-five minutes of driving ahead on a narrow two-lane state road. When I got up to leave, I reached for my attaché case on the chair beside me. Douglas also rose while staring at the case.

"K. K.," he said, looking at me quizzically. "Now I know why you look familiar. You're Karl Kornhauer. I've seen you on some panels on CNN and PBS, haven't I?"

"I suppose you could've," I replied.

"Karl Kornhauer," Douglas said again. "I sure never figured to see you at our little airport."

Turning toward the kitchen, he shouted, "Hey, Bob, come meet a celebrity."

After being formally introduced to the manager, we got into further conversation about Plainston. Bob, a tall, thin white man, was a native of Prairie Grove. He had a working wife and two children.

"We mostly just let Plainstans go their own way. We've got nothing against Plainston."

I interpreted his "we" as representing the Prairie Grove majority.

"This is a free country," Bob went on. "People can do as they please so long as they don't hurt somebody else. I guess some people have sort of disappeared in Plainston, but nobody has ever charged anyone there with kidnapping or murder or torture or anything like that. The FBI has been in there several times, and surely they'd have found out if anything really bad is going on. Personally, I wouldn't want to live there. It's just too different. But there are lots of folks waiting to get in for good."

We exchanged more pleasantries before shaking hands.

As I walked toward the door, Thelma, who'd mopped her way in that direction, got in the last word, actually more like a volley.

"It's my Christian duty, Mr. Cornhusker," she said in a whisper, "to warn you not to let them heathen sun-worshipin' Plainston folk lead you astray. They're just plain evil."

"Thank you for the advice," I said with a smile as I exited the cafe.

Then I got into my bright-red rental car and headed for Plainston.

Chapter 2

The Miscreants

Plainston was about thirty-five miles southwest of Prairie Grove on an old state highway first built in the 1920s, then many times widened and resurfaced. It had been rerouted in the 1970s so that now a highway sign with an arrow indicated that Plainston was two miles ahead on a side road. I turned right, drove a short distance, and then pulled to the side of the road for my first survey of this mysterious place.

Plainston lay below in a broad valley, the flood plain of what had originally been a major tributary of the Ohio River. Then a decade of recurring earthquakes in the 1820s had heaved the land about, changing the course of many rivers. The bigger river had carved a new channel which now flowed through Prairie Grove. Plainston's modest little Sugar Creek had furrowed its own channel in the old river bed. All of that I'd garnered from my research.

Now, however, I actually saw Plainston in the dim light of a blustery January evening. Its four square miles were girded by a twelve-foot high concrete wall, vine-covered and hardly discernible through the surrounding belt of trees. Except for its height and some outlook turrets, it appeared hardly different from the walls commonly built around upscale suburban developments. The surrounding moat was only occasionally visible, its outside banks thickly planted with evergreens, deciduous trees, and bushes.

The city itself appeared not unusual, except for the dominating dome of the Temple in the center of the city. The Temple was often mentioned in the reports I'd read, described in one as "an interesting feature—eclectic and non-sectarian." Constructed almost entirely of native wood and limestone, it had been designed and built wholly by Plainston volunteers.

Plainston's other unusual feature was unusual only in its geographical context: high-rises. With relatively cheap land available, seldom would high-rises be built in a Midwestern city of its size. Four were clumped fairly closely together on the campus of Plainston University. That in itself wasn't unusual, for many universities had modest high-rises. I'd seen several as I'd driven by Prairie Grove's State University campus, but I'd seen none anywhere else in that city, which was about three times the size of Plainston. Eight other high-rises were evenly spaced outside the Center, which I knew from sketches of the city's layout was surrounded by retail stores and Plainston's famed craft shops.

Plainston was now a planned city, having grown from fewer than 2,000 inhabitants in 1900 to what its planners in the 1970s had decided to be the cut-off limit of 50,000 total population. It had reached its limit in the early 1990s and had held that constant—to the dismay of the hundreds, if not thousands, on Plainston's glacially-moving list of applicants for permanent residency.

As I'd read about the small city I was now seeing for the first time, I'd wondered why Plainston hadn't simply expanded beyond its walls—torn them down if need be. Urban sprawl it was called—and it was what American city dwellers, who equate growth with health, wealth, and happiness, had been doing for years. I again wondered about Plainston's failure to expand as I surveyed it now, snugly bound by its eight-mile wall.

After scanning Plainston for several more minutes from that elevated vantage point, I proceeded on toward my possible mission to discover what this unique community was all about. Some lines from a poem I'd read in an American lit class years before came to mind—something about wondering who would be offended if I built a wall which kept some things in and some things out.

The road wound down into the valley through a series of fairly sharp twenty-mile-per-hour curves. It flattened out about half a mile from the city gate, which was guarded by a field-stone gatehouse with entrances on two sides, one marked Visitors, the other With Passes. Pulling up at the latter window, I said, "I'm Karl Kornhauer. I've been invited here to—"

I was interrupted by a warm smile from the gatekeeper, who, ignoring my identification and pass, said, "Oh, yes, Mr. Kornhauer. We're delighted to have you. Mrs. Gray is expecting you. She's in the next building to your right. We're glad you've come."

When I stopped at the designated building, a young girl stepped from the guard booth. With a smile, she said politely, "My name is Susan. Please give me your car keys."

"Oh, I know," I said gruffly, pretending bad humor. "You ecological Puritans with all your divinely cleansed smog-free air. Commandment One is 'Thou shalt not pollute Plainston.'"

With mock gravity, she responded in kind. "Ah, yes, Pagan. Thou shalt not defile our sacred atmosphere with fumes of petroleum. Thou shalt be transported thither via electric cart, ecologically solar-powered."

This might've been a canned riposte, but she made it sound spontaneous. I couldn't help but grin as I disembarked and gathered my luggage. An attendant slid behind the wheel of my car and eased it around the corner into a multi-level parking garage. I walked toward the building.

A woman about my age with fine features and a slight build met me at the door. She smiled warmly.

"Mr. Kornhauer, I'm so glad you made it. I'm Mrs. Gray."

I hadn't yet introduced myself, but apparently the first sentry had notified her of my arrival. That was amazingly fast communication. Was that good or bad? I was feeling ambivalent already.

"What will you have to warm yourself—coffee, tea, cocoa?"

I opted for coffee and settled into a comfortable lounge chair. We began with small talk about my trip and about the upcoming primary elections.

After a short time, she said, in a somewhat apologetic tone while pointing to a camera I hadn't seen, "This may seem a bit unusual to you, but we Plainstans are very strong for recording oral history. We like to record our guests on video. Do you object to being entered into the Plainston oral-video archives?"

Mildly flattered and only a tiny bit suspicious, I agreed. She flipped a switch to activate two cameras high on the walls. We then started talking, somewhat guardedly, about Plainston.

I'd just raised some questions from my reading and the airport café conversations when a red light started flashing, accompanied by a clanging alarm. Mrs. Gray ran to the door, with me close behind, and flung it open.

The girl sentry raised her arms and screamed, "Stop!" as an army-style Jeep with four occupants streaked past. It sped across the bridge and into a sort of tunnel, which extended about forty feet from the end of the moat bridge to the city gate. Suddenly, at each end of the well-lit tunnel, heavy nets dropped simultaneously, effectively trapping the Jeep and its transgressors inside. They climbed out of the Jeep—two young men, who were cursing, and two girls, both waving their arms and shouting somewhat hysterically.

We followed two security officers, who walked somewhat leisurely across the moat bridge. Without side arms or billy clubs or any other arresting paraphernalia, they calmly talked to the enmeshed culprits. The group was first Mirandized and then informed that they'd committed the serious crimes of forced entry and trespass—crimes especially serious since 9/11 and the subsequent national concern for security and protection from terrorists. The group had committed some other minor misdemeanors, which, when listed, convinced the four that they were in "a heap of trouble," as one of the girls said.

"That you surely are," an arresting officer said in a surprisingly kindly voice. "But if you behave yourselves and work with Mrs. Gray here, who is legally qualified to negotiate your appropriate sentencing, you can get out of this without it going onto either a police record or a driving record. Do you understand?"

Somewhat sullenly, they nodded.

"Now understand this. If you make any attempt to escape or treat Judge Gray with anything but the courtesy and respect due her, you'll get a lot deeper into trouble. Understand?"

There was more silent nodding.

"We'll impound the Jeep until you and Mrs. Gray get this thing settled."

With that, the rear net was raised, and the four miscreants walked meekly back across the bridge and into the admissions building behind Mrs. Gray. I waited to see how the garage attendants would disentangle the Jeep from the forward net. They did so easily, then drove the undamaged vehicle into the parking garage.

Back inside, Mrs. Gray invited me to sit in on her negotiations with the accused, who were lined up on an oversized sofa, drinking cocoa.

"It's a little like attending a trial," she said to me, "but without adversarial lawyers making appeals to a jury. It's solidly democratic, just unconventional. But it's highly efficient and economical. Judge it for yourself."

She seemed to be challenging me, sensing, perhaps, my unspoken questions about these unorthodox proceedings.

I studied the four young people as they sat on the sofa while Mrs. Gray asked some simple questions and wrote down some basic information. Hank, the oldest at nineteen, was tall and rather gaunt, dressed as were the girls in denim and leather. He looked scruffy, needing both a shave and a haircut. He had his arm around Rosie, a pretty, round-faced, pink-cheeked girl, who was a full head shorter than he was. She was wearing bright-red leather knee boots, which provided the only color to the group's attire. Adele was the youngest at sixteen. Her hands, holding an inhaler, were visibly shaking. Rick, her boyfriend, was dressed in all black leather—a jacket, pants, knee-high boots, and a cap tilted at a jaunty angle—all of which set him apart as perhaps the rich kid.

Finally, Mrs. Gray laid her notepad and pen aside and looked at the four, her eyes moving slowly from one to the other. She said, "You'll notice that two video cameras are focused on you. This is legal now. It protects you from any abusive treatment from me, mean old Judge Gray. And it protects me from any abusive treatment from you. Okay?"

The group once again responded with sullen nodding.

Turning to me, she said, "Mr. Kornhauer, will you be so kind as to act as an independent observer to these proceedings? The law recommends having a witness to verify the accuracy of such."

She sounded very formal and legal. I agreed.

At this time, Susan, the girl who'd yelled "Stop!" at the speeding Jeep, entered and sat down at a computer. I wondered if she were the modern equivalent of the court reporter. She began by entering the four names from Mrs. Gray's notepad into the county data base to see if anyone had a previous police record. None of them had, but they were more than a little upset as Susan typed. Mrs. Gray allayed their fears.

"Don't worry, kids," she said in a motherly voice. "Nothing that goes on here goes into the county or city records—or the FBI or CIA—unless you really get out of hand. We keep the records in our own files, safe from prying eyes."

"You mean you won't report this to our parents?" asked Rick. "It's my dad's Jeep, and he doesn't know we borrowed it tonight."

"We won't notify your parents, but if they independently find out what you kids did and demand to see this court's record, they have that right. So keep mum about it yourselves and serve your sentences quietly and fully. That way your secret is safe with us."

That warm-hearted statement melted the last layer of frost on the quartet's attitude. They almost eagerly entered into what Mrs. Gray assured them were genuine legal proceedings. Then she repeated the charges.

"There's no use for you to plead innocent to the charges as none of you has a leg to stand on, so let's skip that nonsense and work from the fact that you will all plead guilty. It's just common sense to admit what we all saw you do. So, one at a time, please stand and to my question, 'How plead you to these charges?' simply reply, 'Guilty, as charged.'"

They all did so.

"Now, do we get sentenced?" asked Adele, her hands still shaking despite being clenched together.

"Yes, and this may be more than a little painful, but be brave. The law is specific about the punishments that a judge may impose. And we don't have much discretion in imposing them; in other words, I can't shave much off the fines. But we can arrange ways for you to work out your fines with public service here in Plainston, if you agree. It's the best bargain you'll find anywhere in the county."

Should a judge try to sell a sentence before it's pronounced? I wondered. This sounded a little outside judicial protocol as I understood it. It was the kind of bargain lawyers might try to get for their clients, but since when did judges get to shed their robes and put on lawyers' togs? Actually, there were no robes to shed as she was wearing a pair of charcoal wool slacks and a blue-and-gray plaid jacket. She was certainly acting the part of a judge even if she didn't look it.

Mrs. Gray's mention of their working out the fines in Plainston piqued the group's interest. But before the sentencing began, Mrs. Gray encouraged them to talk about Plainston. I wondered if she was doing this partly to fill me in on some aspects of Plainston she thought I should hear from outsiders.

Mrs. Gray got their life histories with a friendly interviewing manner. Opening up, they talked freely and frankly about their lives, which, on the whole, were aimless and dominated by the pursuit of exciting, even dangerous, action.

They actually knew very little about Plainston. Their comments were a blend of resentment from being excluded from the city, jealousy of the good life they'd heard about, and general curiosity about what was hidden away behind the wall.

Hank said, "They say your Plainston kids get through school early, like at fifteen or sixteen, and go on to your university and then get good jobs. Me, I'm almost twenty. I flunked out of high school, and I can't get a decent job in Prairie Grove without a diploma. They turned me down here though I told 'em I'd work for less than the minimum wage just to get in on all the good stuff they say your workers get for perks."

Rosie said with a frown, "I've heard that some people come in here and are never heard from again."

Mrs. Gray and Susan exchanged glances and laughed.

Then Susan said in a conspiratorial tone, "We make lots of our visitors into zombies. Didn't you think there was something a little funny-tasting in that cocoa Mrs. Gray served you? It'll begin to take effect pretty soon."

The kids laughed a bit nervously and looked at Mrs. Gray for reassurance.

Sensing their anxiety, she said calmly, "She's kidding, of course, but it's true that some people like Plainston so much they never want to leave. Some don't even bother to keep up contacts with the outside world; however, they certainly can if they want to."

That sounded plausible and seemed to satisfy the four. However, it didn't entirely remove my suspicions. The only other places where I'd heard "the outside world" spoken of in that way were prisons and a cloistered nunnery where my wife and I'd once visited an aunt of hers who'd taken the vows. Why should there be an attitude toward "the outside world" in an allegedly free, though protected, community?

After an interlude of relaxed personal interchanges, Mrs. Gray reassumed her judicial role by announcing, "I'm sorry, but we have to get to the unpleasant business—the sentencing."

After a few moments of silence, she said, "The standard fine for trespassing is $500."

All mouths, mine included, dropped open. Theirs closed and re-opened in a chorus of "You must be kidding!"

But nothing in Mrs. Gray's tone or demeanor suggested she was spoofing.

"Plus a $300 fee for releasing your impounded Jeep," she added.

Hank, forgetting the security guard's warning about disrespectful behavior, cut loose with a string of obscenities.

"I'm sorry, Hank," she responded with what seemed to be genuine regret, "but that profane outburst just cost you another $200. Profanity is verbal pollution. We put pretty stiff fines on all kinds of pollution."

All four glared at her but held their tongues, apparently sensing that she had the upper hand.

"How do you intend to pay these fines? We can take credit cards, or shall we contact your parents?"

Was she kidding, just leading these scared kids on? But she'd made believers out of them. They came alive with a barrage of protests and pleas.

"I don't have that kind of money! That's more than a month's wages!"

"Don't call our folks! They'll kill us!"

"My mom will ground me for six months if she finds out!"

Finally, Hank said, "I haven't even got a job. Where can I get the money?"

When they'd exhausted their appeals and protests, Mrs. Gray, who'd been listening impassively, relaxed and smiled.

"Well, as I hinted earlier, we can arrange for you to work out your fines. We don't have to notify your parents. At a fair wage for unskilled labor, you'll have to work eighty hours to pay off the fines—you can divide that among the four of you—and Hank another twenty for swearing. We'll take a promissory note you all must sign to get the Jeep back tonight."

All of this struck me as extremely high-handed, maybe even illegal. But what could these scared kids do except accept this settlement? While the kids' reaction was one of relief, mine was one of indignation as the idea of indentured servitude—a hundred hours of free labor—floated around in my head.

"Now that that's all settled," Mrs. Gray continued, as pleasantly and matter-of-factly as if they'd just agreed about the dreariness of the weather, "would you like to get inside Plainston legally, maybe have a bite to eat?"

This offer cheered them.

Adele asked, "Can we also spend the evening having some fun after we eat?"

Susan, who volunteered as co-hostess, checked the newspaper lying nearby for some events. The list included a stage play in Plainston Northeast, an operetta in Plainston Southeast, a basketball game in Plainston South, a symphony concert at Plainston University, folk dancing in Plainston Southwest, and a movie in Plainston North which an exchange group had made during their year-long visit to Siberia. That choice drew a loud unanimous "No!"

Rick asked, "Is Siberia one of those Arab countries, or is it in Africa?"

After giving him a frown, Rosie said, "You dork, it's that great big cold area somewhere near Russia."

Changing the subject, Hank asked, "Don't you have any good music here?"

He was likely referring to the electro-space combos popular with most kids in the "outside world."

Susan shook her head. "Sorry about that," she said without sounding particularly apologetic. "We Plainstans have pretty old-fashioned musical tastes. But you might enjoy a combination of Dixieland jazz and barbershop singing. That's at the Beanery tonight. The food's good, too, and it's not at all expensive."

Without more attractive alternatives, the group shrugged assent.

Mrs. Gray suggested we walk to the Beanery, less than a mile distant, but when Adele said she was having trouble getting her breath, Susan called for a minibus, which was dropped off in less than five minutes.

The bus was the most skeletal conveyance I'd ever seen—totally open with four thinly-padded bright-blue bench seats, two small wide-tread rear wheels, a single front wheel, and a rudder for steering.

Susan offered minimal information. "It's our own design. Kids build these in our shop, doing some of their apprentice training to learn basic engineering and mechanical skills. Electric motors are in the rear wheels. Batteries are solar powered."

Susan sat with Rosie and Adele on the front bench, where Susan gave Rosie simple driving instructions. Mrs. Gray and I sat on the third seat behind Hank and Rick, who were quietly grousing to each other about being passed over as pilot.

Aha, I said to myself, feminism isn't just alive in Plainston. It's dominant.

Then we were off, gliding with a quiet hum on the damp road.

Chapter 3

The Beanery

The Beanery was an intimate little restaurant, seating about sixty. Susan asked for a table not far from the small stage where the Dixieland band was already in full swing. We had to wait to be seated until they finished their number. As we walked toward our table, Susan explained that guests are seated and served only between numbers and that conversation is considered polite only during those breaks.

"But for those who wish to eat and talk, there is a half-walled conversation section at the rear," she added.

That sounded like shades of the long-gone question "Smoking or non-smoking?" but here guests were asked "Talking or non-talking?"

Once seated, we followed our hosts' suggestions and ordered the bean specials—bean loaf for me, bean burgers for the kids.

"Specially processed for no flatulence," Mrs. Gray commented as the waiter left.

When the word *flatulence* brought puzzled looks, Susan leaned over to whisper to Rosie, who giggled and passed the word to Adele who, with a blush, passed it on to Hank, and he to Rick. By the time the definition had made the rounds, all of them were trying to stifle their laughter.

Then Mrs. Gray casually remarked, "It's true. You won't fart!"

And the dam burst. Everyone grabbed a napkin to muffle the laughter. There's no better ice-breaker than a good laugh. From that point on, we were a group socially at ease.

We all got quiet as a male and female barbershop quartet began to sing. They didn't use microphones, yet every note, every nuance, every word was perfectly clear. There was no competing table talk, no traffic noise from the street, no kitchen clatter.

When I mentioned the acoustics at the next conversation break, Mrs. Gray said, "All places that feature entertainment here are acoustically designed and built to deliver voice and music naturally. And we all learn to listen quietly since we believe anything worth hearing is worth our complete attention."

For the first time in years, I realized how pleasantly different is natural sound from amplified sound, even when it's in high fidelity.

As we began to eat our meals, a band took the stage, featuring two instruments not in the pure Dixieland tradition, a violin and an oboe. The jazz fiddler was an elderly gentleman who looked the part of the concertmaster of the Vienna Philharmonic. An attractive young lady was playing the oboe. A clarinet and a soprano sax lay close by.

"He's Mihaly. She's his granddaughter," Mrs. Gray whispered to me. "I'll tell you about them later."

With the two orchestral instruments added, the band treated us to Dixieland versions of familiar classics—Strauss waltzes, themes from symphonies, national anthems, and popular folk songs. Being a Dixieland aficionado, I had occasionally heard other Dixieland bands give similar renditions of favorite melodies, but the violin and the oboe gave an especially rich and authentic classical touch without in any way losing the happy abandon and upbeat rhythm that is uniquely Dixieland. I wished they wouldn't take their requisite "conversation break," but when they did, Mrs. Gray started explaining the origins of this delightful innovation.

"The unique sound you're hearing is mainly the work of one of our most beloved imports. Mihaly escaped with his family from Hungary during the 1956 revolution which the Soviets crushed so harshly."

"From Budapest?" I asked.

"No, from Gyor," she answered. "It's a small city on the Danube in northwest Hungary, about eighty miles southwest of Vienna. Since some of his family members were leaders of the revolutionary party, they feared persecution. It wasn't hard to help them escape through Austria because we already had post-war contacts in Gyor near the Austrian border. Gyor has a lot in common with Plainston—"

The band started playing again, and we didn't get back to the story of Mihaly until the following day.

I turned my attention to our young friends, interested in how they were responding to this music since Dixieland and barbershop still appealed primarily to the older generations in "the outside world." These kids had probably been exposed to little else besides electro-space music that was, at least to me, a hideous offspring of hard rock, always played at ear-deadening, mega-decibel levels. Here was comparatively delicate, intricately contrapuntal music with plenty of verve but without flashing lights, screaming voices, and gyrating acrobatics.

At first, the kids seemed puzzled, but as the infectious rhythms gradually broke through the barriers of their heavy-metal programmed minds, they began to smile and twitch, to pat one foot and then both feet, until finally their entire bodies were with it. By the sixth set, they were the most exuberant patrons in the café. Even though we had leisurely finished our meal, we unanimously voted to stay on. We gave up our table to diners and moved to seats in the back where the acoustics were as good as they were near the stage.

About 8:30, the band and quartet came on stage together, and the emcee announced they would do a special number in honor of a guest—"or rather two guests," he said, correcting himself.

The band struck up a tune that brought all Plainstans to their feet. We outsiders, of course, joined them. Mrs. Gray briefly dropped her head and covered her face on hearing the opening bars. The music sounded like a national anthem or a school's fight song, which intended to tug at one's heart strings and to stiffen the spine to go forth and do battle for God and country:

> Plainston, Plainston, proud and strong,
> Help us live lives pure and long;
> May we our duties never shirk;
> Teach us how to love all work.

May we learn to care for others,
Treat all people as our brothers.
Plainston, Plainston, just and free,
Shine your light on our country.

As the audience sang along, Mrs. Gray, who wasn't singing, gently shook her head. I wasn't paying much attention to the words, but the music, which was played in a rich minor key by only an eight-piece band, sent shivers down my spine—my basic criterion for inspired music. The audience was singing lustily in full four-part harmony, sounding more like a cathedral choir than a community sing-along.

At the conclusion of the anthem, everyone applauded as Mrs. Gray and I were escorted to the stage. She was introduced first.

"Most of you know this beloved lady, Lydia Colby Gray, who composed, at the tender age of eleven, both the words and music of "Plainston, Proud and Strong.""

This elicited another burst of applause.

Then the emcee asked her to introduce me, her guest. She did so, complimenting me for my career as a distinguished professor of political science, as a political commentator and columnist, and as the author of a series of works on national politics. She even gave a plug for my last book.

Then she said, "Mr. Kornhauer will be staying with us—for how long depends on how well we treat him. He may decide to find out for himself all about Plainston and us Plainstans. Of course, we expect him to do this without our telling him very much. We'll make him dig it out for himself, and then maybe he'll reveal it to the world."

This brought a knowing laugh from the audience, who were mostly Plainstans, I guessed. This somewhat perplexing restriction on access to information was news to me. We hadn't yet begun to negotiate my possible assignment.

Mrs. Gray then introduced the Prairie Grove four, each member standing and receiving a polite round of applause.

"They, too, will be visiting and working with us from time to time," she said, giving no hint as to why.

Even so, I saw no puzzled looks on any faces of the local populace. Was this a common occurrence in Plainston, this indenturing of culprits?

Hank took advantage of his moment of recognition to express his appreciation to the musicians. "I didn't know there even was the kind of music you guys and ladies play and sing. Kind of spoils me for the space stuff I'm used to. I sure want to come back and hear it some more."

We returned to our seats. Before the music started again, I asked Mrs. Gray why she was shaking her head during the singing.

"Oh, those sentimental lyrics," she said with a groan. "I've been trying for forty years to get someone to write something dignified. We Plainstans really do have better taste in poetry, but some ordinary things have a way of getting frozen into our mores, it seems."

I asked if she'd done other composing. She nodded, but before she could explain, the barbershop singers launched another set, and we were once again immersed in the music.

*   *   *

We left around 9:30. Hank drove the minibus back.

It took Mrs. Gray an unhurried half an hour to make arrangements for the Prairie Grove four to work out their fines. Once again, she promised complete confidentiality about both their criminal escapade and the fines they'd be working off in Plainston.

When the garage crew returned the Jeep, all four signed the promissory note for its release. After handshakes and warm hugs all around, the four drove off, singing one of the folksongs they'd heard at the Beanery—acting as if they were about to begin a new life instead of a period of peonage.

I couldn't help saying to Mrs. Gray, "If you treat all trespassers with such a warm welcome, won't you be overrun with young criminals when the word gets around?"

Mrs. Gray smiled. "We'll risk it. But these kids won't tell."

When I started to ask more questions, she declined to answer.

"There's plenty of time for that later. Here, drink this. It'll give you a good night's sleep after your stressful initiation here. You saw how it tamed those wild ones from Prairie Grove," she said with a perfectly straight face.

I drank it, without totally believing the potion was innocuous. Such is the discomfiting power of ambivalence.

Then she accompanied me in a snug typically-yellow mini-cab with a single seat. She trusted me to drive to the Guest Tower Southwest, where she'd reserved a room for me on the tenth floor, which was high enough up for me to look down on the dome of the Temple. After inspecting the room to be certain all was in order, she invited me to breakfast at her apartment the next morning. She gave me directions and then a friendly hug and a kiss on the cheek.

"I'm so glad you've come," she said as she departed.

Such contrasts, I thought later as I gazed at the Temple. So warm and yet so cool. So relaxed and yet so briskly efficient. So seemingly caring and yet so possibly hard-boiled. So young in spirit yet aging in body. Is she a typical Plainstan?

Once I was in bed, this question didn't keep me awake. The lady's brew did its work.

Chapter 4

Lydia

Mrs. Gray's apartment in Plainston North was a chilly twelve-minute walk along the west bank of the now-frozen Sugar Creek. The sky had cleared about sundown yesterday. During the cloudless night, the temperature had dropped to near zero. The sun was beginning to warm things a bit, helped by a moderating northeast wind that the weather forecasters predicted might bring snowfall by nightfall. I hadn't walked that far in years. My feet hurt, but I liked the feel of the cold, clear air in my lungs.

When I arrived at the apartment, Mrs. Gray immediately suggested we get on a first-name basis.

"I suppose your nickname Kiki derives from your double-K initials."

I nodded.

"So should I call you Kiki, or do you prefer Karl?"

"If you like me, please call me Kiki. If I hear Karl, I'll know I've fallen out of favor."

She smiled. "Please relax and be your natural, charming self, and you'll never hear Karl. You know I'm Lydia. No nickname although I've occasionally been called names I won't repeat."

As she finished preparing breakfast, she invited me to survey her apartment. The living room was fairly spacious with an attractive stone fireplace, glowing and warm. Bookshelves, paintings, small sculptures, and other art objects—mostly the products of local artists, she said—tastefully adorned the room.

"In fact, almost everything in here is produced in Plainston."

"Even the piano?" I asked.

It was a large parlor grand. I expected to see a familiar name, such as Steinway, Baldwin, Mason-Hamlin, or perhaps Yamaha, on the fallboard, but it was a foreign name I'd never heard of—Weinhoff.

"Oh, yes. Gregor Weinhoff was another refugee, this time from Bavaria. We resettled him and his family and a few of his piano craftsmen after World War II. We set him up in a small shop here. Our little piano factory turns out a dozen or so pianos a year. Our grand pianos cost about the same as Steinways and other big names, but some pianists consider the Weinhoff superior, especially for homes and small concert halls."

I sat down and played a few bars.

"Oh, good, Kiki! You can play. Shall we do some duets after breakfast?"

The question seemed more like a gentle command than an invitation.

"Only if you have some about Grade One and you let me play secondo," I said.

During breakfast of hot cereal and whole-grain muffins with naturally sweetened jam, Lydia continued the story she'd barely started about Mihaly—the Hungarian refugee violinist and Dixieland innovator.

"Mihaly was already an accomplished violinist by the age of twenty. His father was an expert maker of violins as well as violas, cellos, and bass fiddles. We resettled his whole family and some of his artisans, who make all our stringed instruments. There are none finer made anywhere else nowadays."

"Any other artistic geniuses in Mihaly's family?" I asked, with an unintentional trace of skepticism.

Ignoring the tone, Lydia responded brightly, "Yes, indeed! His mother was highly skilled in all kinds of embroidery and needlework. Hungarian women are famous for that. She opened one of our first handiwork shops."

Lydia paused to pour another cup of coffee. "Mihaly earned his teacher's credential at State in Prairie Grove and then developed our comprehensive school music program. He organized and led our first community orchestra and then began composing simple classical-type music for young orchestras and bands."

"Didn't you say last night that you have composed more than Plainston's anthem?" I asked.

"Well, yes. And that's connected with Mihaly and Gyor. When I was only seven, I went there with my parents and a 4-H group to deliver some livestock and seed to replenish what they'd lost in the war. Gyor was a distribution center. I stayed with Mihaly's family. They took me to concerts and some cafes where I heard a lot of Hungarian folk music. I fell in love with the minor keys. Lots of folk music is minor, you know."

We talked a while longer about our tastes in music, which were remarkably similar.

But I wanted to get down to some of my basic concerns, so I said, "Why did you ask Max to send me here? What am I supposed to do for Plainston—if anything?"

She responded not with an answer but with a question.

"Why did you come?"

Ah, is this going to be a cat and mouse game? I wondered. Why had I come? It really was more than the chance flip of that coin. I'd have likely come even if it'd turned up tails.

"Well, Plainston is different, damnably and confusingly different. I guess I wanted to see if I could get at the roots of all your differences."

"Precisely!" she said as she beamed. "But you have to do what we call, 'live Plainston' for quite a while before you can fully understand—and feel—the difference between root and fruit."

"The chicken and the egg problem? I see the analogy. Did—and does—Plainston produce Plainstans or vice-versa?"

"That's the right question," she said. "We felt that if you care to 'live Plainston' long enough to fully understand our roots—something no other outsider has ever done—you might write a book about us. We need an objective evaluation of our performance and our objectives. Can't you judge us more fairly than any other well-known analyst around?"

"I can't judge your judgment of my judging ability," I said with a laugh. "But am I to understand that you'd like me to take Plainston's brightly lighted candle out from under its bushel and put it on the world's candlestick to shine its light into all the dark corners?"

"Anything wrong with our wanting you to do just that?"

"I guess not, but maybe I'll find something really wrong with Plainston," I countered. "From my research thus far, plus a tiny bit of firsthand experience, I have some questions about the purity of Plainston's purpose."

"Ah, yes, the so-called Plainston conspiracy," Lydia responded in a mocking tone. "The favorite topic of several free-lance journalists and of certain congenital dyspeptics who love to shout their motto, 'If anything sounds too good to be true, you can bet your bottom dollar it is.'"

"Is it my assignment to judge for the rest of the world if Plainston may be a believable exception—that it's too good not to be true? This sickly old world might perk up from a proper dose of goodness and truth."

I delivered that last sentence in a voice carrying more conviction than I yet felt, but it fit with Lydia's optimistic faith.

"And Dr. Kornhauer is just the trusted old family doctor to prescribe it," Lydia said with a wide smile, apparently convinced that I'd accepted the job.

"But first, it appears that I have to determine, by submitting myself to a rather heavy dosage and lengthy treatment, whether this Plainston potion might be poisonous—or at least have dangerous side effects. Right?"

"Doesn't that make good medical sense?" she responded.

"Yes, I suppose it does."

With my decision made, we shook hands, and Lydia gave me a quick hug. Then the conversation went back to the story of Mihaly and classical Dixieland. "Actually, we call it 'Claxieland,'" she said, "'Claxie' meaning a classical piece. Cute, huh?"

She went on to explain how Mihaly had fallen in love with the Dixieland sound, which he thought was the most truly creative American musical style. As an educator specializing in music, he'd found it had special appeal to young kids interested in music.

After we cleared the table and did the dishes, Lydia said, "So how about a few duets. Want to try some of Mihaly's Claxieland arrangements?"

As I started to take my left place on the piano bench, I noticed a video-camera aimed at us. A rush of anger surged through me.

"Can't a fellow do anything in this damned place without Big Brother watching?" I said, pointing at the camera.

I'd agreed to the taping last night, but she hadn't asked my permission this time.

"Oh, I'm so sorry, Kiki. We Plainstans take our video cameras so much for granted that we sometimes forget how our guests may feel about them. But back in the days of our old Kodaks, didn't you usually feel complimented if your host just up and took a snapshot of you—a memento of your visit?"

She continued without waiting for me to answer. "Actually, the camera is off, but would you like our musical venture to be recorded for posterity?"

Her logical response, delivered so calmly and caringly, smothered my suspicion. I apologized for my outburst and agreed to be further entered into Plainston's archives.

With Lydia playing the treble, which was mostly the melody, we plowed through a book of relatively easy duets, including several of Mihaly's Claxieland arrangements. Then, after complimenting my playing, Lydia suggested we trade places. Unfortunately, my performance on the more challenging primo part significantly reduced the quality of our musical efforts. After three pieces, I asked her to stop taping. Laughing loudly, she accused me of having a fragile ego and turned off the camera.

*　　*　　*

About 11 o'clock, Lydia went to the window, read the outside thermometer, and announced that the weather was warming.

"How would you like a brisk skate on Mill Pond? The ice is a safe six-inches thick, our weatherman reported this morning."

Since I hadn't skated for years, I doubted that my bunions could endure being laced tightly into shoe skates. However, I didn't want to confess to this spry little lady that I had such a disability. I'd guessed her age when we first met to be about sixty, but during our get-acquainted small talk, she'd casually stated that she was sixty-seven, two years my senior. I'd have taken her challenge to skate on Mill Pond even if I'd had a broken leg.

"We'll come back here for lunch, if you'd like, and then I have a favor to ask. You have a rental car here, but there's no use paying that cost when we can supply you with one of our cars a lot cheaper when you need one. So why don't you drive me to the airport in Prairie Grove, turn in your rental car, and catch the afternoon bus back to Plainston? I'm leaving this afternoon for a two-week visit with my kids and grandkids and to do a little Plainston outreach business. The trip to the airport will give us a little more time together."

She seemed to relish that opportunity, and so did I.

*   *   *

We walked to a sports shop where I was fitted with rental skates. Another long city block took us to Mill Pond, a twenty-acre mini-lake created by damming Sugar Creek. The dam furnished waterpower for the Old Mill, which was still grinding grain as it'd been doing for the past 150 years or so. The dam produced some electrical power as well.

We sat on wooden benches in a cozy shed, warmed with a heater, and laced up our skates. Then we ventured onto the ice. I hadn't skated outdoors since leaving my little home town about fifty years ago. Temporarily ignoring my bunion pain, I put my arm around Lydia's waist and we glided onto the ice. There was no "Skaters' Waltz" blaring from loudspeakers, no bumping into beginners, no threading our way through crowds of skaters, no dodging speeders. Dozens of other skaters were out, but there was plenty of ice on which to maneuver.

My legs and ankles responded adequately, but my aching bunions canceled most of the pleasure. After a tour of the pond's perimeter, I feigned being winded and urged Lydia to skate solo. Taking a sail from the shed, she showed me some sail-skating techniques. It looked like fun, but I declined her invitation to try it.

As we started to walk back for lunch a short time later, I couldn't help limping a bit.

"Foot trouble, Kiki?"

I confessed. Honesty seemed appropriate.

"I'm so sorry. But fortunately, you couldn't be in a better place to get help with foot problems. If there were a Nobel Prize in podiatry, several of our specialists would be in the running. They've been working on bunions—a universal curse for us bipeds—for over twenty-five years. Their treatments, including laser surgery, help about 98 percent of their patients. I'll make an appointment for you before I leave."

I couldn't very well refuse her offer although several specialists had told me over the years that surgery wouldn't likely do me much good.

"And while you're at Health Services, you might want to get a general physical. Ask them about a program to take off your extra pounds and get you back in shape. You're much too young to be out of breath from skating as little as we did."

I felt the color rise in my cheeks. Who is she, I asked myself, to criticize the state of my health and to presume to prescribe treatment? Is this genuine concern for others or bossy over-mothering?

I limped back to her apartment, where she insisted on my using a foot massage contraption her late husband had used before he got a full recovery from some laser treatments. I did get a little relief.

Lydia scheduled an appointment for me the following afternoon, which caused me to wonder why, if these specialists were so good, they weren't booked up weeks in advance as are big-city specialists.

After a light soup and salad lunch, Lydia ordered a mini-cab to carry us back to the admissions building. We loaded her luggage into my rental car and headed for the airport. During the drive, we exchanged more personal information. We had much in common.

Her husband, Don, had been killed when on volunteer guard duty. A group of Prairie Grove rowdies had run him down as he'd tried to stop them from entering the city. That was before the tunnel with the nets had been built.

"It seems odd why some people—kids, especially—seem determined to run our blockades," she said softly.

I shared the loss of my beloved wife, Marie. She'd died in a head-on crash with a drunk driver who was speeding onto the off ramp.

Lydia had three children and four grandchildren, compared to my two children and four grandchildren. She had a sister in San Francisco. My older sister had lived in Southern California before her death.

Lydia was unusually well-informed about politics. She'd read much of what I'd written and seen some of my television appearances on panels.

"Max assured me you were quite intelligent and very well informed," I said, meaning to pay her a compliment.

She wrinkled her nose playfully and said, "Ah, and you agree with him because I've read what you've written and listened to what you've said."

"Of course," I replied. "What else could be that important?"

She rolled her eyes and grinned. I hadn't matched wits with a woman since Marie had died.

The trip to the airport was far too short.

* * *

I waited to see her off. Giving me another hug and another kiss on the cheek, she said again, "I'm so glad you've come. And I hope you decide to stay."

Smiling, I offered to meet her return flight, but she hadn't yet scheduled it.

"But I'll look you up the minute I get back. I promise. See you soon."

I watched her walk away.

Then after I turned in my rental car, I followed the directions Lydia had given me for taking the airport shuttle to the County Courthouse Square in Prairie Grove, where I'd catch the four o'clock bus back to Plainston. While waiting, I replayed more verbal sparring we'd done when she'd told me about the bus.

"It's our own bus," she'd said, "but pretty conventional with a steering wheel, an internal combustion engine, padded seats—"

"Runs on alcohol and sunshine," I said, interrupting her, "raised, collected, and processed, no doubt, in Plainston."

"Of course," she said with a laugh. "Would we have it any other way?"

I was smiling when I boarded the bus.

* * *

I got back to Plainston about five o'clock. I used Lydia's bunion massager again for a few minutes with a little relief, then napped until almost seven. I'd had coffee and a sweet roll at the airport café, hoping again to meet Douglas, but neither he nor Thelma nor Bob was on duty. Not yet hungry, I made a detailed survey of my new lodgings.

Larger than the usual motel or hotel room, its sixteen by twenty-four foot area included a kitchenette with sink, a four-burner electric stove, a microwave oven, and an average-sized refrigerator with a freezer. Cabinets were stocked with a colorful set of dishes and tableware for four. There were also pots, pans, cutlery, and utensils for light housekeeping.

An attractive four-page brochure explained that most of what was in the room had been produced in Plainston. The original arts and crafts—paintings, small sculptures and figurines, a hand-woven rug, and a handmade quilt—were for sale. Similar items were available in various retail outlets throughout the city.

The only reproduced artwork, also for sale, was a stylized map of Plainston as it might appear from atop the hill leading down into the city. All structures and natural objects were drawn in three-dimensional perspective without losing the accurate distance and scale of a flat map projection. The map had considerable artistic merit.

I'd seen small maps of Plainston in some of the articles I'd read. I knew from them that the city is divided into six sub-Plainstons: North, Northeast, Northwest, South, Southeast, and Southwest. What I hadn't realized, until I studied this panorama, is that each sub-Plainston is a complete little city in itself with populations of about 7,000. Each little city has its own K-12 school with ample playground space. A Child Development Center and an Alumni Center are attached to each big school building.

Residential areas surround the central business area, called the City Center. Residences nearest the City Center are generally apartment-type buildings. Beyond these are individual homes of various sizes with front yards and often backyard gardens. Some older homes still have garages, but the newer ones most often have small gardening sheds with lots of glass for inside plants.

No one in any of the mini-Plainstons lives more than half a mile from its own school-community center and no more than a mile from the City Center. It's no more than two miles from wall to wall, and the longest distance—the diagonal from corner to corner—is under three. If Plainston's podiatrists can prevent fallen arches and cure bunions, everyone should be able to walk any of those distances comfortably.

Without automobiles, banned in 1991—a planned move that coincidentally went into effect during the Mideast OPEC oil crisis that year—Plainston's planners saved a lot of space for housing and parks by having fewer streets and making those only twenty-four feet wide, just wide enough to accommodate necessary two-way truck delivery and garbage trucks as well as police and fire fighting vehicles. A two-lane road circles the inside perimeter of the wall to service light industry and processing plants.

A variety of trees, mostly deciduous, line every street. There are no vacant lots, but there are several large areas labeled Natural Woodland. The abandoned railroad right-of-way is identified as Original Prairie. Not-to-scale drawings of deer, foxes, beavers, and other indigenous creatures, as well as a small group of Indian tepees, are near the limestone quarry in Plainston Southwest. I assumed that these non-urban items are simply there by artistic license, added to give a nostalgic touch to this predominantly modern urban scene.

I'd spent half an hour examining all the details provided by this visual tour of Plainston, portrayed in the full greenness of early summer, when mild hunger pangs reminded me that it was well past dinner time. I took my chances with the Ranch House, which featured vegetarian chili and The Fiddlers Three Times Three. Since last night's bean loaf had been very good, I trusted that meatless chili would be equally palatable. It was.

The Fiddlers were delightful as well. I spent the rest of the evening there. The Ranch House also provided audience chairs around the perimeter since diners were welcome to stay on without being expected to buy more food or drink. I wondered how they could afford to do that with no cover charge and modest prices for the food. I'd discovered another Plainston mystery to solve.

As I was leaving, two hands firmly gripped my shoulders from behind. Turning, I looked into the smiling countenance of a face I recognized—despite the lines around the mouth and at the corners of the eyes and the gray hair at the temples—a face I'd enjoyed seeing almost daily during my early years of teaching at the University of Illinois.

Chapter 5

Nathan

As I struggled to connect a name with the smile, many years matured, he politely forgave my embarrassing memory lapse.

"I don't expect you to recall my name, Professor Kornhauer. After all, you had hundreds of students over the years. I forget the names of some of my current students between classes. I'm the guy you called 'the quiet one.'"

It all came back to me in a rush of delight.

"Nathan Kincade!" I said, giving him a bear hug. "It's good to see you."

"And you," Nathan replied. "I'm guessing you're here to study Plainston and then explain it to the world. If that's the case, they couldn't have chosen better."

"Thank you, but I want to know what has transpired since you left college with your A average and Phi Beta Kappa key. Have you got time for an all-night discussion like we used to have? My room is nearby."

"Nothing would be greater!" Nathan said.

* * *

Settled in comfortable chairs with coffee and blueberry muffins nearby, I first asked Nathan to catch me up on his life since he'd graduated from college.

"Well, you may remember from our talks during the monthly soirees you and Marie hosted for us undergrads that my dad expected me to become a lawyer."

"But, as I remember, you never wanted to pursue the law."

"Right. And it was you who pointed me in a different direction. After four years in your classes, I knew I wanted to teach."

"And did that change of heart get any help from that lovely Italian coed who always sat with you in class? She was already firmly focused on education."

"Well, yes. She was thrilled when I changed my major to secondary education."

"And how did your dad take your decision to abandon law?"

"Sadly, I never told him. He was a heavy smoker and died suddenly from a heart attack shortly after your farewell soiree for us graduates. Fortunately, Mother wasn't at all upset about my change of plans since she'd been a country school teacher before she married Dad."

"Sorry to hear about your father's passing. Did you ever regret making the shift to education? Lots of idealistic new teachers burn out—can't stand the daily grind of the classroom. Where did you end up?"

"Emilia had signed a contract for primary teaching in her hometown district, a south Chicago suburb. There was a social science opening in the junior high, which included grades 7, 8, and 9 in those days."

"And how did that go? I've often heard that middle school kids are the toughest ones to handle."

Nathan paused and shook his head. "Yeah, I burned out in a hurry. I tried my best to use your style of teaching. I kept my lectures short and then broke the kids into groups of four or five to discuss a few central concepts or questions I'd throw out. But I couldn't get it to work, not with classes of thirty or more kids."

Nathan paused again and sighed. "My six classes often totaled about two hundred kids. I had a hard time remembering their names. I knew almost nothing about them personally. Maybe one in ten showed some interest in history or politics or current events, but you can't build a positive class morale on a ten-percent minority of interested kids. At least, I couldn't."

Nathan told this part of his story in a dull, flat voice. I imagined that he was feeling sadness and regret, not only for himself as a failure but for the failure of the whole teaching system.

"Did Emilia have the same problems with her primary children?" I asked.

Nathan beamed. "Not Emilia! Not with primary tots mostly eager to learn and willing to cooperate with any reasonable level of class control. She loved every kid, loved planning creative lessons and getting to know the parents."

He sat back and lapsed into a kind of reverie. I took a chance on changing the subject to satisfy my own curiosity.

"I remember you and Emilia got married soon after you graduated. What I don't know is how you two—?" I paused, trying to phrase tactfully the question that almost everyone who knew Nathan and Emilia had secretly asked each other.

Nathan laughed. "How we got together?" he said, finishing my question. "How did an ordinary-looking, under-sized, un-athletic guy capture the reigning campus beauty?"

"Tell me the story," I said as I refilled our coffee cups.

"All right," Nathan said. "You remember who was voted Most Handsome Man on Campus?"

"Wilber Bickersley," I said. "By the way, he recently warned his readers in one of his syndicated columns that Plainston is hatching a conspiracy to revolutionize the whole world in league with this upstart third party, the FINs."

"I read it," Nathan said in a less than friendly tone. "I always resented Wilber badgering you in class, always raising questions about either your facts or your interpretation of them. Sometimes, he had enough facts and logic of his own to make me question which one of you was on target, but in the end, I always came down on your side, just because I disliked Wilber. His huge ego wouldn't let him admit to ideas superior to his own. Is that my personal bias, or do you agree?

"I do. I usually felt that Wilber was more interested in winning an argument in order to feel superior than in clarifying a complex problem or imagining a better solution. He's made his reputation as a social critic by identifying genuine weaknesses and, in many cases, downright corruption and crime in any institution, public or private."

"That's it! I always felt that Bic—" Nathan paused and grinned. "Remember how he hated for us to call him that? Anyway, I felt Bic was certain he could find plenty of common clay or even some stinking mud under the feet of any popular or respected idol or group."

"And he seemed to be motivated," I said, "not by the desire to help people by exposing corruption but by the desire to look superior himself by bringing others down."

We continued to discuss the clay in this popular figure and somewhat smugly concluded that Wilber Bickersley himself would eventually topple.

Finally, I said, "So much for de-idolizing Wilber. Now continue your story about Emilia. Wilber is involved?"

"He is." Nathan paused before continuing in a lively voice. "You know that Wilbur had excelled in practically everything he undertook in college—pledged the most prestigious fraternity, lettered in four sports, starred in theater productions, was president of his senior classes and editor of the *Daily Illini*. And, of course, he'd dated every desirable girl on campus, save one.

"Your Emilia," I said with a smile.

"Yes and no," Nathan replied. "Emilia, yes, but mine, no. We'd been friends since we met in your Political Science 101 class our freshman year. I fell in love with her immediately, but I knew I was out of her class. I was barely 5'7" on tiptoe with my hair standing on end. Emilia was almost 5'9" barefooted and almost six feet in spike heels."

Nathan smiled. "I could never figure out why she so often found a seat next to me in your classes. I felt lucky to have a platonic relationship with her, which I didn't want to ruin by admitting I was in love with her."

"So how did you break out of the I'm-not-good-enough-for-her trap?"

"I didn't break out of it. Actually, Wilber Bickersley sprung it, quite unintentionally. It was after your last soiree in May. Emilia and I were leaving together as usual, and Wilber followed us. About a block from your house, he came up and pushed himself between us, which was easy to do since we'd never even held hands."

"Unbelievable!" I muttered, shaking my head. "But go on." "Wilber pushed me away—also easy since he was 6'4" and about 200 pounds of muscle, and I was barely 130 pounds. He put an arm around Emilia's waist and said something like, 'Hey, your prince charming has had enough of this brushoff. It's high time you and I get together and do what we beautiful people are designed to do. Now get rid of this runty twerp.'"

Nathan stopped and took a deep breath.

"He tried to kiss her, but she swung a left punch into his eye and scratched his face. 'You filthy bastard! How dare you call the man I love a twerp!' she screamed."

Nathan smiled before continuing the story.

"They stood facing each other, Emilia rigid with both fists clenched and Wilber wiping the blood off his face and smirking. He finally said very dramatically, 'Now that, my lovely, is the kind of fighting spirit I like in a woman. And I know from experience that it's always the sign of love boiling over.' With that, he started toward her with both arms outstretched.

"You probably remember that Emilia was actually the first generation American daughter of a poor immigrant Italian family. Her father was a common laborer in a slaughter house, and her mother was a housemaid, so Emilia had the strength of the working poor. She'd lettered in soccer and taken the university's required self-protection course, so when Wilber got within striking distance, Emilia delivered one of her famed soccer-goal kicks to his groin!"

At that point, my grin was as wide as Nathan's.

"The mighty Bickersley fell to his knees, groaning. Emilia grabbed a handful of his hair and jerked his head up. Then in a calm but icy voice I've heard only that once, she said, 'Wilber Bickersley, you detestable scum, there will never be anything even remotely consensual between us.'

"Wilber was in too much pain to make any response. We just walked away, leaving him moaning and immobilized."

Nathan sat back, looking dreamily at his now cold coffee.

Urging him to finish the story, I said, "So hearing Emilia tell Wilber that you were the man she loved is what sprung that trap you'd set for yourself. I wonder why she hadn't told you herself since she showed no reluctance in telling Wilber."

"Of course, I was asking myself the same question, so I said, 'If you meant that—that you love me—why didn't you tell me a long time ago?' And she, of course, asked me the counter question, 'Do you love me?' and when I said I did, she wanted to know why I'd never told her. So I gave her my 'not in your league—too short, too unmanly, too plain looking' answer. To that, she responded that she felt she wasn't in my league, I being brilliant and the only heir to what she thought was a family fortune. My dad had inherited some good farmland, which by Italian peasant standards seemed to be a gold mine. She hadn't wanted to end our friendship by injecting any hint that she was after me for economic security."

Nathan lapsed into a pleasant reverie, then added, "Thirty years of marriage, two sons, and a two-year-old granddaughter haven't dimmed the mystery of love."

"That's a beautiful story, Nathan. Now I want to know if you're here to explore and explain Plainston as I am."

"Your assumption is correct. I've tried to achieve what you repeatedly described as the necessary approach of a political scientist. Remember what you told us?"

"As I remember, I probably opined that not just political scientists but all conscientious, responsible citizens should keep an open mind and a warm heart but, at the same time, maintain a kind of optimistic skepticism—and not be taken in too quickly by too-rosy promises or too-dire predictions of failure."

"That's it," he said. "But how can people with that mind-and-heart set get their values translated into political action?"

"I wish I knew, Nathan. But maybe this real-life Plainston experiment—although I doubt if they think of it as an experiment—has some of the answers. That's what this outside observer project hopes to discover. Would you like to take on the assignment?"

"Not as the principal investigator because I don't have the prestige for that, but I've gotten interested lately in Utopian literature, which, on one hand, is pretty dreary in terms of mostly unrealistic, pie-in-the-sky proposals and equally unrealistic actual efforts to set up ideal communities. But what is heartening is that as far back as we have recorded literature, people have dreamed of ways to change society so everyone is happy, fulfilled, and well-behaved. Of course, cynics pooh-pooh such dreaming of perfection. They call any proposal for really radical change in any institution 'Utopian' so that when it arrives at the seats of power and in the court of public opinion, it is already labeled for likely failure."

Even though I was unacquainted with much of the Utopian literature, I accepted Nathan's take on the subject.

He continued. "Don't you feel you may risk your professional reputation if you take on this assignment, especially if your open-minded, warm-hearted political science approach finds it appealing? Wilber Bickersley is already committed to clay-footing any great good you may find in Plainston."

I appreciated Nathan's genuine concern for my reputation. I could sincerely reassure him I was willing to risk it.

"Reputation is what you get by doing your job, not by trying to protect it. If you feel your job is to take on something risky that may have positive results—or may not—doing it is a scientist's ethical and moral responsibility. I've never actually done anything risky in my professional life. I think it might be stimulating. Anyway, I will 'live Plainston' for a year or so before I publish any account, so Wilber will be wrestling with an unseen but not unknown adversary."

That seemed to reassure Nathan. We sat without speaking for a short time.

Then he said, "Now feel free to say no to this proposal, but I'd love to be in on this investigation. Since I gave up public school teaching years ago, I've been on the faculty of a small liberal arts college. What I have in mind is this. You say you're not familiar with the Utopian literature. I am since it's been my main intellectual hobby the past several years. Why don't you send me notes on your Plainston experiences, and I'll compare what Plainston is doing with what's been both theoretically proposed and actually practiced over the ages. Actually, that's why I came here—to see about studying Plainston as a Utopia, but I can't get away long enough to do what needs to be done. I'd like to 'live Plainston' through you."

His proposal delighted me. We talked over the details for quite a while.

Then Nathan looked at his watch and gasped, "I've got to catch the bus to the airport in less than an hour! Here's my card with my e-mail address."

We reached out to shake hands but ended up hugging to seal the deal.

Chapter 6

Body and Soul

Plainston's Russian choir was regularly scheduled for the one o'clock service on Wednesdays at the Temple. On my trips to the Soviet Union, I'd always managed to attend cathedral services that featured a Russian choir. I'd also heard the Soviet Army Chorus and Band on several of their American tours. No other music, choral or instrumental, had a more moving quality, which, I believed, came from the spirituality of their unique cultural history.

At the Temple, I was in for a surprise. From the opening bars of the first anthem, I was transported to a cathedral in Leningrad or Moscow or Kiev. The chorus of over sixty voices was accompanied by an authentic Russian orchestra, replete with accordions and balalaikas. The unamplified acoustics were perfect.

The domed sanctuary, seating about two thousand, was nearly filled. An atmosphere of reverence for the music filled the Temple as colorful pictures were splashed across a huge screen—pictures of Russian cathedrals and religious processions, of the Russian country side, of its mountains, lakes, and rivers. The combination of lovely sights and sounds calmed and uplifted my spirits.

The service lasted only an hour, leaving me another hour to invest before my three o'clock appointment with the podiatrist. I wandered south along Sugar Creek to a wooded area of several acres. A rock wall lined the river bank. I brushed snow off the top and leaned on it, watching snowflakes melt into the river where water flowed out from under the ice over a little outcropping of rocks.

I was impressed again with the natural quiet of this place. There I was, close to the center of a city of more than fifty thousand souls, and yet there were no city sounds. I could've been halfway to Hudson Bay, alone in the Canadian wilderness—except that something was fumbling at a pocket in my heavy jacket.

Turning to confront the pickpocket, I looked into the innocent face of a doe with her fawn at her side. I stepped back, but the doe and fawn fearlessly advanced, the mother deer again nuzzling at my jacket pocket. I stood my ground, apologizing for my barren pockets. Seeming to understand, they lingered as I stroked their wintry fur.

They followed me beyond the edge of their little forest home, still suspicious, I guessed, that I might yet have a hidden goodie in my pocket. They stopped when I reached the street leading to Health Services, which was located on the edge of the university campus.

It was a beautifully designed structure, built of limestone from the Plainston quarry. There wasn't a touch of the unadorned glass-and-steel cubicity of the late 20th century commercial architecture. The building looked solid but friendly and inviting.

An elderly receptionist directed me to Podiatry, 5th floor.

There, the receptionist said with a smile, "Down the hall, third door on your left, Mr. Kornhauer. Dr. Luster is expecting you. She'll be joined by Dr. James and Dr. Walsh for the intake interview."

I wondered if it was a bad sign that three doctors weren't busy or behind schedule. And three doctors to examine just a pair of bunions! At $250 an hour for each one, the current rate for office calls in Washington, D.C., I was already well over my GBO medical insurance allowance. This wasn't good.

Moments later, Dr. Elizabeth Luster entered—a smiling, middle-aged black lady, wearing not a white coat but an attractive long-sleeved blue dress. She wasn't whom I'd expected to meet since she looked as little like a doctor as Lydia had looked like a judge.

Somewhat ill at ease, I opened the conversation with small talk about my deer encounter. "What do you Plainstans carry in your pockets to defend yourselves from being accosted by does and fawns?"

Laughing, she opened a drawer and pulled out a little bag of greenish pellets. "Here. All deer lovers carry a handful of these alfalfa tablets. Even though we regularly feed our deer plenty of alfalfa hay and grain, they've developed a taste for the concentrated version, and people spoil them by indulging their addiction. You can buy these little bags almost everywhere."

Dr. Cecilia James, a young white female, and Dr. Robert Walsh, an elderly white gentleman, had joined us by then. Only he wore a white coat. They all sat in comfortable, upholstered chairs without notebooks in hand. Looking up, I spotted the ubiquitous video camera pointed at me. They noticed my glance.

Dr. James said, "Cameras are standard operating procedure here. They allow us to give our full attention to our patients. No two of us take exact notes, and we can't always read what we do take. The video replay settles any questions we may have, but if you'd rather we not use the camera, we'll douse it and get out our note pads."

I thanked her for the explanation and accepted the use of the camera, but before the doctors began to ask questions, I felt the need to discuss the cost of this triple consultation. All three smiled.

"You're new here, so you haven't learned that in Plainston you often get three for the price of one," Dr. Luster said. "We three likely live better in Plainston on one-third of what your doctor earns in Washington."

"We get along quite well without owning a Mercedes or a BMW just like everyone else in Plainston," Dr. Walsh added with a benign smile.

Reassured, I relaxed and surveyed the room which looked a lot more like a living room than a doctor's office.

As if reading my mind, Dr. Luster said, "Most of our patients from the outside miss the usual wall display of our professional credentials. We prefer to hang art on our walls. We keep our credentials in binders. Here are mine."

She handed me a leather binder in which I found a collection of documents and diplomas. I felt like a fool, but when I tried to apologize, Dr. Walsh assured me that questioning their competence was a sign of good mental health.

"We welcome patients who challenge us. The passive patients expect some kind of healing power to flow from us to them—somewhat like the old idea that kids learn by having teachers and text books pour knowledge into their empty little heads. So please ask questions about anything at any time."

After I promised to do so, Dr. Luster punned, "So, shall we now get down to the business afoot?"

Her colleagues and I groaned.

For the next fifteen minutes, they asked me about my life in general. Then when I removed my shoes and socks to expose my ample bunions, all three doctors sounded both sympathetic and encouraging. They took plaster casts of my feet from which an expert Plainston shoemaker would fashion a pair of soft leather shoes. They gave me a bunion massage gadget, which they assured me was superior to the one Lydia had given me, and recommended special exercises. The ultimate cure, however, if I wished for more than just relief, would be gradual surgery. They also suggested ice-skating as an excellent therapy.

"You are assuming I can ice-skate and even like to skate," I said, "or did Mrs. Gray forward that bit of personal information?"

"She did. She thinks that without bunion pain, you'll be a fine skater," said Dr. Luster.

"And did she also suggest that Health Services take off my extra pounds to get me in shape for more vigorous skating?" I asked, partly in jest but also partly from annoyance at Mrs. Gray taking my private life in hand.

Dr. Walsh laughed. "Lydia is always genuinely concerned about our guests' health, and she's so certain that we can make any specimen of humanity into a perfectly functioning organism she recommends us to everyone."

"Incidentally, her special concern about your feet," Dr. James added, "is partly due to our success with her late husband, Don, and we've made considerable advances since we treated him years ago."

In the end, I had no reason not to sign up for the full treatment, which would likely take not over six months, depending partly on how well I cooperated. Urging me to get a complete work-up and a total exercise and diet program, they were pleased to make the necessary appointments for "the works" the following day.

Before I left, Elizabeth—we'd moved to a first-name basis quickly—gave me a ten-minute hand massage on each foot and showed me how to manipulate the new foot massager to simulate her manual massage. Then she gave me a video disk of exercises that were in effect dance steps, set to music. We danced around in our bare feet for another ten or fifteen minutes as she taught me the basic steps. Finally, she performed a bit of laser surgery, which in a few seconds took off a fraction of a millimeter slice of bone—an entirely painless procedure.

It was after five o'clock when I left Health Services, carrying the video disk and a newer twelve-pound model of the foot massager.

Once back in my room, I spent the evening learning to give myself a massage and practicing the dancercises. I probably overdid it all, but when I retired, I was convinced that my feet were in good hands.

*   *   *

At two o'clock on Thursday, a two-doctor team spent well over an hour getting my sixty-five-year life history—on video, of course. They put me through some ingenious calisthenics while measuring various responses. They seemed to be enjoying their work, done unhurriedly and with full explanation of the what and the why of it all. I received my results immediately since my performance data were fed directly into their computers.

"You're in pretty good shape for a sedentary Pagan," said Dr. Julia Chen.

I decided it was time to challenge this Pagan label, which I'd been called several times. Even though the tone had been light and good-humored, I thought it worth a question or two.

"What exactly makes me a Pagan?" I asked with a frown.

"Oh, sorry," Dr. Chen said apologetically. "You seem already to be so much a part of us that I forgot not to use our in-house idiom. Pagans are un-believers, and most of our visitors don't really believe in or understand Plainston—what it stands for and what we're trying to accomplish. So Pagan has become our shorthand for most outsiders. I hope you can believe, however, that we do love our Pagans."

She delivered this little homily with a light touch that I found moving.

"I will wear my Pagan badge humbly, knowing now that it is bestowed with love, and I will wait patiently for the light of truth to dawn," I said, hoping they'd appreciate my feeble but sincere attempt to match her light tone.

*   *   *

I met the podiatry team on Friday for a trial fitting of my new shoes, which felt wonderful. Pleased with their fit, the shoemaker said both my shoes and my skates would be ready Monday afternoon. All this left me wondering how these people could work so fast. One would think they had no other patients.

Dr. Walsh did the laser surgery on Friday.

"We'll take off a little wider slice this time," he explained. "Actually, we need not directly reduce your bunions much, unless you want to do so for aesthetic reasons. Your pain is mostly from what years of tight-fitting shoes and bunions together have done to the basic structure of your feet. If you faithfully follow the exercise program, that should solve your problems."

*   *   *

For the next couple of days, I massaged my feet on a regular schedule, danced around in my bare feet, and ate only prescribed food, much of which I bought fresh and prepared myself.

Waiting around for my new shoes and custom-fitted skates to be delivered at my appointment with Dr. Elizabeth on Monday was like being a kid who knew he was getting his first bicycle but who had to wait until his birthday to get it—and had to be a very good boy in the meantime.

When Monday finally arrived, I tried on the new shoes. Such comfort I'd never felt before. The shoes seemed not to touch my bunions due to a cushioning layer of synthetic material. Padded inserts on the insoles gently pushed the various bones into their proper positions and kept them there. Altogether, I had foot comfort I hadn't known since going barefooted in my childhood days.

With hope, tinged with a bit of doubt, I walked pain-free to Mill Pond on Tuesday. A small horse-drawn snowplow had opened paths through the foot deep layer of snow. Skaters had a mile or more of five-foot wide paths of pristine smooth ice to skate on—concentric circles with intersecting paths across them.

*   *   *

Blessed be advanced podiatry! I continued an hour of skating daily for the next two weeks. The pond stayed safely frozen, but for variety, I also skated once in Plainston's year-round indoor ice rink.

I worked steadily toward making my dream of skating pain-free with Lydia come true. I found myself counting the days until she'd return.

Chapter 7

Wilber

One night in early February, as I was leaving the Beanery, a voice behind me said, "Kiki, I'm so glad I've found you."

I turned to face another former student from my early university teaching days, Wilber Bickersley—all six feet four of him, disheveled yet still handsome.

"I knew you were in town. We've got to talk."

It wasn't an invitation; it was a command—a command from someone that I'd never liked but someone that I'd once admired in a limited way. That admiration, however, had waned in recent years. As Nathan and I had discussed just a few weeks before, Wilber's forte was unearthing the clay in the feet of any individual or institution or governing body—and he was good at that. But he seemed to be unwilling to go a step beyond finding the bad to suggesting ways to improve our society. He was also quite closed-minded to any suggestions made by others, and his ego was fed by all the attention he'd received over the years. For Wilber, being right was first and foremost, and at this stage in his life, he was convinced that he was right all the time.

"And why must we talk?" I said, trying to hide my annoyance.

"I have to get out of town."

"That sounds like a line from a bad Western," I said.

Ignoring my attempt at humor, he continued, "I came here several weeks ago for the same reason you did, and I was just getting a good start with my investigations when I met this art teacher a couple of days ago at a restaurant where some of her students were hanging their paintings. I was impressed with their work. After we talked a while, she invited me to her teaching studio, which is part of her apartment, to see more of her students' work. Well, when I saw this almost life-sized painting of this lovely lady in just a bit of clothing, I assumed it was an artistic come-on and acted accordingly, if you know what I mean."

I was quite sure I knew what he meant, but I said nothing, and he went on with his story.

"Well, she later claimed that I'd tried to assault her. I was arrested, but two days later, a hearing officer—with that artist woman's consent—agreed not to file assault changes if I'd leave town by midnight tonight. My pass has been lifted, so I'm very soon to be out of this crazy place!"

This echoed both what Nathan had told me about Wilber's behavior with Emilia years ago and the same high-handed legal treatment of an outsider that I'd witnessed with the Prairie Grove trespassers. Only this time, he was being kicked out rather than roped into community service.

"So what does this have to do with me?"

"We need to talk somewhere that's not bugged so that I can tell you all that I've learned. Let's go back inside the Beanery where the music will cover up what we say. I don't want you to be duped like I was in the beginning."

With some reluctance—and just a bit of curiosity—I followed Wilber to a table which seemed to suit him near the exit in the talking section. I was torn between wanting nothing to do with Wilber Bickersley and wanting to hear him out. After all, he'd established a reputation for digging into questionable activities, especially those of a conspiratorial nature.

"All right, what's so important?"

Without preliminary comments, Wilber began to unload his major findings and his interpretations of their meanings. He repeatedly apologized for having to say "I think" and "probably."

"Dammit, I was just about to pin these things down for sure, but now I can't get the facts firsthand. And that's why you've got to help me expose this thing."

I didn't swear allegiance to his cause, but I decided to let him talk. I even jotted down some notes. Conspiracy was the dominant theme in what Wilber was saying.

"They've got an unbelievably widespread and efficient national and international organization of real fanatics who will do anything to spread the Plainston plague."

I didn't stop Wilber to ask him to define his terms, such as *plague*, but it was apparent that I was in for a lecture full of loaded, emotionally charged words.

He then blasted the Plainston connection to the Future Is Now political party, claiming that FIN members are the political front for Plainston.

Next on his list to attack was Health Services, especially their connection with Native American medicine men and their information about the use of herbs. He said, "They can put stuff in medicines that will affect how people think and feel—mind and mood altering drugs that keep people so quiet and obedient."

That attitude continued to appear in his comments about Plainston having its own water system and growing much of its own food. Control food and water and thus control behavior was Wilber's reasoning.

Wilber did have some good words for the education system which admittedly turns out a lot of very bright kids, but he seemed to see even that as part of the conspiracy.

"They start these kids in child development centers so that the school is the dominant influence during those critical years. But the worst part is that the kids who do escape these walls and get good educations on the outside come trotting right back here to waste their most productive years rather than achieving fame and fortune on the outside. Then lots of them leave when they are middle aged to work in centers on the outside which are like malignant tumors growing all over the country."

Then Wilber launched into the charge that some people who'd come to Plainston had just disappeared—"probably not killed but imprisoned in some way," he said. "I was just about to find a man you knew from your university days years ago—Lancelot Lewellyn. Remember him?"

I did. He had a nickname related to his initials similar to mine—"LL," he was called. Our paths had crossed at various conferences since he was a professor of political science as was I. He'd also written some books about national politics. I didn't realize that LL had gone to Plainston.

"I've found out that he is still here but totally incapacitated in some way. You need to investigate, Kiki. Something is wrong with a man being kept in a vegetative state. I'm guessing they are using him as a human guinea pig to test some sort of herbal witchcraft or some drugs. Whatever it is, it's not right."

Wilber wasn't quite done even though midnight was approaching.

"You know that they control the media here with a television station and several radio stations. The *Gazette* is tax supported and provided free to everyone. There are national papers in the library and other stations available, but most people use the ones from here.

"And here's a really scary item. Every morning about 7 a.m., there's a special broadcast on the television station that gives the elite of the city their marching orders for the day. Since it's in code, they have a special gadget on their sets that translates it for them, making sure that they hear just what Big Brother wants them to hear."

Who this—or these—Big Brothers might be clearly disturbed Wilber. There was an elected government which he felt was the front for the unknown real power in Plainston. There was no City Hall or mayor's office—just a council of eighteen members, three from each section of the city, with a chairman who ran the open, informal meetings every other Thursday evening, moving from school to school. Wilber was convinced that there was an unknown power behind this simple government.

After a final attack on religion and the Temple where all religions are respected—"very unnatural," he said—Wilber begged me to continue his research, assuming that my findings would support his.

"Find Plainston's brain center, Kiki, and we can save the world!"

The prospect of saving the world in league with Wilber Bickersley didn't thrill me. Seemingly aware of my reluctance, he added a few more comments to strengthen his conspiracy theory.

"I'm guessing that you were welcomed to Plainston as I was with a meeting with Lydia Colby Gray at the admissions building. Then you went happily to some place to eat. Lydia invited you to breakfast the next morning. And you played piano duets."

"I suppose you played primo," I said, trying to hide my irritation. I couldn't imagine Wilber playing second to anyone.

Ignoring the interruption, Wilber went on. "Did you ice-skate or swim or hike afterwards? Did she refer you to Health Services? I confessed to high blood pressure."

Wilber couldn't have dragged the word *bunions* out of me if he'd had me on a rack with my feet to the fire. But he knew he'd hit a nerve.

Before he could punch any more holes in my view of Plainston and Lydia Gray, I looked at my watch and said, "You'd best be getting out of town or your carriage will turn into a pumpkin."

I wondered if my weak attempt at humor would cover up the boiling emotions I was feeling. I desperately wanted out of the same room Wilber was in. Finally, he stood, wished me well, and left. I didn't return the sentiment.

Minutes later, I left the restaurant with a heavy heart, wondering if all I'd felt about Lydia was a sham. At least, he hadn't mentioned any hugs.

Despite all my conflicting feelings, that night I dreamed of skating without any foot pain—with Lydia.

Chapter 8

One Who "Disappeared"

As I settled into my routine in Plainston, one particular item on Wilber's conspiracy list kept gnawing at me. At the airport café, Bob, the manager, had mentioned the same thing—people who'd gone to Plainston and then disappeared. I decided to find Lancelot Lewellyn.

At the university library, I got his basic biographical information: his birth date, parents, education, long-term employment at the university, publications, and so forth. He'd never married, and no siblings were listed. The most recent article I could find indicated that he'd taken his sabbatical leave to study Plainston, "hoping to either disprove or prove conclusively the rumors that have surrounded that small city for decades," he'd written.

That had been about three and a half years ago. I found no later updates about Lancelot Lewellyn.

When I approached one of the librarians about more current information, she assured me that Professor Lewellyn was indeed still in Plainston and that he would enjoy having a visit, despite his failing physical condition.

"His mind is sharp, but he can barely utter a clear word," she said. "The kids will help you communicate with him. He's in the Alumni Center South which is attached to the school there."

I walked to that Alumni Center, which is a euphemism, I'd read, for a senior citizens' center—Plainston being their Alma Mater. I expected to find LL sitting in a wheelchair surrounded by other incapacitated elderly, all vacantly watching television. However, that wasn't what I saw. Some of the residents were hunched over chess and checker boards; others were knitting; several men and women were skillfully carving comical little figurines, such as those which decorated my hotel room. Several children looked on, talking about the whittling and asking questions. There were three wheelchair occupants being read to by young children from the school which was connected to the Alumni Center by a covered walkway. No uniformed nurses or other caretakers were visible. The upbeat atmosphere was that of a lively social club.

I introduced myself to an elderly lady sitting alone and asked about LL.

"Oh, yes," she answered brightly, "LL spends most of his time over at the school library. Give him all the time you can spare. He loves visitors."

I spotted LL as soon as I entered the library. He was sitting in a wheelchair, dressed in a light-blue shirt, a matching tie, and a tan corduroy sports jacket. He was a rather small, spare man with sharp features, a high forehead, and thinning hair. Though his head drooped to one side, his eyes were very bright and squinting intently as he listened to a slight girl with dark braids who was reading to him. Three other children, all about eight or nine, I guessed, surrounded him.

An older boy, about twelve, with a dark complexion and features suggesting some Native American genes, came over and stood beside me, facing LL.

"I'm Roger Thorton," he said. "I help with interviews."

"Hello," I said. "I'm Karl Kornhauer, called Kiki, of the Global Betterment Organization. Professor Lewellyn and I met years ago at—"

I stopped speaking as LL raised his eyes to meet mine. A hint of a smile crossed his face.

"He remembers you, Mr. Kornhauer, and he's very glad to see you. He knew you were in town and was hoping you'd visit us. But before we visit, he thinks it's best if you see the video he made. It'll answer a lot of questions he now has trouble answering himself."

Why wasn't I surprised—being offered a video to explain something in Plainston.

Roger and I went to a little soundproof cubicle on the other side of the library with a disk Roger had gotten from the front desk. In seconds, I was seeing and listening to a younger-looking Lancelot Lewellyn. And for the next fifteen minutes or so, he explained the last several years of his life.

It was true that he'd originally come to investigate this walled city, but he'd also come for another reason he'd shared with no one when he left the university. He'd begun to have some disturbing physical symptoms the months before he was to take his sabbatical—stiffness in his legs when he walked and trouble forming words clearly. Using the internet, he'd found what he feared, amyotrophic lateral sclerosis, Lou Gehrig's disease. Saying nothing to anyone at the university, he'd left for Plainston.

Once there, he'd begun to "live Plainston," finding it a place of peace and tranquility. When his symptoms worsened, he went to Health Services for confirmation of ALS. With the help of the medical personnel there, he'd made decisions about the rest of his life, which he knew would be limited since most ALS patients lived for between three to five years after diagnosis.

LL ended the video lightly with the assurance that no one had kidnapped him; no one was forcing him to stay on the "inside." He'd notified the university that he'd be retiring, due to health reasons, instead of returning after his sabbatical. He'd chosen to divulge no details. LL wanted to live with caring people, he said, who'd keep his life private as he degenerated into a being who'd likely lose his ability to speak, who'd likely drool and gag and struggle to breathe towards the end. He wanted to keep up with the world without the world keeping up with him.

After the video ended, Roger explained how several students his age had learned to understand what LL said when most others couldn't—a combination of listening carefully and knowing what LL's interests were. Younger children read to him every day—sometimes what he was interested in and sometimes material the kids were interested in. All knew that one day soon, he wouldn't be able to sit in a wheelchair since his muscles were deteriorating rapidly. He'd already lived almost four years since he'd noticed the first symptoms of ALS.

When Roger and I returned to the little circle of readers, space was made for me. I saw the hint of a smile again as I began to talk to LL. I explained that I'd also come to "live Plainston." Roger said that LL approved. When I mentioned my conversation with Wilber Bickersley, even I could read a change in LL's face, one showing disapproval. LL looked toward Roger who leaned in close as LL made whispering sounds.

"He wants you to have access to the material he gathered before he was confined to a wheelchair and could no longer leave the Alumni Center or the school."

I smiled broadly and thanked him. Then I explained what I'd learned about Plainston so far in response to the many questions the kids asked me.

It was well past noon when a young woman appeared and said that LL was due back at the Alumni Center. I'd heard no bells; no students had left our circle for lunch or another class. Now they rose, replaced their chairs around nearby tables, shook hands with me, and left as LL was wheeled from the library.

Roger said, "Please come back. He'll be very interested in your reactions to Plainston—all of us will be."

*   *   *

Back at the university library, I asked to see LL's material. It was rich in details. Now I had two outside sources to include in my assessment—Nathan's information about Utopian experiments and LL's comprehensive work, which described how Plainston was so different from other cities of its size—or any size, for that matter—and Plainston was truly different in many ways.

LL began his paper with Plainston's "no growth" policies. The idea of non-growth is certainly foreign to most other towns and cities, but the early Plainstans had decided what was enough growth to encourage diversity and some degree of self-sufficiency and yet keep the city small enough for the quality of life they wished to achieve—thus the 40,000 full-time residential population limit with another 10,000 or so, like me, coming and going for such reasons as to visit, to receive medical treatment, to study the city, to attend the university, and to attend Temple services.

An even more unusual policy is having no cars inside the city walls. As LL wrote, "In order to have a city of about 50,000 souls to function without personal vehicles, it must be compact enough to allow for walking and bicycling as the primary ways of getting from place to place. As more and more people came to Plainston in the early days, Plainstans decided to build up rather than out—thus the high-rises around the center of the city and the apartment complexes scattered throughout the city. Beyond these complexes are single family dwellings for those who wish the more traditional styles of homes. However, without the need for garages and streets wide enough for parking, these cozy neighborhoods take up lots less space than the same number of homes in traditional cities."

Throughout the city are all sorts of green spaces—small parks with playground equipment, basketball and tennis courts, flower gardens, community garden plots for those residents of high rises who still want to exercise their green thumbs. The city is full of all sorts of trees.

LL described the effect as follows: "Deciduous trees such as maples, oaks, and walnuts color the fall landscape with all shades of yellow, gold, orange, red, and rust; spring flowering trees, such as redbuds, crab apples, and Bradford pears, add white, lavender, pink, and rose to the new green of spring. Lilacs and honeysuckle add wonderful smells."

Almost all the landscaping and care of the city is done by volunteers— mostly by people in their own neighborhoods with those in the high rises and apartment complexes volunteering as desired.

The lack of cars also changes the smell of the city. In addition, it means no gas stations except near the gates where people can either keep their own vehicles or rent the ones there. The streets are just wide enough to allow for two vehicles to pass—the rare fire engine, garbage trucks, or a moving truck, for instance.

LL wrote, "Since there are days when no vehicles venture down some streets, they are filled with kids and adults on bikes, skateboards, and roller skates. As I buzzed around the city in the little electric car I rented that first summer, I witnessed many times whole blocks closed off for a neighborhood cookout or a dance—with live music, of course. How wonderful to see so many enjoying the out-of-doors under the stars and a full moon, dancing to a jazz band."

All the walking and outdoor activity help explain another Plainston difference—the overall good health and fitness of its citizens. When LL had first gone to Health Services, he was somewhat taken aback by the few people in the waiting rooms and his visits with two, often three, doctors at a time—the same experience as I'd had. The explanation is basically a simple one. Healthy people don't need to see doctors often. The focus at Health

Services is on prevention and education. If people don't smoke—and almost no one is Plainston does—lots of ill health is avoided. If people maintain healthy weights and eat well, the threat of a whole host of physical problems disappears. If people know how to take care of themselves when they do get colds, trips to see a doctor become unnecessary. When people do have problems, affordable health care is readily available and thus treatment is started early enough to prevent some complications associated with delayed treatment. It was as simple as that.

The other factor that makes the city work is its division into six areas—South, Southwest, Southeast, North, Northwest, and Northeast. Each of these residential areas has a large school for pre-school through high school students with an Alumni Center for the elderly attached. The schools act as community centers with buildings open often for sixteen to eighteen hours a day almost all year round. Most kids are there from eight a.m. to four p.m. nine or ten or eleven months a year. The Plainston schools meet state requirements, just not in the same ways as most other schools with opening and closing dates, exact hours for attendance for all the student population, and so forth. All kids walk or bike to school.

The schools are designed to mix all ages and ability levels with lots of flexibility. The rooms are large centers, each for a different discipline—basic education, language arts, science, math, social studies, art, and music. Each school has a cafeteria area, a gym, and a library. There are no bells, no lines of children going from place to place, no rows of desks or tables, no teachers' desks in front, no report cards sent home every four to six weeks, no promotion from grade to grade.

"In other words," LL wrote, "the schools are completely different from everything most of us know about public schools. The Plainston schools are beehives of activity with kids and adults all over the place. The outcome is now several generations of very bright, very disciplined, very well-educated teens who usually go to college and then succeed in whatever they choose to accomplish."

By the time LL got to the schools, his disease had weakened him to the point where he could no longer write or type. Since he knew his time was limited, he decided to simply enjoy Plainston for whatever time he had left. He ended his description with the following words:

I will no longer attempt to explain Plainston; instead, I will simply 'live it' in all its delightful manifestations. I will go to Temple as long as I am able to sit erect to bask in its beauty, to hear the music, and to listen to the words of love and truth from many different religions. I will not try to figure out why the children who read to me every day are so delightful, so helpful, so caring; I will only enjoy that they are the way they are. I will keep in touch with the doctors at Health Services as my condition worsens, knowing that I will be cared for with compassion.

In other words, I will enjoy this wonderful city and let you others who come to study it try to figure out what has made it this way. If this is a conspiracy, let it win out! I can't imagine how the beauty and peace of this city wouldn't be welcomed wherever its ideals take root.

This is my farewell to academia and to all who know me. LL

*   *   *

I read and reread LL's description of Plainston, which I've only briefly summarized here. Two mornings later, I returned to the school library to tell LL what I intended to do as I "lived Plainston." And that was to try to answer the question of why Plainston was so different. He'd clearly and succinctly explained how Plainston was different, but he hadn't worked on the why. In other words, he'd described the fruit. I would try to identify the roots.

LL was delighted at my response to his work—incomplete as it was. He said, with Roger as the interpreter again, that he fully supported my plan to go for the roots, which was what he'd intended to do when he'd first planned to use his sabbatical to study Plainston—before ALS changed his life and his plans.

I also explained to LL that I wanted to figure out if the "conspiracy" label fit what was going on in Plainston—a topic neither Nathan nor LL had addressed. In doing so, I'd check out Plainston's connection with the FINs, which Wilber had identified as the most threatening aspect of what he'd labeled as a conspiracy.

Again, LL indicated approval of my plan.

As I left the school, I wondered if maybe I could work with Lydia as I sensed she was getting deeply involved in politics since she'd been "living Plainston" her entire life. I relished the prospect of doing some broad-scale political research myself, hopefully with Lydia's help, in the inadequately studied and under-appreciated field of third-party politics.

I began to feel like an old, retired fire-wagon horse which had been re-harnessed for duty.

Now if only Lydia would get back to Plainston.

Chapter 9

The Temple

Lydia mailed me several short letters—three, to be exact—while she was away. The last said her return date to Plainston was indefinite due to her son's family having been stricken with a new strain of influenza—a vicious bug first identified in northern Saskatchewan. She was afraid she might come down with it, but she was more concerned about bringing the flu back to Plainston.

"There are things our beloved walls can't keep out," she wrote, "but stay inside them nonetheless. Don't expose yourself."

Her phrase "beloved walls" made me wonder if it was healthy to love walls—to fear going outside them—to look to walls to protect one from the world's dangers. My first impression, however, was that Plainstans didn't seem to be fear-ridden folk, but would that impression be the same once I got below a surface relationship with any of them?

*   *   *

Correcting my foot problems had dominated my activities during the final weeks of January and the first ones of February—weekly office calls plus my foot massaging, dancercising in my room, and two hours of walking and skating. I always carried deer pellets when I walked and often returned to the same spot of my first deer encounter, but they failed to renew our acquaintance. I saw a fox once and several deer, but none approached me.

Between bunion relief activities, I leisurely sampled more of Plainston's cultural and recreational offerings. Of the latter, I tried roller skating as my bunion pain decreased. I swam often in the heated Olympic-sized indoor pool at the university, which adults shared with the students at specific times during the day and evening.

I also found myself drawn more and more to the Temple. Soft lighting filtered through beautiful stained glass windows, which had been made by an Italian expert who'd settled in Plainston after World War II.

A dramatic encircling mural in muted colors traced humankind's gradual development of the religious mind and spirit—from cave people's drawings, believed to have had worshipful significance, to portrayals of modern religious crusades for social justice. Images of positive accomplishments and religious inspiration were shown above an indistinct line: humanitarian campaigns to improve prisons and insane asylums, the abolition of slavery movement, the formation of the Red Cross, the elimination of child labor, and the civil rights marches and triumphs of the 20th century. Below it, the dark side of religious fanaticism was graphically depicted: cannibalism, human sacrifice, holy wars, the Inquisition, the burning of heretics and witches, imperialism that traded Christianity for land and resources, and slavery upheld by theological rationale. Beautiful cathedrals and shrines above the line, torture chambers below it. Humankind striving upward toward peace and justice and equality and love above the line, humankind sinking into savagery and exploitation and materialism and prejudice below.

Although dedicated to all religions, the designers had agreed not to show representations of religious founders. There was no Hindu avatar, no Moses descending Mt. Sinai with the Ten Commandments in hand, no meditating Buddha, no manger scene nor Jesus preaching nor Christ on the cross, no Muhammad fleeing Mecca. The mural emphasized religion in action—how followers turned their leaders' exhortations and examples into everyday life. All services were devoted to that concept.

Theological, philosophical, and psychological interpretations of the contradictory human tendencies shown in the mural—to reach for the heavens yet to sink to hellish behavior—were left to the ministers of the various denominations scattered throughout Plainston. The Temple area itself, covering about twenty acres, included several chapels and study rooms provided by the major religions and some of their denominations. Any religious group not large enough to need its own sanctuary was allowed free use of the school facilities and other public meeting rooms for services and social activities.

The larger churches with congregations of several hundred or more active members took turns providing programs at the Temple on a regularly scheduled basis. Some churches specialized in religious drama, some in dance, and some in a kind of coordinated musical-visual program like the one I'd first experienced with the Russian choir, which was sponsored by an interfaith group. All Temple services and programs, which were supported by contributions, were video-recorded on high fidelity discs available to everyone.

The outpouring of optimism that had ushered in the 21st century had included passionate appeals for our nation to return to God and to reestablish our roots in the faith of our fathers. Plainstans, in designing their Temple, had included the faiths of the fathers worldwide, a true ecumenical spirit.

Plainston's unusual investment in religions puzzled me. My basic reason for being there was to identify the roots of Plainston's unusual flowering and to determine, if possible, if its fruits were individually and socially beneficial—and replicable. The Temple's central location, its powerful appeal to Plainstans and the city's visitors, its congregations from two hundred to two thousand throughout the day from 7 a.m. matins to 7 p.m. vespers—all pointed to religion as Plainston's taproot. I decided to dig for it.

* * *

The religious editor of the *Plainston Gazette,* Peter Hammill was a man about my age, I guessed. He welcomed me warmly. Since he'd read some of my books and syndicated columns, we easily fell into a stimulating conversation about the relationship of religion and politics in 21st century society.

However, my ignorance of religion, both in theory and practice, made me a poor discussant. My interest in religion hadn't gone much beyond my concern for the rapidly increasing influence of identifiable religious blocs on elections—how would the Jewish or Catholic or fundamentalist evangelical groups affect elections and legislation directly? But that practical interest hadn't led me to examine the roots of the personal religious life or the effects of a strong religious commitment of its members on a modern community as tightly knit as Plainston.

Pete was remarkably tolerant of my inability to make any reasoned judgments about why most politicians seemed reluctant to include in their political platforms even such basic religious concepts as the well-demonstrated fact that material prosperity doesn't bring happiness.

"Aren't most political and economic problems basically problems of moral and spiritual values?" Pete asked.

"I suppose politicians think that working from moral precepts somehow violates the separation of church and state," I suggested.

"That's only partly true," Pete said. "Politicians don't hesitate to inveigh against murder, libel, thievery, and such that are prohibited by the Ten Commandments as well as other religions and moral codes. Why then don't they also promote brotherhood, community service, and a simple life style that would solve a lot of ecological and waste disposal problems and that would also give people some leisure time to enjoy the pleasure of being alive?"

"Maybe it's because they can't pass laws that make people believe and live that way."

Peter agreed. "Precisely! That's what religion is supposed to do—lead believers to want to live by those values."

"So why," I asked, "are Plainstans so much more interested and active in religion than most people?"

Pete paused a few moments, then smiled.

"Well, Kiki, it would take all the fun and meaning out of your visit if any of us were to tell you the answer to that question. Aren't you here to do your own digging to find our roots?"

Pete's gentle put-off irritated me slightly, echoing Lydia's advising the Beanery patrons not to tell me too much.

"Why is it an investigative reporter can't get straight answers from knowledgeable sources? Am I supposed to spend a year attending Temple services thrice daily and listening to every parson sermonize to find out why Plainstans spent years and untold donated dollars to build a truly beautiful temple on twenty of the most valuable acres in the middle of town?"

My tone was a bit sharp.

Pete took my question in good humor. "Because that would be secondhand knowledge," he said. "Hearsay isn't acceptable in the court of law or in the court of public opinion. We Plainstans don't put much stock in important knowledge unless we get it get firsthand. Just live a normal, Plainston-style life and see where it leads you. It will take a while to discover what that life style is, but you will learn by doing, not by being told."

That seemed as far as Pete was going to go in revealing the roots of Plainston, so I shifted the topic some and asked some specific questions about church attendance and paying the preacher and doing missionary work. Pete had statistical answers at his fingertips. He said that over 80 percent of Plainstans are registered church members. Attendance at their services runs from 70 to 95 percent of the membership. Roughly 60 percent of church members attend at least one Temple service each week, and they mostly attend services presented by religions or denominations different from their own. Musical programs are Temple favorites, followed by drama. Informative, narrative, and descriptive programs, which are on the lecture side, are least favored, but they still earn audience rating of over 7 on a 10-point scale. Last year, the average attendance for each of the forty-nine live services per week—seven per day seven days a week—ranged from 226 to standing room only for the most popular music and drama performances. The average attendance overall was 712 per live service.

As I looked at the copy of those figures Pete had given me, I brought up a new, though distantly related, topic.

"Has Wilber Bickersley ever visited you?" I asked point-blank. "You know he's charged Plainston with being not a 'puzzle' but a 'conspiracy.'"

"Oh, yes. He barged in here only a few weeks ago with a long list of questions about religion in Plainston, all of them loaded against the whole concept of the Temple—interreligious harmony and cooperation in helping people achieve their spiritual goals. He asked for all those statistics I just read to you. He couldn't believe that with two-thirds of our people active in Christian denominations that they would stand for, let alone actively participate in, our Temple program. Calling it pantheism, he said, 'You people are condoning and promoting the worship of all gods!'"

Pete rose and walked to the window looking toward the Temple.

"Can you guess what most interested him about our Temple? It wasn't what Plainstans consider its contributions to their spiritual growth. No. It was the golden ball with the planets and moon surrounding it. You know about that, I suppose—Plainston's biggest secret?"

I did. It was almost always mentioned in the general descriptive articles about Plainston, cited as an interesting example of the advanced scientific work going on there.

"Here. Have a close-up look," Pete said as he handed me a pair of powerful binoculars.

I brought the lenses into focus and located the apex of the Temple's steeple. There in the pale light of a late-afternoon February sun was a miniature solar system, not constructed to astronomical scale but complete with the golden globe as its Sun and the eight planets with their circling moons as well as Saturn's rings and little Pluto, which had now been downgraded from planet to asteroid, barely visible beyond Neptune. The planets were roughly proportional in size, but their orbital distances from the sun were not as they revolved around it at differing speeds.

"Can you see the supporting wires which carry the electrical currents that keep everything in proper motion?" Pete asked.

I'd been looking for them because other observers claimed there were no such channels of support and energy. Properly mystified, I reported seeing none.

"Neither could Wilber. And that infuriated him," Pete said, mildly amused. "It infuriated him further that I wouldn't confirm whether there are invisible wires—whether the secret is the discovery of how to manufacture invisible current-carrying wire or whether it is the discovery of some way to create and control a no-wire electromagnetic dynamic field. Wilber said, 'Anyone with the powers to do whatever you people have done to create that contraption—'"

Pete paused, then shook his head slowly and added, "He sneeringly labeled that beautiful little replica 'a contraption.' Anyway, Wilbur said that if Plainston could create such a thing, we must have the power to conquer, even destroy, the world. He went farther and charged that, in his words, 'Your refusal to share it, as all ethical scientists and humanitarians do, is a sure sign of evil intent—a conspiracy!'"

Pete shook his head again. "I can still see his eyes ablaze, his fists clenched as he damned Plainston! Do you think he is a fanatic, or does he genuinely pursue God's truth?"

"I don't know about him now, Pete," I replied, trying to be objective, "but when he was a student of mine, he had a pretty thorough grasp of essential facts and a logical framework to support his position. But even then, he had some of the traits of the fanatic. He's made his professional reputation by exposing a lot of corruption, deceit, hypocrisy, and downright felonious activities in various parts of our society. I admire his sharp mind, but I've never felt he had a warm heart."

Pete nodded assent.

I continued, trying to be even-handedly judgmental. "I do agree with Wilber that Plainston does have a problem with this secrecy thing. Why don't you explain what goes on up there around that spire? Or have your pantheon of gods decided to do this for you as a reward for your pantheism?"

I hoped a touch of levity wasn't out of place. It wasn't.

Pete grinned. "You may be surprised at this, but that's exactly what some critics say. When something is beyond common belief, any explanation is better than none. When folks can't believe Plainstans are smart enough either to make invisible wires or to create a controlled magnetic field, they'll attribute the undeniable reality to an unearthly force, which they label as divine if they like us or evil if they don't."

"But we humans are the question-asking species," I said. "Isn't it natural for us to suspect evil intentions and purpose from secrecy? Who hides good news?"

I was about to convince myself of Plainston's evil designs.

"We're not really hiding anything," Pete answered calmly. "We put our little solar system up there for all to see as a challenge to the scientific community to duplicate it, with or without wires. The laws of the physical universe are out there for any interested person or group to discover. So are the laws of the social and moral universe."

Pete resumed his seat and changed the subject.

"We were all so sorry to hear about the loss of your wife in that tragic accident. How are you coping with that loss?" he asked gently.

Since I hadn't been coping well with that personal tragedy, I welcomed an opportunity to talk about it with a person I felt might have some comforting insights into the confusing relationship of life and death. But first, I wanted to get an answer to a question.

"You said, 'We all were sorry.' Who do you mean, and how did you hear about it? The accident wasn't widely publicized to my knowledge."

"Oh, thousands of us Plainstans have been your fans ever since your monthly column was syndicated. Our own *Plainston Gazette* has carried it for years. But several years ago, a group of us unanimously decided that you were the commentator we wanted to take on the job of formally introducing Plainston to the world. We were all immensely relieved when Lydia learned that you were staying on with the GBO after losing Marie."

"Well, I did consider an early retirement after her death, but she wasn't the kind who'd let tragedy destroy her desire to fulfill what she felt was her purpose in life. After a few months, I realized she'd want me to continue to try to fulfill mine, even without the support she'd given me for almost forty wonderful years."

We were both silent for a short while.

"All religions and cultures have their unique beliefs about death," I said, trying to sound intellectual and unemotional. "And since we're all faced with it, everyone eventually has to come up with his or her own attitude toward it. Have you Plainstans reached some common agreement on the meaning of death, some explanation for tragic death, some ideas about life after death?"

Pete's face took on an especially benevolent expression as he started to talk about what he plainly regarded as a beautiful experience. He said, "We haven't done any formal polling on the subject of death and a possible afterlife, but I'm pretty sure very few if any Plainstans, especially our life-long, native-born residents, fear or resent death. And I think most accept the idea that life is a form of energy that is indestructible by physical death. It just continues in a different form in a different environment."

"Heaven or hell?" I asked, partly in jest.

"We haven't polled Plainstans on that question either," Pete replied, "but my guess is that no one believes in a fiery eternal hell. It's never presented in any Temple service, except in a dramatization of some classical story or myth. Since people talk freely about these ideas, you can ask anyone about his or her beliefs about death and an afterlife. All the people I've talked with have very positive, upbeat concepts of life beyond the grave."

"How do your sick and elderly receive a doctor's prognosis of an incurable disease?" I asked, this time in all seriousness.

"Our elderly, especially those born and raised here, seldom develop incapacitating illnesses, but if they do, they seldom linger long and rarely in a vegetative state. We don't practice euthanasia, but no one asks that we artificially prolong life. Our own people seem to develop a sense of when it's time to move on. They die peacefully in their sleep or when they're playing chess or watching television. They may not continue a conversation with a child they're reading a story to."

The idea of young children, such as the ones I'd seen reading to the elderly in wheelchairs in the Alumni Center, witnessing death rather horrified me.

"Oh, Pete, kids aren't mature enough to handle that experience."

Pete responded calmly, "Isn't death as natural in the life cycle as birth and growth? We celebrate death as we celebrate birth. As you know, all modern religions, along with most of what we call primitive ones, postulate an afterlife."

Pete paused, then added, "Much of the grief over someone's death is from our sense of personal loss. Children grieve when their elderly friends in the Alumni Centers die, but children learn about death from their real-life experiences with the pets and the plants that they care for and from stories they read and hear. Children can understand the facts of life and death when they are presented in honest, caring ways. As you said, it's a great mystery, not just death itself but the possibility—the probability, most of us think—of an interesting, pleasant afterlife. That's a reasonable possibility, don't you think?"

Not prepared to discuss the questions of life beyond, I said, "I'm concentrating on trying to live this earthly life happily."

Pete nodded and said, "We concentrate on life, what makes it meaningful and joyful. Even though no minister here preaches hellfire and damnation, neither are we heaven-looking, waiting for our rewards in the Great Beyond. Plainstans believe that it's possible to create the essentials of heaven here on earth."

Pete paused, then laughed. He went to the window and looked at the Temple.

"I almost told you what you're supposed to dig out by yourself."

I sensed that Pete knew perfectly well that his words didn't convey the whole meaning of what Plainston is all about. He knew that I'd have to "live Plainston" for some time to put personal meaning and full understanding into those words.

As we shook hands, I felt that I'd just met someone who would become a very good friend.

*   *   *

The five o'clock service had already begun in the Temple when I slipped into a back seat. The vesper service was for meditation. As the soft organ music soaked into my soul, I slipped into a meditative mood, feeling at-one with the music, the people around me, and the Temple.

Walking back to the Tower, I hoped this new feeling wouldn't demand that I achieve saintliness—that I should feel brotherly love for Wilber Bickersley, for example. After pondering that for a few minutes, I decided not to waste my energy. Instead, I'd concentrate on Lydia.

Chapter 10

The Epidemic

After my visit with Peter Hammill, I looked with more interest at the *Plainston Gazette*. Big city journalists tend to look with disdain on small city newspapers. I had to admit that I hadn't bothered to look at the copy of the *Gazette*, which was delivered daily to my door. Instead, I'd been buying the *Washington Post* in the Tower lobby.

The following morning, I read through the *Gazette* during breakfast. Almost all the articles were by *Gazette* reporters. Capital news came from the paper's own Washington correspondent, and foreign news similarly had a *Gazette* by-line. From over forty years of experience in national and international reporting, I recognized the accuracy of the reports, which often showed evidence of deeper digging than merely summarizing official government or agency handouts.

Pete's page on religion wasn't just announcements of church meetings or uplifting homilies but thoughtful commentaries on the moral aspects of the news as well as reports about the many humanitarian projects worldwide.

I dropped in on Pete later that morning to express my admiration.

Pete chuckled. "So we're credible?"

"Most definitely."

Pete then asked if I'd been reading the articles about the new strain of flu that was beginning to appear around the country. I said I had, adding what Lydia had told me about her family's illness.

"It's a really bad strain of flu—one that the fall vaccines can't protect you against," Pete said. "There are some cases here already. It has traveled faster into the country than the new vaccine can be prepared. Health Services just now has enough vaccine for a city-wide vaccination program which is starting today."

"Was that announced on your special TV program for the elite?"

"What do you mean by that?" Pete asked, sounding perplexed.

"Wilber Bickersley claims that you have coded morning TV announcements aimed at just certain of your 'elite' citizens, whom he calls your co-conspirators."

"Oh, that!" Pete replied with a wry smile. "Wilber is a half-baked newshound, but he's partly right—but not about elite co-conspirators. Do you have time for me to explain where Wilber got that notion?"

"Of course," I said.

Pete said, "Most Plainstans of all ages get involved is various research projects at some time, which must be kept secret to prevent persons serving as controls from changing their normal behavior. Experiments need control groups to get comparative results. To maintain secrecy, on-going instructions for the experimental volunteers are given in code on a special television channel. That way printed instructions won't fall into the hands of the control subjects or anyone else, for that matter."

Pete's explanation made sense to me.

"Why didn't someone explain that to Wilber?"

"Because we simply don't trust him. Wilber tears down something he thinks is wrong without regard to its relationship with other things which may be all right. Whoever was talking to Wilber either didn't notice his tag color or was color-blind."

"Aha!" I responded, in a tone partly triumphant but partly disappointed. "So you do in some way mark us Pagans in order to control our access to Plainston's secrets."

"Of course, we do," Pete replied matter-of-factly. "Plainston is an incorporated private entity. We have a legal right to identify our visitors, just as all corporations have when they issue identification tags to their visitors, especially since security measures have been increased since 9/11."

I looked at the color of my tag and then at Pete's. Both appeared to be the same dark green.

"What's the difference between yours and mine?"

"Mine has a white ring, which identifies a person as a permanent resident, a verified Plainstan. Your dark green identifies you as someone we can trust with information."

"That sounds complimentary. And what must I do to become a verified Plainstan—to earn the white ring, which is for purity, I suppose?"

Pete laughed. "Just continue to be the kind of person we've been admiring for years." He paused, then added with quiet sincerity, "The person who can fully understand and explain Plainston to a skeptical world."

Picking up the earlier thread of our conversation, he said, "But to answer your previous question about the flu vaccination program. It was announced publicly on our 7 a.m. local news broadcast. The coded instructions to our volunteer vaccination subjects would've been on the special channel at 6:30."

"If you'd been in this project, what would you've done to get your directions? Wouldn't a lot of subjects get them mixed up or forget them, with no written record to refer to?"

"We all learned early in school to pay close attention and then rehearse spoken directions until they're clearly in mind. Subjects can also call the station and get a repeat."

I was becoming more and more impressed—and a bit incredulous. "You Plainstans are quite beyond belief!"

"No, Kiki. We aren't beyond belief. You are, at the moment, beyond believing. That's why we lovingly call you Pagan," Pete said with a grin, "and we can't afford to lose such a valuable Pagan, so please get your unbelieving self over to Health Services pronto and get that first flu shot."

*   *   *

Believing in the competence of Plainston's medical personnel, I headed to Health Services. There was already a line, moving, as in banks and post offices, so that a patient went to the next of six open stations. Each station had a nurse and an attendant at a computer terminal. Three doctors were supervising. Dr. Chen, one of the doctors in charge of my general overhaul, motioned me to the third station. An attendant called up my medical records and handed a printout to Dr. Chen. She spent about a minute reviewing my life history, then gave directions to the nurse who measured the dose and applied the needle.

Dr. Chen explained, "We think a single shot could be too much, so we're starting with a smaller injection to give your immune system a chance to call up the troops for a bigger battle, if necessary. It may make you a bit ill for a day or so, much like a mild flu attack. Then you should return next week for a stronger shot. Frankly, we're having to experiment a bit, but the Center for Disease Control has approved this approach. Now go on about your business, but don't do anything physically strenuous."

Handing me a pamphlet, she added, "And stick to this diet until this flu thing blows over."

*   *   *

I attended a Temple service before eating lunch at the Hennery where the waiter explained that the starred items on the menu were the ones recommended by Health Services to help build immunity to the flu.

I noticed that below his name tag, he was wearing an additional tag which featured the medical profession's caduceus, the twin snakes coiled around a winged staff, inside a large V for vaccination.

"You must've gotten up early to get the call. You probably got it on the experimenters' special channel," I said in a casual tone to test his reaction.

He looked closely at my name tag. Then reassured by its dark green color, he smiled to acknowledge my right to be trusted with some degree of knowledge of the conspiracy.

"I didn't since all of us food servers and the medical people were given flu shots weeks ago when the first vaccine was available in limited quantities. Some had apparently already been exposed to the flu and got sick despite the vaccinations. The flu weakens people too much for them to work for a while. The rest of us will carry on when the epidemic really hits. Sounds bad, doesn't it?"

I agreed that it did.

*   *   *

After lunch, I returned to my room where I obediently spent a quiet day reading, napping, and watching television.

Around 9 p.m., Lydia called from Kansas.

"Are you all right?" she said, sounding worried. "Have you had your first flu shot yet?"

She was relieved to hear that I had.

"Thank goodness! The Health Services personnel will do their very best, but this is no ordinary epidemic, Kiki. The death rate in cities like Minneapolis, Denver, and Kansas City has been appalling—by far the worst since the flu epidemic during World War I. You know how bad that one was, don't you?"

"Refresh my memory. I don't know the facts—just that it was bad."

"It was. According to a news story I read yesterday, half the U.S. soldiers who died in the war died from the flu. Overall, 28 percent of Americans were infected—675,000 died. Worldwide, the number of deaths was somewhere between 20 and 40 million. It was a scary disease. A person could be healthy in the morning and dead by nightfall—often from pneumonia that caused suffocation." Lydia paused, then added softly, "I shouldn't be talking about this since fear never helps anyone."

"That's all right. I'm tough."

"Please stay that way, Kiki. Reports are that over ten percent of the cases have been fatal so far—and not just the weak and elderly. The vaccine isn't protecting everyone either since this new strain is mutating as it travels. We've all been desperately ill here, but we'll be coming back to Plainston whenever the doctors here determine we're no longer contagious and are strong enough to travel."

"The whole family? Why come back here?" I asked.

That made no sense to me. Lydia's son, Will, and his wife, Vangie, had three children.

"Because Plainston will need all the help we can muster. Believe me, Kiki, much of the town will likely be down with this flu, pretty much all at once. It hits hard and fast. The vaccinations will likely help some, but many will get the flu because they've already been exposed or the vaccine just doesn't fully protect. The only hope for adequate care of the sick is that everyone doesn't get sick all at once. Those who've responded to the vaccine and those who've already recovered from the flu can take care of those who are ill. You just lie miserly in bed and ache all over for days, hoping the fever doesn't rage so high as to kill you."

I was learning that Lydia believed in straight talk. We chatted a bit longer before saying good-night.

* * *

With disquieting visions of a 21st century black death sweeping through Plainston, I retired. My bad dreams were interrupted about midnight with some typical aching in my joints and a temperature of almost 101. Was this my predicted reaction to my first shot, or had I already contracted the dreaded Saskatchewan flu?

I dropped off to sleep again and slept through until a little before nine when I awoke feeling pretty normal. My symptoms had probably been only a "mustering of the immune troops" as Dr. Chen had suggested.

About ten, Pete Hammill called to inquire after my health and to report that he'd had a similar reaction to his first shot.

"Our immunologists are glad to hear that the side effects are short-lived. They predict the next round of shots will be no worse."

"But what if someone gets the real thing before the series of shots is over?" I asked, ever the wary realist.

"That worries our doctors, of course. They know of no effective treatment beyond what they've told us about eating well, resting a lot, keeping a positive outlook, and watching your temperature. If it's over 104, get in the tub and cover yourself with water as cool as you can stand until the fever comes down. What's good about a high fever is that it seems to stop a virus, but these Saskatchewan buggers don't play by the rule book, and we can't risk brain damage from a high fever, even we poor old geezers whose brains burned out years ago," Pete concluded with a chuckle.

"You've got a few cells left worth saving, Pete," I said.

"Since you got up late, you missed the TV information that suggested that everyone stay at home. Kiki, if you need food or any essential supplies, call 711, and they will deliver it."

"Who are 'they'? I thought you said everyone is supposed to stay at home. Who's available to run around being Good Samaritans?"

Pete paused. "Okay. Here's an example of how things work secretly in Plainston. Please don't pass this on, at least not yet."

After I promised to keep the secret, Pete explained how Plainston had prepared for the plague.

As soon as the Center for Disease Control had prepared a vaccine, Plainston Pharmaceuticals got their allotted breeder batch and went to work preparing serum in quantity. First, they vaccinated the food workers and all medical personnel. Next, when more vaccine was available, they asked for a group of over three thousand volunteers to get the two shots. It was necessary to get, if possible, a cadre of healthy individuals, who'd keep the economy going at its minimal level and tend the very sick. If the plan worked, the three thousand would provide one healthy person for about fifteen Plainstans and Pagans like me.

Pete said, "This has been done rather secretly because Plainston's health practitioners believe that fear has a debilitating effect on the immune system. Although Plainstans have been fully aware through news channels of the Saskatchewan threat, they don't seem to be worried. Everyone feels secure because they know that everyone cares. That's active faith in each other. Our basic religion teaches that—and we practice what we preach."

*   *   *

I didn't get a chance to get the second flu shot because a real Saskatchewan bug invaded my body and drove off my inexperienced flu-fighting corpuscles. I awoke two mornings later, alternately sweating and chilling, with every joint aching. Even the thought of food made me nauseous. When my fever had risen to 104, I struggled out of bed to pour a tub of cool water in case I needed to take a plunge. Then, I called 711 for emergency help.

I was reminded to unlock my door. Pete had said once that Plainstans generally don't lock their doors, but the Tower was inhabited mostly by Pagans who generally locked their doors against each other. But not after the epidemic struck.

Help arrived quickly in the form of nineteen-year-old Jason, a tall, thin young man with tousled sandy hair and intense blue eyes. After checking me carefully, he phoned his report into the Health Services computer: temperature, pulse, blood pressure, and severity of headaches. I rated mine at 5.5 with 7 being considered almost unbearable.

Despite feeling so sick, I was much impressed with the professionalism of this young man. I asked if he were a trained paramedic.

"Oh, everyone who's spent more than a couple of years in a Plainston school is practically a paramedic. Almost any eight-year-old here can take your pulse and read a sphygmomanometer. It's a good thing, too. This flu epidemic may get out of hand. In just two days, we went from less than a hundred sick to about two thousand. They're having a terrible time with it in Prairie Grove. People there expected they could go to a hospital, but those were all filled up within the first forty-eight hours after this thing hit last week. Prairie Grove didn't make realistic plans to meet this level of emergency. We've heard that they expect their death rate to be over 10 percent. We think we can hold ours to below 5 percent."

As he helped me into the cool bath, he confidently assured me that I wouldn't be among that 5 percent.

"They will be mostly the already ill or very frail elderly people. You younger healthy ones still in your 60s and 70s are pretty sure to pull through, especially if you have no heart problems. This new strain of flu has been especially hard on the heart. Some persons who seem to be over it suddenly have a fatal heart attack. But don't you worry. Your heart is strong."

Jason gave me confidence in myself and in the care I was getting. He seemed certain of his knowledge, yet he wasn't a pre-med student; he was majoring in botany and plant genetics. As I lay in the cool water, I asked him how he got his knowledge of medicine in general and of this flu epidemic in particular.

"We get interested in how things grow and develop from the time we're old enough to tell the difference between things which are animate and things which aren't," he said. "From then on, natural curiosity about this amazingly complex body we're given to live in for four score and ten years or so takes over. And you know, in science, every question raises a few more, so, over time, we collect a pretty good store of knowledge about human physiology and disease. It's fascinating stuff, isn't it!"

He stopped to take my temperature.

"103.8, not bad. About this Saskatchewan flu," he continued, "we meet every morning at six in the campus auditorium to get a briefing from the Health Services personnel about how things are going and to get answers to questions we raise. We have access to the Health Services staff twenty-four hours a day for any special problems we run into. We volunteers are on call for twelve-hour shifts."

"And all this is unpaid volunteer work?" I asked.

Jason nodded.

"But aren't you missing your studies? What about your grades?"

"In the first place, we don't have grades. We take exams when we're ready to pass a class. After this epidemic is over, we'll simply go back to school and pick up where we left off. Nobody loses anything by taking time off for any worthwhile project. That's true for the kids still in public school, too. Over five hundred of them were involved in the pre-vaccination program—a dedicated bunch of kids."

"And they can do what you're doing?"

"Sure can. Some of the fourteen and fifteen-year-olds are as competent and reliable as any of us older volunteers when doing the routine stuff. Think about it. Is there anything I've done for you at nineteen that a fourteen-year-old couldn't have done as well?"

"I'm sure I couldn't have done it even at nineteen. Besides, no one would've trusted me if I'd tried," I said with a laugh.

"They would've trusted you, and you'd have been perfectly capable if you'd grown up in Plainston," he answered confidently as he helped me into a clean pair of pajamas.

Then, before he left, he put one hand on my forehead, took my hand in his other hand, and was silent for a few moments. His eyes were closed.

"Are you praying?" I asked when he opened his eyes.

He smiled. "There's no extra charge, and prayer might help. We try everything since there are no known negative side effects from a little prayer. Ever try it yourself?" he asked gently.

"Not since God didn't give me the pony I asked for on my fifth birthday. Oh, I know. You praying folks say He answered my prayer—that I should learn to take no for an answer. But I think the lines of communication have been cut."

"They're easily repaired. Anyway, the forces we try to tap are not 'out there.' They're your own untapped inner resources, put there, no doubt, by the Creator. And it doesn't hurt to drop in a word or two of gratitude to the Creator for making them available."

"Okay, Doc, if you prescribe it, I'll try a little dose maybe every day or so to get my system used to it. Since prayer is a foreign substance for me, my body might reject it."

"Not a chance," he said with a laugh. "And there's no danger of overdosing."

After Jason left, I said what may have passed for a little prayer to my inner resources to join up and support my embattled immune legions. Then I dropped off to sleep.

Jason dropped by two more times that day to check on me—praying silently before he left each time.

Despite my little prayers and his, my inner resources apparently didn't get the call—or they were too unpracticed to be of any help. When I awoke late the next morning, my fever had roared past the 104 mark. I called 711 and struggled to get to the bathroom.

Within minutes, another volunteer arrived, one of the young teenagers who looked to be about fourteen.

"I'm Gregory," he said. "Jason couldn't come because he's with an older man whose heart is acting up."

This young fellow quickly turned on the faucet, took my temperature and other vitals, and called them into Health Services. Using a thermometer to measure water temperature, he adjusted the cold in-flow. After he helped me into the cool water, he again took my temperature.

"Keep concentrating on the 104 number," he instructed in a confident tone. "Keep telling your fever, 'Go back to 104. Go back to 104. Go back to 104.' You've got the power to take it down to where it will do as much good fighting the bugs as it does at 105. The cool water will help, but what really takes it down is you saying, 'Go down to 104! Stay at 104!'"

Despite his serious, confident tone, I burst out laughing.

"That's good, too," he said. "Laugh a lot. Laugh at anything. Especially, laugh at those darn little Saskatchewan bugs and say, 'Go away, you nasty little Saskatchewan aliens. You've got no visitor's pass into America.' Just laugh 'em right out of yourself."

He paused after this vigorous pep talk, then asked, "By the way, were you laughing at me? I was dead serious about all that."

"Well, don't you see anything funny about a boy, young enough to be my grandson, coming into a strange bathroom to tell a shivering old man he's never met before and who may be about to kick the bucket from a raging fever, how to save himself by soaking in a bath tub and yelling with a thermometer in his mouth '104! 104!'? What could be funnier?"

Though he seemed to be a truly serious lad, he laughed sympathetically and said, "Yeah, I suppose it could be funny to you. But it's what I've been doing all day and some of the nights for the last five days. After you've done the same thing over and over, it's not funny anymore. Things that are funny are usually somehow new, sort of unexpected. Like a joke is funny because, all of a sudden, the ending is really different from what you expected. But when I answer a call, nothing is really different or surprising—it's just people sick with this awful flu."

He paused and frowned thoughtfully before adding, "Now if I answered a call and the person died while I was there, that would be different. But I wouldn't laugh."

"What if I were to die while you're here? How would you handle it?"

He pondered a few moments, then said, "Well, I'd call in right away to report your death. I'd be awfully sad, not so much for you but for your family and friends who'd miss you. I'd also feel bad because I couldn't save you. But the doctors told us in training that two or three thousand people here may die from the flu. And since there are around 3,000 of us volunteers on duty—well, you do the math."

He paused again, his head bowed and his eyes closed. Then he raised his head and spoke directly to me.

"But, you know, death isn't a bad thing. It's just the end of life here on earth, and we sort of graduate to another level. I don't think any of us here in Plainston are afraid of death. Yes, I'd have a strange feeling if you'd die while I'm here, but I could handle it, I think."

Suddenly, he looked at me with alarm. "You're not going to test me, are you? You are feeling all right now, aren't you?"

I threw back my head and laughed.

* * *

Whether it was the cool water or Gregory firmly ordering my temperature to go down or the laughter, my fever did obediently abate to 102.5. He helped me out of the tub, toweled me dry, and sat me down in my easy chair. Then he put clean sheets on the bed and helped me climb back into it. Before leaving, he again phoned in my statistics. He also called and left a message for someone in the Tower to pick up my sheets, which would be washed in the laundromat and then returned.

My fever stayed between 103 and 104 for the next four days before finally breaking the next day. It took another couple of days for my joints to quit aching. I was as weak as a kitten, as my grandma used to say. I'd eaten no solid food—only drunk the liquids Jason and Gregory had forced me to take. I was glad the apartment was small because it took all my strength to get from the bed to the easy chair to the bathroom.

Jason still dropped in once a day to check my vitals, but he was needed elsewhere for people who were much sicker than I was at that point. When my appetite returned a bit, I started eating applesauce, dry toast, bananas, and chicken soup, but even the slightest physical exertion, like eating, exhausted me. I was sleeping twelve to fourteen hours a day. When up, I became a sofa sloth with only enough energy to watch television—dramas, news, panel discussions, old movie classics, and Temple services on Plainston's channel. Besides Jason, an attendant came by every day to supervise a shower and to bring me more freshly made soup and other food.

I hadn't seen a doctor or a nurse the whole time I was sick. I did get a call from Dr. Chen, who'd been monitoring the reports my volunteer attendants had phoned in. She apologized for not seeing me, but the doctors had been making house calls only for patients having unforeseen difficulties. I was doing well, she said.

* * *

Then, several days later, my final recovery started when I opened my door, after hearing a gentle knock, and looked into the smiling faces of three generations of Plainstans: Lydia Colby Gray, her son Will, daughter-in-law Evangeline, and three grandchildren, ages twenty-one, seventeen, and twelve.

Even before introducing me, the eldest Gray gave me a hug and a kiss. Then, hands on my shoulders, she said, "Oh, Kiki, I'm so glad to get back and find you still here. It's not just to cure your bunions and get over the flu, is it? Are you staying for us?"

I didn't ask her what she meant precisely by "us"—Plainstans, in general, or the two of us, in particular? Either way, I reaffirmed what I'd decided after visiting Pete Hammill.

"I'm staying. Yes, I'm definitely staying."

Chapter 11

Recovery

The Grays, the first multi-generational Plainston family I'd met, spent a lively hour with me. They were as interested in finding out all about me and my family as I was in getting their various activities and interests sorted out.

Will Gray, the middle child of Lydia's three, was a good-looking man in his mid-forties, a professor of agronomy, specializing in plant breeding. His wife, Evangeline, called Vangie, was a professor of plant pathology. They were on a two-year exchange with agronomists at the University of Kansas in Lawrence.

"We've sown our seeds of reform in Lawrence," Will said, using an agricultural metaphor, "but the soil there isn't as hospitable to educational and societal reform as here in Plainston, but we think with tender loving husbandry, we'll get a crop eventually."

"You'd think it would be easier in a university town," Vangie added, "but no bureaucracy is more entrenched than the unelected intellectual elite. As long as you're working in their tradition and building on their theoretical bases, you'll be listened to. But the university's school of education isn't exactly hospitable toward our restructuring proposals. And that, of course, is our basic goal."

My antennae sprang into action. Plainstans did have a "goal" beyond their own walls—Vangie had just said so—and it involved education. I studied Will and Vangie, trying to envision them as "conspirators" with all the negative connotations that go along with that word. I couldn't.

The topic of conversation shifted to the youngest generation.

The Gray grandchildren, after getting me to tell about my grandchildren, sketched their current lives. Anne, a lovely girl of twenty-one, had already earned her master's degree in plant genetics and was starting on her doctoral. That rang a bell. Jason, my flu attendant, was interested in plant genetics. I mentioned him to Anne.

Blushing lightly, she said only, "I know Jason Crawford."

"Actually, Anne knows Jason quite well," Vangie added. "We expect them, eventually, to provide us with grandchildren."

"Mom!" Anne said, her face turning rosy as everyone laughed.

Andrew, seventeen, was following Grandmother Lydia's musical footsteps. A sophomore in music school, he was majoring in composition and trying to interest his fellow students and his instructors in Dixieland and Claxieland, with limited success.

"My professors think we debase the classics with the instrumentation and innovation. I think it's a warm, friendly tribute to their enduring appeal. Mihaly helped us learn first to love them in their original form. Isn't humor a form of loving?" He paused, then added, "That's how we feel about Claxieland."

Twelve-year-old Alexander, called Alex, complained about the University Lab School. "They don't really give you individualized instruction like they claim they do—they just give you a little more time to do the stuff all the other kids are assigned to do. And they wouldn't let me go on with my own pet project in electromagnetic fields that I'd started with some kids back here. My folks got me some of the basic lab equipment to work on it at home, but that's not nearly as much fun as working with other kids."

After we talked a while longer, Lydia suggested they do their special family rendition of "The Wabash Blues," with a chorus of simulated instruments as the Mills Brothers would've done in their salad days. It was delightful.

I asked for an encore, but they declined due to the late hour. Having driven straight through from Lawrence, they were tired.

"We're all still recuperating, too. Can't risk overdoing and having a relapse. But we did have to see how you're doing," Lydia said.

We gave hugs all around, and everyone departed for that good night's sleep we all needed.

*   *   *

Having the Grays in town speeded my recovery. Each of them dropped in frequently for a brief visit. They all became volunteer attendants since more and more Plainstans continued to come down with the flu, which had a virulence that wasn't abating. I also felt well enough to volunteer my services. I was assigned to report on nearby Tower guests, who the doctors felt weren't in any serious danger.

The Tower serves regularly as outpatient quarters for outsiders who come to Plainston for special therapies. Some observers have charged that Plainston has "a hospital without beds." That isn't true. Plainston has a 200-bed hospital for patients who require 24-hour nursing care and regular doctor visits. However, if patients are ambulatory, they are advised to live normally in the Tower and to get involved in Plainston life as much as possible.

When I'd first met Dr. Chen, she'd told me that they seldom took on patients who couldn't stay in Plainston long enough for that kind of involvement to take effect. She'd said, "It's also why we have such a high rate of satisfaction. In fact, we sometimes have a hard time dismissing patients. The Tower probably has a hundred or so malingerers who insist they need more treatment, but what they really want is Plainston's 'inspiring tranquility,' as one patient put it."

*   *   *

The flu epidemic petered out in Plainston towards the end of April, but it swept outward in all directions from its upper Midwest start and continued to infect people all across the nation until well after Thanksgiving. The strain also seemed to change and grow stronger as it moved from place to place. All those infected seemed to have the high fever and body aches, as I'd had, but many experienced a dry, wracking cough and difficulty breathing as well. Death resulted most often from uncontrolled fever, pneumonia that sometimes followed when the body was so weakened, or heart problems. The national news reported that some were dying from reactions to drugs used to control the symptoms.

When the national statistics had all been gathered and published the following year, no city of Plainston's size had a death rate as low as Plainston's. Even so, many skeptics found fault with the methods of data collection and their interpretation, and most ignored the plan Plainstans had implemented to handle the epidemic: Health Services had vaccinated health care workers, food servers, and volunteers as soon as possible. A home care system was organized with volunteers available to check the progress of the illness, to help with basic tasks for the patient, and to provide food and drink as needed. That left the hospital beds available for those who developed complications. Schools had closed for about a month while Plainston television had devoted most of its daytime programming to material for the school kids. The live Temple services had been suspended as well with reruns of previous programs broadcast on television. Besides ignoring Plainston's plan to cope with the epidemic and the basic good health of its residents due to diet and life style, the media also ignored the low death rate from the flu—only 3 percent of those infected had died. That percentage was remarkable when compared to the 10 to 15 percent death rates experienced in most urban areas.

One death, however, did garner some attention—that of Lancelot Llewellyn, who'd died fairly early in the Saskatchewan flu epidemic. LL had written a directive for the Health Services doctors when he'd first become wheelchair bound. He wanted no treatment for anything beyond pain control. When the fever came, he went to bed and died in his sleep—his lungs too weak to fight.

A couple of weeks after I was well enough to leave the Tower, I went to Plainston South where I'd first met LL and asked to see Roger. He was the first person to use the words "by choice" to describe LL's death. Roger's eyes were bright as he told me about seeing LL, his face so peaceful in death.

"You know," he said, "LL dreaded the indignity of being unable to hold up his head and drooling like a teething baby. He knew all about what he faced with ALS. He was already too weak to take his own life—which he didn't really want to do anyway—so he let the flu end it for him."

"And you're okay with his choice not to fight?"

"I am. I miss him, of course. How could I not after spending part of every day with him for several years? But I believe he'll live again in a new, strong body. I can't feel sad about that."

Roger's moving words left me unable to speak. I reached out to grasp his hand.

Moments later, he said, "Come see what some of us are working on."

As we walked toward the Social Studies Center, he said, "A group of us are using the many hours of video from LL's years here in Plainston and making a ninety-minute documentary about him—his work and ALS. You're going to be in part of it."

Roger explained how the project had come about right after LL's death when several of the students were watching some recent footage. They'd gone to Miss Ellen, one of the social studies teachers, with the idea. She'd given the project an enthusiastic stamp of approval.

"Now we're finding clips and writing the narration to hold the whole thing together. The last step will be actually making the disk."

He paused, then added with a grin, "I'm hoping the group will choose me to be the narrator."

Later, when I expressed my amazement at the quality of the film and the students' understanding of LL's sophisticated concepts, Miss Ellen shrugged and explained, "These kids have been doing videotaping since they were about seven or eight years old. They've been asking questions of us adults and older students since they learned to talk. If kids' sentences don't begin with 'Why?' we feel we've seriously neglected them."

"Don't you have a hard time keeping ahead of them and being sure you give them the right answers?"

With slightly raised eyebrows, she said, "We teachers don't try to stay ahead of our students. Keeping up with them is enough. And we certainly don't regard it as our responsibility to answer all their questions."

"Then what do you do?"

"We help them clarify their questions and then suggest where or how they may find answers."

I smiled. "But this is an advanced group, isn't it?"

"No," she said with a laugh. "Just run-of-the-mill, garden-variety Plainston kids."

I recalled some of my earlier misgivings about the system. For instance, Lydia's two older grandchildren were ahead of schedule in their schooling—Anne at twenty-one already pursuing a doctorate and Andy at seventeen a sophomore in college. I also remembered hearing Hank, the Jeep driver who'd tried to crash into Plainston, say that kids here finish high school at fifteen or sixteen. At the time, I'd wondered what kind of pressure cookers were these schools. But that metaphor didn't fit because I wasn't seeing signs of pressure.

Ironically, the lack of pressure bothered me. Teachers weren't policing the place or teaching classes or keeping the kids on task.

I definitely needed more time in the schools.

*   *   *

The Prairie Grove Four didn't show up until late April to work out their fines. Sadly, only three of them reported. Adele was missing. Both she and her mother had died from the flu. No one had been available to go to their home and care for them when their fevers got too high. The flu had attacked Adele's already weakened, asthmatic lungs.

"A lot of people in Prairie Grove died because no one was there to help," Rick said bitterly. "A whole family would come down real sick all at once and maybe so would their neighbors, and there wasn't anyone around to know how sick they were and to help them. I wish Adele and her mom had been in Plainston. Maybe you could've saved them."

*   *   *

I'd been curious about what kind of work Lydia would assign the group.

"We always find work connected with the schools," she said.

"Always?" I asked. "Is having kids work out their fines standard Plainston practice?"

I hadn't yet rationalized Lydia's high-handed, perhaps even illegal, treatment of these kids. She sensed my disapproval.

"Plainston's been in the business of parole rehab for years," she replied, a bit defensively. "Oh, I suppose you feel the kids didn't receive their civil rights since they had no lawyers. Are you going to make a federal case of my handling of the situation?"

"I might if you can't justify it."

"Well, it was a judgment call. These kids looked like good candidates for the Plainston rehab program, which would be more preventative of future crime than punitive for their trespass infraction. They didn't have any police records yet, but couldn't you tell it would be only a matter of time until they'd do something seriously unlawful? If we'd gone through the usual routine of formal booking, a hearing, and a court appearance with their parents involved, the whole matter would've snowballed for the kids, and in the end, they'd probably have gotten about the same punishment I gave them."

"So you get them involved in your schools, somehow," I said. "Won't that expose your Plainston kids to bad influences?"

Lydia laughed. "How could these three fairly ignorant, aimless souls have any attraction for our kids, beyond eliciting their sympathies and a desire to help them? What kind of kids do you think our schools nurture that they'd take this Prairie Grove trio as models?"

Lydia sometime took on an irritating, school-teacherish tone. I wasn't used to being lectured like a schoolboy who hadn't studied his lessons. Besides, when I couldn't answer her questions, she answered them for me.

"Our students will instruct them but in, what will seem to you, an odd sort of way. We'll put Hank and Rick in the auto mechanic shop, where kids learn auto repair, mostly for electric cars. Rosie, I'm certain, will like working in the Child Development Center.

"And since the shops and the Child Development Center are open on Saturdays, they can come then if they wish and stay on after they've put in their required hours to get involved in other activities. Hank wants to learn to play a guitar, so we'll provide a student to teach him."

I sat with my mouth open, listening to this course of "punishment." Plainston didn't need these extra hours of work from these kids. This was all a front for an educational program—and all from the goodness of the Plainston heart. Or if there really were a dark conspiracy, as Wilber Bickersley charged, was this a trap for these kids?

Unaware of my recurring suspicion, Lydia continued. "Sad to say, we've found that young Rick is on drugs. We hope we can get him to enter a formal drug rehab program at Health Services. His losing Adele to the flu has hit him really hard. We'll have to watch him closely. Our main hope is to get him here full time after his school is out for summer vacation. Our schools run year 'round, you know."

That much I did know.

And so the Prairie Grove three arrived and immediately began to work to pay off their fines—Hank, who was out of school, coming a bit earlier each day and staying a bit later, and Rosie and Rick coming on Saturdays. The rehab was working perfectly, it seemed, just as Lydia had predicted, even Rick's involvement in the drug program.

Score one for Lydia, the Plainston judge. Score zero for me, the skeptic.

*   *   *

It was early June before my doctors considered me sufficiently recovered from the flu to resume my exercise program. Shortly after that, Max called to ask if I could suspend my Plainston investigation and instead cover the upcoming Congressional elections. I really wanted to see how the FINs would fare in their first nationwide campaign. Some political pundits were predicting that the FINs might get enough seats in both houses of Congress to effectively hold the balance of power, and I knew some Democrats and Republicans who were taking them seriously. It promised to be a lively and probably dirty campaign, which I couldn't miss covering, so I told Max I'd hit the campaign trail in early July.

I spent the final three weeks of June feverishly catching up on national politics in general and FIN activity in particular. The editorial staff members of the *Gazette* were generous with both their time and their facilities. The main library subscribed to the major newspapers, magazines, and professional journals. Because the Library of Congress had been computerized and made available to all libraries nationwide, I was as well-equipped in Plainston to do the essential background research as I would've been at the GBO headquarters near Washington, D. C.

I took time for a daily walk to the ice rink and spent at least half an hour skating. Lydia and I had several evening meals at the Beanery, enjoying Mihaly's Claxieland.

Every minute I spent with Lydia made me want to see her even more, but every so often, Wilber's description of his first day with her, which mirrored so perfectly my first day, caused me to question her motives and her sincerity. Did she treat all male visitors to Plainston the same way? I needed to know if I was just another visitor or was I special. I needed to know before I fell totally in love with her.

So, shortly before I was to leave for Washington, I asked bluntly, as we walked back to the Tower after supper, "Do you treat all male visitors the same way?"

"I don't know what you mean by 'the same way.'"

"Wilber told me that when he came last winter, you had him come for breakfast, you played duets, you went skating—"

"Oh, that," she said, interrupting me. "This is jealousy I'm seeing, I hope."

Now I was totally mystified. We stopped beneath a street light and faced each other.

"You want me to be jealous?"

"Not exactly 'want,' but if you're jealous, it means you care for me."

Words didn't come, so I hugged her on a perfect June evening in a wonderfully peaceful town.

* * *

I had an evening flight back to Washington, so I made a date to spend the day with Lydia. I invited her to breakfast at my apartment, serving her exactly the same breakfast she'd served me six months previously. We talked a bit about why I'd come to Plainston. Then I asked her if she'd like to play a few duets, suggesting Beethoven's Fifth, which I'd been practicing on a keyboard I'd rented.

"Primo or secondo?" I asked, wondering if she was catching on.

"Oh, I'm a little rusty. I'll take secondo."

We got through the first movement in pretty good form. After complimenting her on her playing, I suggested we trade places for the second and third movements. She agreed, not yet revealing whether or not she was aware of the rerun of our January meeting.

After Beethoven's last crashing chords, I went to the window, remarked on the weather, and suggested we go ice-skating.

Lydia couldn't restrain herself at this obvious replay.

"Oh, I'm sure Mill Pond is frozen thick enough. Let's go."

She threw her arms around my neck and kissed my cheek.

"And then—"

"Oh, no," I said, interrupting her, "that's my line. 'And then we'll come back here for lunch. I also have a favor to ask of you.'"

She interrupted me. "Please let me have this next line, Kiki, since I'd already planned it. 'Will you take me to the airport?'"

"'So we can have a little more time together,'" I put in before she had a chance to finish quoting the well-remembered dialogue.

We walked to her apartment to pick up her skates and then on to the ice rink in Plainston West. She noted that I no longer limped.

"Dr. Walsh tells me they consider you one of their best patients."

"And all because of your prying into my personal life," I growled.

"Complain, complain," she said, suppressing a grin. "You Pagans are forever ungrateful."

I put my arm around Lydia's slim waist, and she put hers around my slightly slimmer one, and we took our first long step together onto the smooth rink ice. It was the dream I'd had on my second night in Plainston some six months earlier—painlessly ice-skating with Lydia.

But this reality far outstripped the dream. Without foot pain and with all the practice I'd had before the flu, I skated pretty well. We executed some fancy turns, skated backwards, and did a few dance steps, all without bumps or falls.

Lydia let me dominate the script from then on. I duplicated the lunch she'd served me. I called the mini-bus, but she insisted on paying for the rental car. On our drive to the county airport, we talked mostly about our families, the upcoming elections, and the prospects for Hank, Rick, and Rosie.

Then at the airport, we waited silently in the check-in line. As we moved away from the counter, Lydia broke the silence.

"Shall we write a new script for this parting, Kiki?"

I paused and looked her full in the face. Then I kissed her.

"I'll miss you," she whispered.

After a final lingering hug, I walked toward the security lines and then to the tarmac to board the little plane.

As the little commuter plane took off to return me to "the outside world," I pondered the prospect of trying to predict how a national Congressional election with three parties might affect 300-plus million fellow Americans—realizing, suddenly, that the prospect appeared both less important and less challenging than trying to figure out what makes a mere 40,000 Plainstans so delightfully and mystifyingly different.

Chapter 12

Politics

The Saskatchewan flu was still ravaging the East Coast when I arrived at the GBO headquarters in early July. It'd already claimed the lives of three staff members, and about half of the remainder were absent. Max, who looked ghostly pale, had just returned to work.

"How did you get through this damned flu and come out looking so healthy?" he asked. "Are Plainstans really as strong as some people claim?"

I gave Max the comparative statistics.

He replied with a touch of his usual warm cynicism. "How do you account for the big difference between them and us? What gods do they pray to?"

Although he headed an organization sponsored largely by philanthropic foundations, Max wasn't himself a bleeding-heart reformer. He'd been made executive director not for his love of humanity but for his managerial talents. Even though he was by no means a misanthrope, he fit well the Plainston stereotype of Pagan, the unbeliever. Even so, he sincerely respected people who had idealistic beliefs and optimistic attitudes.

I sketched Plainston's highly-organized, efficient care program. "It was a model of community cooperation of highly competent people." I paused before adding a postscript that I couldn't remember ever adding to a report, either verbal or written. "And they care a lot."

Max looked at me quizzically before asking, "You think that really made a difference?"

"As a very practical matter, yes. A teen-aged kid likely saved my life. He came into the apartment and had me yell, while I was in a cool bath, '104! 104!' to convince my fever to come down. We don't know how many people elsewhere died from not having someone come in to help, but nobody in Plainston died from neglect. That we know full well."

I was almost belligerent in defending Plainston.

Ignoring my tone, Max smiled weakly. "Yeah, I know what you mean. A neighbor looked after me, or I probably would've died. I was sicker'n hell—still am. And I didn't even know the guy more than to say 'Good morning.' He's a bachelor, like me."

Max paused then asked, "Everybody's like that in Plainston—really caring?"

His tone sounded almost pleading as if he were hoping I'd say yes. Had his brush with death mellowed him? When I thought back to his tone of voice when he'd asked about the gods they prayed to, I realized he hadn't sounded sarcastic.

"Everyone I've met—yes," I said. "I can't vouch for everyone, obviously, but my feeling is that Plainston is truly a very friendly place."

"That's good," Max said wearily. "You know, we could use a lot more friendliness, couldn't we?"

I'd been so immersed in genuine friendliness for the past six months that I'd almost forgotten that it was a rather rare commodity in "the outside world," especially in the aggressively competitive capital city.

During the next few hours, Max and I mapped a strategy for my covering the major candidates and the FINs, and we sorted out what would likely be the major issues in the upcoming campaign. He let me do most of the talking while he sat with his head in his hands, mumbling assents to most of my proposals. He seemed to be still too weak to contribute much.

After I'd exhausted my store of creative strategies, he looked up and asked, in a genuinely concerned tone, "Kiki, do you think you can get your mind off Plainston long enough to do this job right?"

That was Max at his insightful best. He could often read a person's unspoken thoughts. At that moment, however, I felt I could read his mind, which was on Plainston. Suddenly, I realized that Max needed Plainston, desperately—for spirit as much as for body.

I reached for his phone and dialed the only Plainston number I'd memorized. Lydia answered.

"Can Plainston handle another Washington Pagan who is likely to perish without your tender loving care?"

That roused Max from his near-stupor. "Hey! What goes here? Gimme that phone."

He grabbed it out my hand and asked, "Who's this?"

The answer brought a bright smile. "Oh, is that you, Lydia?" he said, sounding as if he'd known her all his life.

I reached over, punched the speaker button, and said, "Listen, Lydia, I don't know how you seem to know everybody in the world, and, at the moment, I don't need to know. But what you need to know is that this old buddy of yours is a very sick man, and this city is no place for him to get well. Now tell me you'll get him a seat on the next plane out of Washington and make the necessary transfers to get him to the county airport."

"I've been trying to get Max to Plainston for years," Lydia said happily, "and if we practically have to kill him with the flu to get him here, so be it. Now don't argue, Max. Kiki and I know what's best for you. See you soon."

Much to my amazement, Max made not the slightest protest. He was booked on the next plane out.

On the way to Dulles, Max filled me in on how he and Lydia had met.

"Lydia and Don were doing a stint at Plainston's Washington headquarters. You know they maintain a kind of lobby here?"

I did know a bit but nothing of Lydia's connection with it.

"She interviewed me soon after the GBO was established in 1996. That was before you came on board. She asked the sharpest questions, but ones nicely put, about the media's influence on culture, especially what she considered its overemphasis on bad news and its neglect of good news. She briefly described Plainston, which was obviously her idea of good news. She said enough to interest me. Even so, because the GBO was focusing mainly on international issues, I never took time to visit Plainston, but when you joined us, Lydia kept closer track of us, especially of you."

Max was silent for a while before commenting, "Great lady, Lydia." Then without looking at me, he asked, "Something going on between you two?"

The question made me wonder if he hoped I'd say no. Misapprehension swept through me. Might Max's willingness to drop everything at a moment's notice and head for Plainston be due to a personal interest in Lydia?

"Married to my work," he'd always said to explain his bachelor status.

But at that moment, I had an uneasy feeling that he might not have that attitude etched in his allegedly stony heart.

*   *   *

The national flu epidemic was ravaging the ranks of the candidates. All parties were wrestling with the problems of nominating back-up candidates in case their nominees were to perish or become too ill to campaign vigorously. Because of the threat of cardiac arrest from overexertion after initial recovery, candidates couldn't safely put in the usual sixteen-hour days on the campaign trail, and volunteers lacked the energy for much door-to-door canvassing. I had to revise my predictions and commentaries continually as the lists of candidates changed.

Shortly after I arrived, Lydia suggested that I move my headquarters to Plainston Place in Coral Hills, a small community about six miles from the capital.

"Plainston bought a huge old farmhouse there back in the 1950s and made it into a hostelry for our school kids and others who went there to observe the national government in action. We still use it for that, but it's also our ear to the ground. We lobby—we pry into things," she said in a conspiratorial tone.

So a few days later, I moved out of my temporary apartment and into the spacious Plainston Place in Coral Hills, which was as peaceful and efficient as Plainston itself. The Place was on a five-acre parcel of ground, meticulously kept by Plainstans who came to visit and work. The professional staff, two senior members who'd been at the Place for over thirty years, knew as much about the inner workings of Congress as most professional lobbyists I'd known. The Plainston operation, I learned, was highly respected in many bureaus—much feared in others.

"We've contributed more than is generally known to many of the investigations that cleaned up some pretty messy bureau operations," the senior staffer said, "but we don't want exposure. We're pleased to turn over our findings to agencies that have the power to make corrections and reforms. That includes some of our crusading newspapers."

Most bureau activity is under the media's radar guns, which are aimed mostly at the struggles to get legislation passed. Plainstans, on the other hand, had been focusing primarily on the day-to-day operations of bureaus and administrative agencies.

Before I started on my coast-to-coast campaign, Lydia gave me a list of names and addresses of Plainstan émigrés, who not only invited me to stay with them but also met me at airports, taxied me to meetings, fed me delicious food, and helped me organize the information I was gathering with assistance from the librarians in Plainston and many others. After a hard day's work, we'd gather in their communication room to have a conversation with Lydia and the political volunteers back in Plainston. Max was almost always among the conferees.

"By the way," she said one evening, "our doctors have prescribed a six-month rest cure for Max. He can do his essential GBO work right here. We've got a crew doing for him what your cadre is doing for you. Don't you think it would be a good idea to move the whole GBO operation to Plainston?"

I could hear Max in the background, laughing appreciatively. My apprehension increased. I didn't wish Max any bad luck with his health, but I'd have felt much more comfortable if he'd been back in Washington—and not so close to Lydia.

*   *   *

Soon I realized that I was visiting outposts of Plainston's national network, a most impressive organization established in every state capital and major city. Spacious headquarters were usually in a large old three-story house with either a dry basement or a useable attic, which housed their communication equipment. The people at the headquarters, although strongly individual, all bore the Plainston stamp of exceeding good humor combined with firm dedication to their cause of making some fundamental cultural changes in a society threatened with decay, possibly even destruction. The residents were mostly couples of late middle-age or older, born and raised in Plainston.

"Plainston wouldn't ask us to sacrifice our children by taking them out of our schools there," explained the wife of one Sacramento couple in their late fifties. "And anyway, we had to get expert enough in our professional fields to get good jobs to cover the high costs of living here."

"Even though most Plainstans contribute to the cost of running this operation," her husband added with a laugh, "none of us is going to die rich."

I risked asking a root question.

"Why do you leave the peaceful security of Plainston to battle it out in this hostile 'outside world'?"

I repeatedly asked the émigrés that question, and I always received the same enthusiastic response, stated with a humorous twinkle in their eyes, "The conspiracy!"

Then most of them added, "We believe Plainston can save the world."

Soon I was staying exclusively with these "conspirators," enjoying every minute of my time with them. They were all deeply involved in politics, working intently in the Congressional campaigns, vigorously backing the third-party FIN candidates or supporting the most worthy Democrats or Republicans if there was no FIN opposing them.

I had access to extensive files my hosts and my helpers back in Plainston had collected on the backgrounds of all candidates. My GBO reports crackled with sharply-drawn contrasts between candidates.

Some commentators, reading my weekly column, accused me of partiality toward the FIN candidates, all of whom eschewed low-road politicking. Instead, the FINs insisted on presenting well-reasoned proposals for national legislation. The mass media, both television and print, often focused on personalities and trivial issues, but the FINs persisted in presenting their platform proposals, defined in down-to-earth language that connected these promises with believable benefits to the general population. Gradually, the level of the campaigning rose a few notches above mudslinging—perhaps because no FIN candidate ever slung any.

* * *

About three weeks before the election, I was asked to be on a panel to ask questions for a debate among three candidates in Chicago. Unfortunately, so was Wilber Bickersley. Because he'd failed to locate me the previous day, when we did meet shortly before the debate, he accused me of hiding out.

"Hardly hiding," I said. "I'm staying with my daughter and her family."

"Well, let's meet after the debate to catch up."

Unable to think of a reason to say no, I reluctantly agreed to do so.

When we met a couple of hours later in the bar of the hotel where he was staying, I asked how he'd weathered the flu.

Though he said, "No problem. Took it in stride," his face, pale without television makeup, and the circles beneath his eyes said something else.

I admitted to lack of stamina—working eight to ten-hour days, not the twelve to fourteen-hour ones of campaigns past.

Suddenly, Wilber cut off the small talk to get to what I'd guessed was his reason for wanting to meet in the first place—Plainston.

"Well, I guess your brains haven't turned entirely to mush from your six months in Plainston. How have you resisted their blandishments?"

Wilber had badgered me when he was my student, often challenging my facts and opinions. But now that he was on equal or superior footing with me—he was, in fact, a more widely known commentator than I—he felt free to challenge me without restraint.

Trying to control my rising temper at his ill-concealed sneer, I replied simply, "Mostly by ice-skating and massaging my bunions."

Ignoring that obviously inadequate explanation, he lunged ahead.

"It really hurts me to think my respected old professor would fall for Plainston's stuff," he said, feigning pain. "Haven't you tried to expose their doctors who consort with herbalists and medicine men from all over the world?"

"My purpose in Plainston isn't to expose anything, Wilber," I replied as calmly as I could. "I'm interested in finding the roots of Plainston's obviously different social organization."

"And what have you found so far?" he challenged.

"In six months, they've practically cured my thirty-year bunion problem. They put me through an exercise and diet program that has taken off almost fifteen pounds—with some help from the flu, I admit. They likely saved my life from the flu attack. Overall, I've never felt better in my life. How could quacks accomplish all that? And how could quacks manage to lose less than 3 percent to the flu?"

He sneered again. "How do you know that? Did you visit every mortuary during the epidemic? Has any independent health agency come to Plainston to verify their claims?"

I snapped back, "And did you witness the same all across the nation? Maybe the death rate nationally is even higher than reported."

Ignoring my response, he launched into a tirade, citing all the things that could be wrong with Plainston—things he'd seen on his few short visits and had read in the same literature I'd briefly scanned. He talked as if he were a prophet preaching to the multitudes to save them from iniquity.

"Suppose that all that you seem to believe about Plainston's goodness and benign intentions are true," he began. "It would still be disastrous for the United States, in particular, and world, in general, to take Plainston as a model. It's ridiculous that 40,000 people with a history of about sixty years of what they consider to be revolutionary progress think they can influence billions of people worldwide with cultures rooted in thousands of years of development."

After I made no response, he continued. "For the sake of argument, suppose the United States were to copy Plainston. Do you realize what that would do to our economy? Take our auto industry that produces one or two cars per family. Plainstans have fewer than a thousand cars, and since they ride bicycles or walk mostly, they never wear out their cars."

I remained quiet, so on he went. "And Plainston's claim to be almost self-sufficient simply isn't true. Plainston succeeds in meeting its people's needs by being part of the national and international economic system that manufactures all kinds of things Plainston imports to make their own things. Plainston piggybacks on this worldwide economy."

Then he launched into an extended attack on Plainston's dual money system, their bartering of labor to supplement their cash income. Looking at him, I wondered what drove him to such intensity of opposition. My inability to answer his economic charges, which were mostly new to me, also bothered me.

Sensing that he'd cut fairly deeply into my new-found faith in Plainston's truth and goodness, Wilber's approach changed to his well-known ability to charm people by appearing to have a genuine concern for their welfare.

"Kiki, old man, like I said before, I'd hate to see you waste your reputation by becoming an advocate for this social experiment, no matter how noble. It would be all right if Plainstans were content to live their own little lives apart from the rest of us. But no, your Plainstans are going to suffer from their hubris—their feeling of superiority and confidence in their having achieved the ultimate truth for mankind. I'd feel really bad to see your shining image tarnished by association with them. Why don't you pull out now? Give them their rightful due, if you truly believe they deserve it, but for God's sake don't get involved in their conspiracy. It's sure to destroy you."

If that appeal had come from anyone but Wilber Bickersley, it might have struck home. For a moment, I almost believed that he had my welfare at heart.

"Thanks, Wilber, for your concern and your insights. You may be right."

That massaged his ego. He warmly shook my hand. Then as we parted, he patted me condescendingly on the shoulder as if I were a child who needed to be shown the error of his ways. That final patronizing gesture restored my familiar, deep dislike for the man.

*   *   *

Two days later, Wilber Bickersley devoted a column to developments in Plainston, headlined "Respected Critic Loses Objectivity":

> After spending nearly six months in the vaunted micro-Utopia of Plainston, fellow commentator Karl "Kiki" Kornhauer has become a pawn of that admitted conspiracy. Although his investigation of Plainston has been limited by treatment for his painful bunions and a near-fatal attack of the Saskatchewan flu, he has been sufficiently convinced of Plainston's innocence to join their conspiracy.
>
> Since midsummer, he has been the guest of Plainston expatriates who have settled in state capitals and strategic cities. These Plainstans are interconnected in an extensive global communications network. Most of Kornhauer's information about candidates has been gathered by Plainston operatives at these outposts and others in Plainston. It is noteworthy that this subversive network most often supports third party candidates.

This commentator sincerely regrets the loss of an objective voice so sorely needed in this complex, strategically important election. Kornhauer came near death from the flu and is not fully recovered. Thus his need to rely on others' opinions and data and to use secondhand information is understandable, but it cannot be professionally condoned. Kornhauer should either withdraw from further commentary or publicly admit that he has become a spokesperson for a very narrow and possibly dangerous minority group, the members of the Plainston Conspiracy, who are using the third party FIN candidates to further their cause.

Additionally disturbing is the fact the Kornhauer's immediate superior, the able and highly respected executive director of the Global Betterment Organization, Max Baum, is himself a long-term patient recuperating under the care of Plainston's Health Services. Baum continues to direct the GBO's operations from Plainston, where he expects to remain until after the fall elections.

* * *

Max was furious, Lydia reported.

"Can't we sue the bastard?" he raged.

I calmed him by saying, "Everything Wilber wrote is true, in an odd sort of way. It's his innuendos that libel us, but you can't sue for innuendo. I think we should ignore the attack. It might even backfire. We could get some positive publicity from it."

In fact, only a few newspapers dropped my weekly commentary. In the dog-eat-dog media world, several commentators felt they would score more points attacking Wilber than joining him in attacking me and Plainston. All this happened in late October, just prior to the November election. Wilber himself was labeled as biased against third party candidates, so his attempt to knife a competitor was regarded as a normal tactic in the political game as played in the media.

Later, when thinking about my meeting with Wilber, I thought about the response I should've made. I should've said, "Wilber, based on my contact with Plainstans, I can't believe that they don't have realistic solutions to the problems you propose. They are intelligent, far-seeing, realistic people, who know it'll take generations to make radical changes in all the ill-fitting elements of our society. But in time, they will offer practical, humane, equitable solutions to the problems you see—solutions that won't destroy any economy or culture anywhere."

I thought about writing such a rebuttal, but I gave up the idea without even consulting Lydia or Max since it was premature. I needed to know a lot more about Plainston.

*   *   *

The midterm election did upset the major parties, neither of which came out with a clear majority in either the House or the Senate. The incorruptible FINs, who weren't "in the pocket" of any special interest groups, would have to be wooed to pass legislation. A new force had entered American politics.

*   *   *

I had a relapse after the election. I'd gone back to Chicago to visit my daughter, Joyce, her husband, Rob, and my grandchildren, Jean Marie, thirteen, and Matt, nine. While there, I suffered a delayed heart condition, peculiar to the Saskatchewan flu. I wanted to return to Plainston, but my family wouldn't hear of it, nor would Dr. Chen at Health Services, whom Lydia had contacted as soon as she heard. Since I wasn't sure I'd get the same attention from Lydia I'd enjoyed before Max's arrival in Plainston, I accepted my family's wishes and stayed on through the Christmas holidays—sleeping late and reading during the day when they were at work or at school, watching Illini basketball and Bears football and playing all sorts of games in the evenings.

Lydia invited all three of her children and their families to spend the holidays with her in Plainston. She included Max in that extended family. I kept wondering if he played the piano and liked to ice-skate.

That quandary dampened the joy of my extended visit with my Chicago family.

Chapter 13

A Love Story

A note that came the day after Christmas cheered me a little. It was from Lydia, inviting me to a New Year's Eve party. Her postscript, however, was more than a bit unsettling. It said, "Max sends regards. Eager to see you. Surprise news to report."

I arrived at the county airport on a drizzly, gray afternoon. Nothing is more depressing than after-Christmas, Midwestern weather that can be warm enough for rain which erodes most of the dirty snow, leaving only pock-marked little piles here and there.

I was hoping Lydia would meet me, but she'd made no inquiry about my arrival time. Douglas and Thelma were on duty at the café, but since I didn't feel up to exchanging New Year's greetings, I caught the shuttle into Prairie Grove, which was blanketed in soggy grayness, and took the five o'clock bus to Plainston.

A sentry gave me the first genuinely cheery welcome I'd had since leaving O'Hare.

"Season's greetings, Mr. Kornhauer. I've been reading all the articles you wrote on the election—lots of us have. Our FINs did all right. Hope you're back for a good long stay."

I thanked him for the welcome. A garage attendant offered to drive me to the Tower, but I liked driving the little mini-cab myself. He loaded my luggage with a cheery "Happy New Year." Then I drove to the Tower's small parking lot from which the cab would be picked up later.

It seemed impossible that Plainston could look so warm and inviting in such dismal weather, but it did. The drizzly rain which made Prairie Grove and the countryside look sodden somehow made Plainston glisten. Without air pollutants to dirty the snow, the remaining patches and piles still looked fresh, and seemed to welcome the rain. I was struck more forcibly than before how the absence of parked vehicles made the streets look inviting, not deserted. The deciduous trees were intermingled with evergreens, which were dripping and glowing with moisture. Lighted windows in the apartments lining Plainston Way cast soft shadows. Old-fashioned ten-foot tall lamp posts, several to a block, with white globes covering the low-wattage bulbs, radiated a twilight glow along the entire street. By the time I'd purred slowly to my Tower, I felt solidly at home.

The desk clerk reinforced that feeling by saying, all in a rush, "Mr. Kornhauer, you're back! When we heard you were coming, we got your old room ready for you. Are you feeling all right? We heard you had some kind of relapse. Anyway, have a real happy New Year!"

I felt that I might, except for those nagging questions about Max.

I didn't call Lydia until the next day, New Year's Eve. Since she was busy preparing for the party, she was brief, saying only, "So glad you're back, Kiki. Hope you're feeling better. Dinner will be at eight."

* * *

I didn't go early. When I did arrive just a few minutes before eight, it was without an appetite. The greeting hostess was Lydia's daughter-in-law, Vangie. The other Gray families had returned to their homes with only Will's family staying to greet the New Year. Vangie gave me a hug and a kiss on the cheek.

"Mother is so happy to have you back. She's been worried about your health, but you're looking pretty good. Plainston will get you back in top form. Happy New Year," she said as she hugged me again.

My eyes swept the room to locate Max and Lydia. When I saw them together, my flu-weakened heart threatened to stop. Max came striding across the room, both hands held out in greeting. He'd never been known to bubble, but he was now near to spilling over with joy.

"Kiki, it's good to see you. Great job you did on the campaign. Sorry we can't raise your wages, but you did the job as a labor of love, didn't you?" he said with a grin.

Love wasn't a word that often fell from Max's lips, but it slipped out now, naturally and easily, as if from familiar use.

I took a deep breath and asked, "What's the big surprise?"

Max's eyes glowed as he said, "You'll do me the honor of being my best man, I assume. Now that's an order, so don't give me that old, 'Let me think about it.'"

I tried to be light-hearted, but it wasn't easy with a leaden heart barely able to beat.

"I'd rather be a bridesmaid if the lucky woman is who I think she is. Am I right?"

I was looking at Lydia, who stood watching us from across the room. Turning, Max motioned for her to join us.

There was something a little strange about her as she moved toward us, but I figured that she couldn't help but feel some embarrassment at seeing me again. She didn't hug me but instead held out her hand.

"Kiki wants to be a bridesmaid," he said with a grin, "but don't you think he'll do better as the best man, Lisbeth?"

"Lisbeth?" I said with a gasp.

She laughed a Lydia laugh. Then she gave me a Lydia hug and a Lydia kiss on the cheek.

"Didn't Lydia tell you she had a twin sister?" Max asked, surprised at my astonishment.

"No, she didn't. A sister, yes, but I can't remember hearing the word *twin*," I said, making a record recovery from cardiac arrest. "I guess this is another example of Plainston's penchant for keeping secrets." I took a deep breath and added, "Does the world deserve to be so doubly blessed?"

Max laughed. "See, Lisbeth. I told you that you'd hear a multiple 'P' alliteration among Kiki's first three sentences. Did you catch his 'Plainston's penchant'?"

She had and hugged me again.

A pair of arms encircled me from behind. Breaking the hold, I turned to face a radiant Lydia. She fell into my arms as she said, "Aren't they beautiful!"

And then she kissed me twice.

Taking my arm, she led me to dinner where I discovered that my appetite had returned. The food was delicious. The company was wonderful. The conversation was lively. I was almost as happy as the newly betrothed couple.

During dinner, the conversation naturally turned to the upcoming nuptials.

"Lydia, why don't we make it a double wedding?" Lisbeth suggested.

"I'm not that old-fashioned," Lydia said with a laugh. "Anyway, I'm just hanging onto Kiki until something better comes along. After all, he's still a Pagan, you know, and we Plainstans vow not to marry outside our faith."

"And we Pagans," I replied, "have our pride and honor, haughty miss. There are limits to how far we Pagans will demean ourselves just to satisfy our primitive urges. I shall not swallow Plainston's pious platitudes for all the alleged joys of matrimony."

Lisbeth grinned. "You're right, Max. Kiki alliterates even better in threes," she said.

*　　*　　*

During the meal, I garnered bits and pieces about Lisbeth's life. She and her late husband, Phil, were both native Plainstans. They'd gone to San Francisco on a Plainston "outside world" experience soon after their marriage. He'd joined a real estate firm, where he'd quickly developed into a top salesman.

Liking the Bay Area, the young couple stayed. Phil made a modest fortune in real estate, most of which they funneled into the conspiracy. They paid off the mortgage of the Coral Hills Center and took care of taxes. They spent a month or more each year doing volunteer work there.

Some years later, Phil, who was six years older than Lisbeth, became actively involved in the world ecology movement. He was appointed to a UNESCO committee working on reclaiming the Brazilian rain forest which was being devastated by farming. On one of the few trips he and Lisbeth didn't take together, he contracted a rare tropical disease and died in Brazil.

For a while, Lisbeth stayed on to run the operation in San Francisco. Then when she was in the midst of planning a move to Coral Hills near Washington, the flu epidemic hit the West Coast. The only place where she felt she'd get the care she'd need if she became sick was Plainston. She'd arrived there only a few days after I'd left in July and before Max had arrived to recuperate.

Actually, Lisbeth and Max had known each other for a long time. Max had interviewed Lisbeth and Phil years ago when he was with the *Washington Post*. When in Washington, they'd often invited him out to Coral Hills for a leisurely evening.

That explained why Max had been so willing to go to Plainston when Lydia and I'd proposed it. He knew Lisbeth was planning to go there—they'd kept in touch after Phil's death.

"I've been carrying a torch for Lisbeth for over twenty years," Max confessed.

"Oh, you poor, timid man! Why didn't you speak up?" Lisbeth said with a laugh. "We could've worked out some kind of polygamous arrangement. Phil was very fond of you, too."

I had no idea how much seriousness underlay this kind of banter. As far as I could tell, Plainstans weren't prudes, just private about their personal lives. Max and Lydia's outburst of laughter that followed Lisbeth's suggestion was infectious. I joined in.

Then, wiping her eyes, Lydia said to her sister, "Like that would've happened," which indicated that Lisbeth had a sense of humor rather than an unconventional view of marriage.

Lisbeth and Phil had been unable to have children, but they had "parented" in a different way by helping hundreds of children find homes, especially some "mixed" children, who'd been abandoned by their black and white GI fathers and their Vietnamese mothers both during and after the war. About two hundred had been resettled in Plainston and another hundred among some emigrant Plainstans. If a child proved too difficult for these outpost families and their local schools to handle, that child would be resettled in Plainston.

"We reasoned that if our Plainston schools and the total community are as good as we claim in shaping and reshaping kids' behavior, we ought to take on the toughest challenges," Lydia explained. "We feel we've succeeded, even with some of the real toughies in their teen years."

The rest of the evening flew by as the conversation jumped from topic to topic. About ten, we stopped talking long enough to enjoy a wonderful cherry cheese cake Lydia and Lisbeth had made from their mother's recipe.

Then, following a long-time Plainston tradition, a few minutes before midnight, we turned out the lights and gathered around the living room windows to gaze upon the beautiful, glowing dome of the Temple just blocks away. Holding up our goblets of sparkling cider, we toasted in the New Year.

*   *   *

Lydia flew back to San Francisco with Lisbeth in early January to help prepare for the wedding and for the move to Lisbeth and Max's new home near Washington, D.C. I flew out a few days before the ceremony.

After an elaborate church wedding on Valentine's Day and a sumptuous banquet, the newlyweds flew to Washington to resume work.

"The rest of our lives will be our honeymoon," Lisbeth said.

She'd already bought a house she liked in Suitland, only a few miles from the Coral Hills headquarters. Max liked it—actually, he liked everything Lisbeth liked—and they were happily ensconced by spring. Their home became a second Plainston outpost, concentrating on communication with their overseas outposts in national capitals and major cities worldwide.

If Plainstans were planning a global assault, they certainly had their communication channels ready. My goal, however, wasn't to ferret out information about Plainston's global reach but to find its home roots. What nurtures these remarkable people, so light-hearted and yet so deeply committed to some great purpose, both for themselves as individuals and for all humankind? I was hardly nearer the answer to that basic question than I'd been when I'd met Lydia over a year ago.

The only progress I'd made was in tearing out most of the weeds of doubt which had weakly sprouted from seeds sown in my mind by both my prior few weeks of reading reports and later from Wilber Bickersley's impassioned denunciation.

The deepest-rooted weed was the possibility, so often mentioned by fair-minded critics, that Plainston may be good and proper for Plainstans but not as a viable model for society at large. The spindliest, most shallowly rooted weed was that I might be risking my professional career by continuing the investigation, especially if I were blind to its basic faults. I hoped this latter ego-centered weed would just wither away while I was digging at the roots of the sturdier one.

I recalled what my teen-aged paramedic had explained while helping to bring down my raging fever: "You can't help if you don't know how. Being willing isn't enough. You gotta be willing and able!"

That pretty well encapsulated the typical Plainstan's philosophy of life. That lad's willingness and ability were fruit. But what were the roots?

Chapter 14

The Marketplace

After returning from the wedding in San Francisco, I began organized digging. After pondering how to get at the roots, I decided to check out Wilber's accusations about the economic system—Plainston's remarkable across-the-board prosperity, apparently based on its dual money system which Wilber had declared was illegal.

"I think you might understand if you put your mind to it," Lydia assured me during one of our daily phone calls. She suggested I contact Ed Grossman, one of the senior social studies teachers at Plainston North.

I did so the next day. I figured I'd have to catch Mr. Grossman between classes or maybe have a noisy lunch with him in the cafeteria or a quick chat in the teachers' lounge. I thought he'd give me some things to read or maybe a video since Plainstans are so adept at taping.

But what I expected to happen didn't happen. By now, I should've been prepared for the untraditional.

Ed Grossman was not in class, not monitoring a hallway or an outside playground, not in a teachers' lounge, not holed up somewhere making out lesson plans or grading papers. Instead, Ed Grossman was seated in an upholstered, executive style chair in a small but very attractive private office, talking to a student who was also sitting in an upholstered chair.

His office was one of two glass-walled offices on one side of the large social studies room, which itself didn't look like a classroom. It more resembled a mini-museum with dioramas of historical development and accomplishments, display cases of artifacts, dolls dressed in national costumes, and busts of famous men and women of different ethnicities and eras. Paintings of historical events, many done by students, covered one wall.

Notably missing were rows of student desks facing a teacher's desk as well as dusty blackboards or shining white boards. Instead, there were, scattered among the displays, round tables of various heights, accommodating up to six students. Study carrels were on the periphery. Students were reading, writing, talking quietly, and moving around at will. They were of all sizes, indicating they were likely of mixed ages as well. Another teacher, a young Asiatic woman, was in an adjoining office in conference with four students. Two other adults were in the big room—one at a table outside Ed's room helping a single student, the other in conference with a group of five students at a round study table.

After a few minutes, Ed Grossman came out of his office to greet me. "Very pleased to have you visit, Mr. Kornhauer."

Noticing my puzzlement at what I was seeing, he added with a chuckle, "Not quite the same as when you took social studies, huh?"

Because Ed Grossman looked to be about my age, I said, "And for you, too, I'd guess. Didn't you sit through those boring lectures and recitations and read those dull history and geography texts when you were in school?"

"Not me," Ed replied. "I had the good fortune to be born and raised here. We've had this kind of schooling for many years though not until recently in facilities this nice and efficient. But the freedom to follow our own interests and to work together and to help each other—that's been our education style for almost a hundred years."

When he paused, I was again reminded that I was to figure out Plainston's history and roots myself. Ed seemed to know that was my goal.

"I understand," Ed continued, "that Lydia recommends you take our economics course, Plainston-style? Come in and we'll talk about it."

Once we were seated, he said, "So you're ready to try to fathom the mystery of Plainston's prosperity? We've found is best to learn that subject through an intensive simulated experience. Books, videos, and discussion are of some value afterwards, but the introduction to Plainston economics is a twenty-hour experience in two contrasting economies: traditional and Plainstan. Do you have twenty hours—four hours a day for five consecutive days—to invest?"

"If that's the price, I'll have to pay it. Valuable knowledge never comes cheap."

"You're in luck, then. A simulation starts next Monday at 8 a.m. in the basement of the First National Bank downtown," Ed said.

*   *   *

On Monday morning, I arrived at the bank promptly at 8 a.m. My fellow students were a mixture of mostly first-timers with a few repeaters, who were fulfilling the requirements to be narrator or guide. In addition, these older students had to pass an exam which "is about the equivalent of a final in a college course in money, credit, and banking," Ed had said. "You'll be in very competent hands."

That was apparent from the outset. The students, fourteen in all, ranged in age from eleven to sixteen.

Our guide, Manette, a sixteen-year-old black girl with sparkling dark eyes and a halo of black hair, sketched the program. "You're going to experience a tiny slice of ordinary daily life under different economic systems. What will be hard is trying to forget all you know about our modern life. Forget who you are, and put yourself into your part. We're supposed to have fun with this, but take it seriously at the same time. Any messing up what others are doing will get you kicked out!"

She paused to let that warning sink it, which seemed unnecessary as everyone struck me as being totally serious. Suddenly, it occurred to me that perhaps the warning was aimed at me since I could imagine some adults—Wilber Bickersley, for example—taking delight in trying to sabotage being educated by a bunch of juveniles.

Manette continued, "We don't start way back when our ancestors were hunters and gatherers of seeds, roots, berries, and nuts—and probably went hungry a lot of the time. We start when people had settled down to raise different kinds of food and make different things—back when they needed to trade with each other."

Our narrator, a curly-haired, freckle-faced fourteen-year-old lad named Paul, read a brief account of early civilization at the level of primitive barter. Manette followed with directions.

"You'll find your name and your specialty along with the props you'll need at the tables over there. Read your directions to find out who you are and what your problem is. Then you're on your own to figure out how to solve it. But you must follow a principle: You must be honest and fair. You'll be trading what you've raised or made or what you can do—your skills. The idea isn't to get just what you think is a fair bargain but to get a reputation for being a fair and honest bargainer. You've got to operate above the line."

Everyone smiled knowingly at that Temple-based phrase.

As directed, we all went to the designated tables to find our new persona. I was to be a shepherd. On this warm day, I was to take a ewe, ready to lamb, to market and to trade her for food—potatoes, cabbages, carrots, and herbs—and a new water jug. My wife also suggested I get a headdress and a trinket for her. A props' aide handed me a cord attached to a life-sized, real-wool, stuffed ewe on wheels. To make me feel warm enough, she gave me a heavy, coarse, chestnut brown robe and turban.

She said proudly, "One of our kids made these. She spun the wool, dyed it, wove it, and hand-sewed the robe and turban. Nice wraps, aren't they?"

I agreed that they were.

Then the aide handed me a large, roughly woven bag and said, with a slight frown, "For all the stuff you've got to trade for. And your wife will be very upset if you don't bring her those pretty things."

I was already quite warm when my ewe and I started circulating through the busy marketplace. I suddenly realized that I had no clue as to how much a pregnant ewe might be worth in terms of vegetables, household utensils, and jewelry. And what if nobody happened to be interested in sheep that day, and she was all I had to trade? And then there was the demanding wife at home.

You might intellectually imagine the situation, but until you've spent a hot forty-five minutes trying to locate a vegetable producer who might want an ovine mother and child and then deciding how many potatoes are a fair trade, you'll never really understand the inefficiency of direct barter.

We were all glad when that first frustrating forty-five minutes was over. I had finally ended up with three heavy bags of potatoes, heavier than I could possibly have struggled home with, and I still had the problem of trading my excess potatoes for all the other stuff my loving wife had ordered.

After removing our hot robes, we all sat down to share our tales of trading woes. Manette and Paul didn't try to control or direct our discussion. Everyone spoke to the whole group. When Manette judged that we'd come to an adequate understanding of primitive barter on an honest level, she asked each of us to go "below the line" and to imagine how we could've cheated. The "woman" who'd traded potatoes said she could've put some rotten ones and maybe a few rocks in the bottom of the bags. I confessed that I could've hidden the fact that my ewe was old and, although pregnant, had never produced a live lamb. Others in the group invented equally iniquitous ploys.

Manette then asked a simple question: "Which would people keep trying to do, trade honest or cheat?"

Nobody answered immediately. From my sixty-plus years of too frequently finding malfeasance in modern transactions, I was almost ready to answer "cheat" when one of the younger boys said, "I'd never trade again with the apple man because his apples looked good, but they were all wormy."

The wormy-apple man avowed that he'd avoid the cheating dairy man whose cheese was too moldy to eat.

After a few more spoke, Paul asked, "Can you think of a basic law of economics you've learned from trying two ways to barter—being honest or cheating?"

The older students who were repeating the simulation let the first-timers speak their minds.

"Pretty soon, people will quit bartering with someone they know is trying to cheat them," said one beginner.

"Right!" added another. "You have to be above the line, or you'll starve to death!"

"So," Manette asked, "is there a law of economics we can be pretty sure of from this little taste of bartering?"

After a moment of thoughtful silence, Paul called on me. "Mr. Kornhauer, any words of wisdom?"

For an instant, I felt that familiar student's fear of being wrong, but I said, "I suppose any economic system won't work unless people are fair and square with each other. They must've found out pretty quickly that honesty isn't just the best policy—it's the only policy!"

There were smiles all around as narrator Paul read on. "The next step was simply an improved form of barter. It happened that a trader came into the market one day and offered to trade gold ornaments, trinkets, and jewelry. We peasants were all drably dressed with crudely-tooled leather belts and animal teeth and polished stones for necklaces and bracelets. None of our handiwork matched the beauty of the gold items. We eagerly traded for them.

"We discovered how much easier it was to trade our goods and services for small gold ornaments and trinkets. Gold didn't spoil like cabbages or get sick and die like pigs and sheep or sour like milk. We could keep gold and trade it whenever we wanted to or needed to. It didn't lose its trading value. But we discovered it also had some drawbacks. Can you imagine what some of these were?"

No one answered right away.

Then an older girl who'd taken the class before said, "As I remember, the main trouble with bartering gold jewelry and other gold items was that they were all different sizes, shapes, and weights. Some were real artistic—they had an emotional appeal that made them worth more to some people."

An older boy continued, "And the people who made the artistic stuff wouldn't trade it for just anything, like a few heads of cabbage or a bag of horse feed."

The first-timers began to catch on to this quantity-quality dilemma and offered a few examples. One said, "I wouldn't trade two of my piglets for a bracelet that I thought wasn't worth more than one."

Another one added, "I'd refuse to spend a week doing carpentry repairs on a woman's house and barn in exchange for a small scarf she had woven even if my wife liked it."

Bargaining services for goods became more contentious with traders seldom feeling they'd made a mutually fair bargain.

After Paul filled in the historical details, we acted out part of the story. I was made emperor of a large country. From the gold mines I owned, I was to turn out quantities of gold trinkets to pay for the materials and labor needed to run the empire. The government employees took their gold trinkets to the marketplaces and traded them for food, clothing, and other people's work as well as entertainment. But they still ran into frustrating bargaining problems even though they were trying to be fair and honest. So they came to me, the emperor, with appeals for some still better way to barter.

I pretended to have not the foggiest notion about what to do. As before, the experienced repeaters waited for the younger, less experienced members to suggest a solution. They finally asked me to issue small chunks of gold, all the same size, shape, and weight and marked with my seal; however, simply arriving at the solution of bartering with same-size, non-jewelry gold wasn't enough. The drama continued. The script called for me to order a quantity of such small objects to be distributed at the next pay day.

Half the students were in my employ; the other half were the farmers, artisans, and other laborers needed to run the empire. They would trade their goods and services to my empire employees for their gold pay. Everyone then faced a new version of the original trading problem. My gold-paid workers wanted to give up as few of their pay pieces as possible to get the goods and services of the workers, who, of course, wanted to get their hands on as many gold pieces as they could because they could use gold, as well as their services, in bargaining with each other. We were instructed not to call these standard gold pieces "coins."

When we learned that we hadn't solved the bargaining problem by getting regular size-and-weight pieces to trade, we discussed why it was so hard to solve. Again, the least experienced players analyzed the problem and suggested solutions with never more than gentle leading hints from the more experienced players.

One young man said, "Well, it's still about the same problem we had at the very beginning. We had to decide how many gold pieces we'd trade for whatever we wanted, whether we were buying or selling. I mean, I had baskets I'd made, and I didn't know what they were worth in those new little pieces of gold, and I needed the gold for a leg of lamb and a new robe."

"How did you decide what a basket was worth in gold pieces?" Manette asked.

"That was really hard for both of us. The woman really needed the basket, but although she was an empire employee, she didn't have a lot of pieces for her work, so she didn't feel she could give me as many pieces as I needed. Both of us sort of gave in a little to finish the deal. Then I didn't know how much I'd need for the leg of lamb and the new robe."

"Why didn't you know?" Paul asked.

"I didn't know how many gold pieces other people were using to get what they needed."

It fascinated me to hear these kids trying to solve this basic problem of fair trade. All of them—buyers and sellers alike—had held off closing a deal until they'd inquired around as to what the other merchants and workers were trading for their goods and services. It had taken over an hour for those kids to establish a fairly uniform value for the gold pieces and all the different things they were trading for, but I doubt if a group of adults could've done it any faster or any better.

It was impossible not to let our current knowledge of money lead us to the solution for the problem. But that firsthand, living experience of trying to establish the value of money gave us an operational understanding of a basic problem of a money economy.

Manette asked the central questions: "How did you finally know what those gold pieces were really worth? And why would you trade things you can eat or wear or really need for little pieces of metal that you can't eat or wear or use for anything except jewelry?"

"Because we knew that other people would trade them for the stuff we really wanted and needed," one young girl said as we all nodded in agreement.

"Didn't you accept them in trade when you had something really useful to sell because they were gold—a precious metal?" Paul asked.

We all thought about that for a while.

"I guess in the back of my mind I might've thought, Yeah, I can get myself a nice set of earrings out of those gold pieces," said a young lady who made and sold shawls, "but I already have all the jewelry I want. I needed the gold pieces to hire a fellow who makes chairs. I need more chairs."

"And I took 'em," the chair maker responded, "because I could trade 'em for a nanny goat. We have a new baby, and she needs goat's milk."

The kids were really into the spirit of the drama.

"You all believed you were trading real gold, didn't you? Would it've made any difference if the pieces had really been common iron or lead with a thin layer of gold on the outside? Would you have traded them the same way?" Manette asked.

The room was silent again as we all thought about her questions. Then gradually a larger truth dawned on us. We realized this was a question about the intrinsic value of money.

"So long as everybody else will take it, it doesn't really make any difference," one student answered confidently.

Manette rephrased the question: "So what gives money its value to you?"

A tentative answer came quickly from an eager young boy, who said, "Other people willing to trade you something good for it."

We all sat back, satisfied and thoroughly convinced that money gets its value not from its worth as a consumer item, such as an apple or a bottle of milk or an hour's work someone does for you. Money is valuable only because everyone will trade it for goods and services.

An experienced member of the cast finally summarized what we'd learned: "Money is the most efficient method of exchange. It doesn't need to have intrinsic value. Its value is always determined by others' willingness to trade things that do have intrinsic value."

When a young boy asked what *intrinsic* meant, an older teen answered, using an analogy. "A postcard you can write on is useful. It has more value as paper than a flimsy paper $100 bill. But that $100 bill is a lot more valuable than a postcard because you can trade it for things you need or want. Even so, the $100 bill is just a piece of paper. As that, it has less intrinsic value than the postcard which is useful as a piece of paper."

The boy had the concept pretty clear in his own mind, but I'm not sure it cleared it up for everyone else. I saw some puzzled looks.

Paul said, "Don't worry, kids. By week's end you'll be saying 'intrinsic' and knowing what it means as well as you know that $1.50 buys your favorite snack bar."

"I think I know right now!" a rosy-cheeked girl, the youngest of our group, said. "The snack bar is intrinsic 'cause I can eat it. The $1.50 is nothing but just money! I can't eat it."

We laughed as we clapped for that clarifying example.

When Manette dismissed us at noon, she said, "Nice as money is as a medium of exchange, it has a down side. We'll tackle the major problems with money tomorrow."

*   *   *

The problems we wrestled with the second day dealt with keeping the amount of money in circulation in balance with the amount of goods and services for which it served as the medium of exchange. We started the day with each of us being given the same amount of money to spend and a fixed amount of goods and services to spend it on. But when the amount of goods and services changed—either increased or decreased—that played havoc with prices, savings, and debt.

We experienced inflation when production held steady but the amount of money increased—through counterfeiting, the discovery of rich gold and silver lodes, the printing of a lot of paper money, and the speeding up of the rate at which the money circulated.

Conversely, we had to go through deflation, *a la* the Great Depression of the 1930s. That hit us when we had an influx of new people. We started the day with ten of us, each one of us equal to one hundred people to make a village of a thousand. Then the reserve five students came in to increase the town's population to 1,500, but they didn't bring any new money with them, so we all had to get along with our original amount of money. These people all did productive work or offered skilled labor, so we had to buy their products and pay for their labor out of our limited supply of money. As a result, we had to offer less money for goods and services, which depressed the prices we used to get for our goods and services. If we had debts we'd taken on at the former price level, they were harder to pay off when our earnings were less than what they were when we'd gone into debt.

Although there was plenty of work for these new people to do, we didn't have enough money to pay them at the same level as when there were only a thousand of us. Thus many of the newcomers and some of our own original townsfolk became unemployed, living by begging or doing odd jobs.

These experiences took intensive acting out for four solid hours, after which we were convinced of the truth of that centuries-old statement, "Who controls a nation's money supply rules that nation."

We were eager to learn more and to tackle the basic question: What is the best, most natural, possibly foolproof way to fairly exchange goods and services?

During the next three days, we came to understand the dual "money" system of Plainston, a concept applicable to economies everywhere.

The simulations started with us as westward pioneer settlers, staking out farmland, clearing forests, draining swamps, and breaking the prairie sod. We were all doing about the same things on our farms, so all we traded was labor—helping build houses, barns, fences, roads, bridges, a schoolhouse, and a church. I helped a neighbor shuck his corn, and he helped me back the same number of days. Our wives traded quilting and nursing and child care.

We began to see that the value of goods was based primarily on how much labor went into producing them. When we did begin to specialize—I became a carpenter and traded my work for the blacksmith's—we expected to trade hours about equally. This, however, was much harder to do when trading food. How many human hours does it take to produce a pound of butter or a ham or a bushel of corn? But underneath the dollar price of goods, we began to see that it was the labor involved in their production and distribution that we were really exchanging.

Plainston's economy is based on the concept that labor is the proper basis of a rational, equitable money economy. There are only twenty-four hours in a day. An hour of labor can't be counterfeited or magically spewed out of a printing press. It can't disappear in bank failures or be stolen from a Brinks truck. We discovered that so long as the earth provides the raw materials for labor to work on, labor provides its own medium of exchange.

When new settlers arrived on our frontier, bringing new skills, the community was enriched without needing an influx of new money. The new arrivals added their hours of work and were paid in equivalent hours of work transformed into food, clothing, shelter, medical care, schooling, and such. The more labor available, the richer the community.

Plainston, of course, traded with the outside world and had to pay for outside raw materials and finished products with U.S. currency. They got such money by selling Plainston products and services to outsiders.

Within Plainston, the "currency" was the hours of work people put in for their neighbors. Computerization made the bookkeeping manageable. Plainston hours were, of course, good only for Plainston-made goods and services. By Plainston being as self-sufficient as practical, about three-fourths of all Plainstans' basic living expenses could be paid for by their labor, an average of twenty hours per week. Additional hours—usually about ten per week—earned workers regular wages which they used for goods and services outside the walls. Visitors like me added more currency to the economy as we paid for lodging, food, entertainment, and services.

The rich variety of skilled labor which Plainston had imported and developed was its source of wealth. Free time was for most Plainstans their most prized possession. Because everyone worked efficiently, the essentials of comfortable living were produced with about thirty hours a week for an individual.

* * *

The bank treated us to a delicious lunch of lasagna and salad on the final day of our economics course—not the usual end-of-course celebration I remembered from my college days when some of us burned our notes and rushed to the book store to sell back our texts. Since we'd become a close-knit group, the conversation was mostly personal and light.

As we all headed back to the school, the conversation centered on the course. Those who'd repeated it stated what new ideas they'd gotten, and new students were already expressing their eagerness to take it again. What most impressed me about this group was their genuine interest in each other. They'd listened patiently to one another's explanations and carefully questioned others to help clarify their thinking. When a beginner would finally see the light, their faces glowed. Sometimes, there would be hugs or more often a burst of applause. They were the happiest group I'd ever spent twenty hours with.

Once back at school, I thanked Ed Grossman for arranging this experience.

"You know, I already knew just about everything we covered this week, but the quality of the knowledge is wonderfully different. I need to find out if I've finally found Plainston's roots," I said with a smile. "I'll be seeing you later."

* * *

The week's course was followed by my studying additional material which Ed Grossman gave me. Plainston's system had been in evolution for fifty years; many very good minds had refined it in both theory and practice. Contrary to Wilber Bickersley's allegations, Plainston's labor-barter system wasn't illegal. The system had been cleared with the IRS. Plainstans paid local, state, and federal taxes as did other American citizens.

I became convinced that the system, in its essential simplicity, was technically sound. Plainstans' basic beliefs about work and wealth were admirable: Unless disabled, we all should produce as much as we consume. The earth's resources are limited, so we must husband them carefully. Material goods are necessary but not sufficient for happiness. The wealth of a community is the public services it provides. Contributing to the public good makes life better for all. The simple life gives time to enjoy living. We work to make life worth living, not just to make a living.

In a world dominated by competitive greed for material wealth far beyond an individual's reasonable needs or capacities to enjoy, how did Plainston produce such reasonable, caring, intelligent people?

Despite it being highly successful, Plainston's economic system was top growth, which richly fed its roots. I was now convinced that I knew where to find those roots.

Chapter 15

Utopia or Not

I decided to stop, take a deep breath, and review what I'd already discovered by "living Plainston." Even though I'd technically had the assignment for a little over a year, I'd been away from Plainston for about six months, covering the election, and I'd lost another month or so with the flu and my recovery. Even so, I felt that I could draw a number of accurate conclusions about Plainston. It was time to begin writing those down, creating book chapters and article topics to describe Plainston's unique features.

I started with my conviction that people in Plainston are kind, caring, relaxed, happy individuals. I'd met no one who didn't fit that stereotype. I was convinced the cause wasn't from something imposed from outside—no additives in the food or water, no secret mood-altering medication from Health Services—as charged by some columnists, led by Wilber Bickersley. I found no mind control from the Temple. The people are simply genuinely good human beings in every sense of the word.

Plainstans are also healthier than the outside population, but no one forces them to eat a better quality of food. No one stops them at the gate to search shopping bags for cookies or potato chips or sugared colas. Actually, residents pass in and out of Plainston at will. Some work at jobs outside the walls. Many travel frequently or visit extended families. No one is forced to come to Plainston or to stay there. Plainston "lifers" are "lifers" solely by choice.

Religious tolerance is also totally unforced. Participation in Temple services is completely voluntary. To donate or not donate is a totally private matter. According to Pete Hammill, no records are kept of who attends or volunteers or donates—only how many.

The decisions to limit the size of the city and to build a wall around it are still accepted by the post-wall generations as the best way to maintain the life style and values that had evolved over several generations following World War I. There are no plans to change the no-car policy. Walking and biking seem to be as natural to Plainstans as breathing.

In a world where change generally equates progress, Plainston is remarkable in its unchanging structure.

*   *   *

I'd been in regular contact with Nathan Kincade since our meeting a year before. After discussing his findings about American Utopian societies at length, we'd reached a tentative conclusion about whether Plainston belongs in that classification as defined as "intentional communities created to perfect American society."

If you were to list those ingredients that make modern American society imperfect, you'd likely include crime, teen-aged pregnancy, high school drop-out rates, unemployment, obesity, pollution, corruption, greed, poverty—and the list goes on. Inside the walls of Plainston, those problems hardly exist—or don't exist at all—I couldn't fully judge that firsthand, having "lived Plainston" only a matter of months.

So if Plainston, by definition, is a Utopia, why has it succeeded for generations when most Utopias fade in a relatively short time? Nathan thought he had the answers. His examples and reasoning were convincing.

For one thing, there is no charismatic leader who directs all facets of the community. In fact, it isn't clear who runs Plainston. I'd been reading the *Gazette* faithfully, but there was no mention of a mayor. Wilber had also failed to find what he dubbed "the Big Brother" who runs Plainston. However, he'd noticed, as I had, that the South Tower elevator had a top 13th floor button that needed a key to operate it. Wilber was absolutely certain that the "power" was hidden up there.

During one of my conversations with Pete Hammill, I asked point blank, "Who has keys to the 13th floor of the South Tower?"

I'd expected Pete to turn white with fear or red with anger or assume an innocent expression of naiveté, but instead he laughed heartily.

"I wondered when you'd get around to asking about that. And I'm glad to see that you've lost your Pagan status so that I can fill you in."

I had, in fact, been given a new badge shortly after taking the marketing course. Lydia had simply handed it to me and said, with mock formality, "I hereby dub thee 'Plainstan.' Having abandoned your status of Pagan, you now can enjoy full Plainston citizenship and the knowledge thereof."

When I asked who'd made the decision, she'd simply shrugged and smiled. The questions just kept coming about Plainston!

"Why don't you come with me on Friday about eleven o'clock to see the 13th floor?" Pete said.

And with that simple invitation, I joined the Consensus.

*   *   *

On Friday, we walked from the newspaper offices to the South Tower— an unusually mild early March day, filled with the promise of spring, with newly arrived robins pecking at the moist gray-brown grass for morsels and just the hint of warmth in the light breeze.

At the Tower, we entered the elevator where Pete pushed the button for the 12th floor. When the elevator stopped there, he inserted a key into the button for the 13th floor, and the elevator rose one more floor. We stepped into a room that covered the entire upper story. Men and women were emerging from small offices scattered around the periphery. The aroma of chicken and vegetables filled the air. This very diverse group of about fifty mostly elderly people who met for lunch every other Friday was the Consensus.

Several individuals came to greet me. The first one who shook my hand looked quite familiar. In just seconds, I recognized him as another one of the "disappeared" whom Wilber had mentioned to me.

"Aren't you a former science writer for *National Tech Services*—but I don't recognize your name?" I said, looking at his name tag.

He hesitated, then smiled. "I am, but you're right about the name. When I made the decision to stay in this beautifully different place, I decided to take on a different name. I'm an orphan. I have no idea who my family is or how I got my original name, which I didn't even like, so I created a new name here. I chose Kenneth because I had a great third-grade teacher with that name and Terra for the earth because I'm an ecologist. I went back to the old custom of having a surname that reflects one's occupation."

Several others who approached me were also people who'd come to visit Plainston and had then stayed. One was a Nobelist in bio-chemistry, a woman near eighty. She'd dropped out of the rat race of publish-or-perish at the university where she'd worked for years and come to the University of Plainston about thirty years ago. She'd used her prize money to set up the bio-chemistry lab there.

A writer was another example of an outsider who'd come to visit—he was especially interested in the schools since he'd decided to write a book for young people about man's pre-history. Since he'd already cranked out a series of best-sellers for adults, his agent and publisher were pressuring him for more of the same. Instead, he'd chosen to "disappear" in Plainston, once his publishing contract was fulfilled.

"I spend most of my time at the schools with the kids who are helping me with the book. We've been working on it for over a year now. Never enjoyed writing so much before."

A handsome, aging black man with a white beard and hair, Professor Harrigan, had come to Plainston when he was young to visit his uncle who was working on the wall. He'd ended up working that summer beside him.

"That wall itself seemed a kind of crazy idea, but the feelings and dedication—well, even a kid like me felt that the ideals behind it were admirable—even the idea of sacrificing a higher standard of living for the greater good. I ended up becoming a professor of philosophy some years later, and because of the Supreme Court desegregation decision in the mid-50s, I had a bright future, as a black man, in academia. But that meant grinding out several papers a year—and knowing that I was accepted by many only because I was the token black the university needed. To make a long story short, I came back to Plainston to visit my uncle when he was dying, and I ended up with a job at the schools, developing a way to bring philosophy to kids younger than college age. And I've been here ever since."

The people around us applauded.

Soon, everyone began to move toward the huge, oval table in the center of the room. No one seemed to be in charge. No one told us where to sit. As the newcomer, I was introduced by Pete and encouraged to ask questions as we ate, which I did. Most answers confirmed what I'd already discovered—always a good feeling.

What I understood the Consensus to be was a body of persons from all sorts of background and disciplines who met to discuss how individuals and society interacted—a sort of philosophy of life.

Ken Terra said, "We've mostly been examining every facet of life in Plainston, comparing it with other life styles we know about and adopting, if we can, their best features and eliminating, if we can, the negative elements."

When I asked if there was any interest in the FINs, I was greeted with a round of applause.

The rest of the time, I just listened to the variety of topics discussed. It was a delightful meeting.

On the way back to the newspaper office, Pete explained that the day-to-day operations of the city are handled by a council that meets monthly—or more often if needed—at the schools, rotating among all six. The regular council has three or four members from each section of the city for a total of twenty or so. Each section decides who to send to the meetings, which are always open and run very informally. Any council member or resident can write on the board where the meeting is being held an item that needs to be discussed. For example, a recent issue was the overpopulation of deer. Various solutions were proposed—tranquilizing and removing to areas outside the walls, fencing the garden plots so that the increased number doesn't negatively affect the residents so much, and looking into a method of birth control for the females. Pete said that at the next meeting various members as well as interested residents will present the costs, labor, effects, and such of each solution. Discussion will follow until agreement is reached. Once a solution is implemented, the issue will be revisited several times to see if further changes need to be made.

I listened intently to Pete's long explanation. Then I asked, "But what keeps the various sides from being unable to reach agreement?"

I was thinking of the failure of our own government to reach consensus on all sorts of issues, especially ones related to budgets and expenditures.

Pete's answer was a simple one. "Plainstans have a commonality of values and the desire to have a city that is good for all—the sort of Three Musketeers slogan, 'One for all and all for one.' They will talk until they can agree on a solution."

It was hard to imagine a world without special interests, but Plainston seemed to have created one.

*   *   *

So in a city with no single leader, no factions supporting one cause or another, no desire to make decisions that aren't for the good of all—there are no problems of succession, no problems of jealously of control, no problems of a leader becoming too powerful or even an unbalanced megalomaniac—James Jones and the tragedy at Jonestown as the worst of the worst examples of that.

Also, since people have complete freedom to come and go, there are no unsatisfied residents, no dissidents to form sects as happened in New Harmony, Indiana. There is no forced socialism. People choose their work inside or outside the walls. People handle their own money and the barter hours they earn. No one says a resident has to work at least twenty hours a week or can't work more than forty.

Plainston doesn't attract eccentrics like some at Fruitlands, founded by Branson Alcott and Charles Lane in 1843. Nathan explained just how far beyond the norm some of the practices there had been. A group called "body purists" didn't wear cotton because of its reliance on slave labor or wool because the sheep were sheared without their consent. The residents were vegetarians, but they didn't eat root plants since growing and removing those would disturb the earthworms and other organisms in the soil. Since many at Fruitlands viewed labor as a non-spiritual activity, the commune couldn't grow enough food. Members became malnourished—and no doubt discouraged—and the community collapsed in less than a year.

Plainston also allows total freedom of religion, so again there is no single religious leader, no doctrine and practices all must follow, no need for converts. The Shakers, for example, had survived for years even with a policy of total celibacy. However, eventually, the groups declined due to a lack of converts. In Plainston, people are free to marry or not, to have children or not, to live their private lives in total privacy.

In the end, Nathan and I decided that Plainston is a Utopia because it is "an intentional community." It is walled with certain restrictions inside, such as a limited population and no cars, and it strives to "perfect American society." However, the elements that have so often led to the failure of historical American Utopias are missing in Plainston—the single powerful leader, a single religion or philosophy for all, a lack of tolerance for others' ideas, and a need to control residents.

Several questions remained: What has made Plainston the way it is—and has been for generations? Is the label "conspiracy" a fair one? Can Plainston be replicated elsewhere?

*   *   *

I shared all my thoughts in detail with Lydia during our frequent lunches and our hand-in-hand walks. She mostly smiled and often said, "I'm so glad you're here."

She helped me only by agreeing that Plainston's economy, its spirituality, and its healthy life style are the fruits. She agreed that I still needed to find the roots, but she wouldn't confirm that I thought I now knew where to find them.

Then one afternoon, after I'd been writing my findings for several weeks, she said, "I think it's time for you to read *Plainston Chronicles, 1919-1951.* It's a collection, mostly of letters, which tell firsthand about the origins of the Plainston you are now 'living.'"

She refused to tell me more, and so I tackled the thousand-plus pages of two volumes, becoming immediately immersed in the story that began with Mrs. Grace Muenster, a World War I widow, and Ten Maples, a one-room country school.

When I finished reading *Plainston Chronicles*, I knew for sure what my next step should be in discovering what makes Plainston tick.

Chapter 16

Digging for the Roots

I spent the last days of March at the Tower. A late winter blizzard made staying inside very enjoyable as large snowflakes battered the windows, propelled by fifty and sixty mile-per-hour winds. I knew huge drifts must be piling up outside. Since Plainston had buried its utility lines years before, we lost no power as other Midwestern cities did during the storm. Satellite television reception was an off-and-on-again affair, which hardly disturbed me at all as I worked to organize the next phase of my "living Plainston," this time in the schools.

Since I'd laid in a good supply of canned soups, cheeses, bread, oatmeal, and other staples when the storm had been predicted, I had no need to dial 711 for help that was available for anyone who ran into trouble while being snowbound. It was possible to get around outside on foot, just not at all pleasant.

In one of our frequent phone calls, Lydia said, "At least when a deep snow comes this late in the season, you know it won't last long since it'll be warming soon."

And she was right. I walked to Plainston North on April 1ˢᵗ—a date which seemed ironic since I was so certain that I wouldn't be fooled by my certainty that I would soon know the roots of Plainston. Residents had scooped out walkways in every block, sometimes in the street, sometimes on the sidewalks—wherever the snow wasn't too deep. Shimmering waist-high drifts were everywhere, with the shoveled paths winding around among them. By the time I reached the school about 11:30, I felt positively invigorated after being inside for several days.

I went directly to Ed Grossman's Social Studies Center and waited for him to finish with three students in his office.

"May I observe your school?" I asked directly.

"You're in luck. Come to the weekly staff meeting at lunch time, and we'll issue you formal permission to explore," he said with a smile as he glanced at his watch. "We'll be meeting in the All Purpose Center in about twenty minutes."

Ed explained that a rotating third of the personnel met on Tuesdays for lunch to discuss issues and to socialize. Since each learning center was manned with between two and four adults, the activities weren't affected in a major way when part of them disappeared for lunch together, especially since both kids and adults had staggered lunch times between eleven and one every day anyway.

Once every six weeks, personnel from all six buildings in Plainston met—again at least one from every learning center and department—during an evening seminar which moved from building to building. The primary purpose of those meetings was to share ideas and discuss problems.

When we arrived at the All Purpose Center, several students in green aprons were shoving some tables together to form a rectangle to seat fifteen—I made sixteen. Once everyone was seated, each person, for my benefit, stated his or her name and the department represented. A nurse, a cook, a maintenance man, and one of the district's social workers were there along with a representative from the Child Development Center, the Alumni Center, all seven learning centers, the library, and the gym.

Then Ed introduced me. "This is Kiki. I'm sure you know all about him—if you've been following Wilber Bickersley's columns. He has bunions, has survived the flu, supports FIN politics, and is now apparently involved in our Plainston conspiracy."

Grins appeared all around the table.

"Last month, he finished our first course in economics, and now he's ready to know more about how his classmates got to be so 'happy and supportive'—his words, not mine. He wants to dig for our roots. Shall we permit him to do so?"

Laughter indicated assent.

When asked, I explained my plan. I would first look at the physical layout of the school—I knew that all six schools had basically the same floor plan and physical organization, so I'd have to do that only once. Then I planned on studying the curriculum at all six schools. I figured on about two days in each building—two or two and a half weeks tops to study the schools.

Some teachers nodded, but others looked at me with raised eyebrows. I should have paid more attention to the latter group. The two weeks turned into three, then four, then five . . . .

As the introductions were being made, two green-aproned teens wheeled over a large pot of homemade chicken and rice soup, which they ladled into bowls as other student workers distributed small plates and silverware. A huge bowl of fresh fruit and a tray of warm bran muffins were passed around.

While we ate the delicious lunch, several problems were addressed. The first was mud. I smiled as I realized that such a topic had never been discussed at any faculty meeting I'd ever attended. The maintenance man, John Anderson, who was also the garden instructor, I learned later, presented the problem. Soon the kids would be outside, first cleaning up the winter debris of dead leaves and twigs, then tending the emerging perennials in gardens all around the building, and finally adding annuals from their own greenhouse stock. Outside work in the spring in the Midwest means muddy shoes. The mats at the side doors hadn't solved the annual problem. John's suggestion was to build cubbies for shoes in the garden shed, which was close to the door the gardeners used. Parents would be asked to send old pairs of shoes for their own kids and maybe extras for kids without a pair.

I learned later what the outcome was for John's suggestion. Others in the five Plainston schools thought the plan was worth a try. Older students at the woodworking shop at Southwest designed and built the cubbies for North. Parents sent in a plethora of old shoes. By the end of May, the plan was deemed a success at North and orders were sent to the woodworking shop for five more cubbies for the other five buildings. Thus, the problem was solved, and much more Midwestern mud was left outside where it was supposed to be.

Item two on the lunch agenda was new students. A pair of four-year-old fraternal twins would be entering the Child Development Center the following week—boys with very different personalities and abilities according to their parents and the pre-testing done in March at North. The brief discussion was centered on how to let each boy progress at his own pace without making the other one feel less able. Since one was ready for the phonics program in the Basic Education Center, the other one needed a reason to also leave the Child Development Center at the same time. That young boy was very interested in animals of all kinds, so it was decided that he would go to the Science Center each day where he'd be introduced to animals through stories read to him by an older boy and where he'd see and be able to handle Bella and Winky, the rats; some newly-hatched chicks; three toads; two snakes; and one very pregnant rabbit, Mrs. Cabbage. The rest of the day, the twins would be together in the Child Development Center. Gradually, the time they spent apart would be increased until each could progress as his interests and abilities allowed.

The other new students coming at the end of the week were three sisters from upstate just entering Plainston's extensive foster care program. The girls' father was in prison, and after a year of trying to cope alone, the mother had dropped out by dropping into the drug scene. For over a year, she'd disappeared for days at a time, leaving her eight-year-old to parent her three and four-year-old sisters. In short order, several decisions were made. The homeroom for all three girls would be the Child Development Center since splitting them up would likely cause anxiety in the beginning. The older one, Jenny, would become a helper there until she felt comfortable leaving her little sisters. A couple of older students would come to the Child Development Center to help Jenny with basic skills in reading, writing, and math.

The nurse and the gym teacher would evaluate the girls' physical condition since the girls had basically been in hiding inside their small apartment to keep anyone from taking them away—their mother's warning when she showed up every few days with a bag of groceries. Early on, when someone from the local school called to check on Jenny's absence, Jenny pretended to be her mother and said they were moving to Nebraska on Saturday to live with their grandmother—and the girls promptly fell through the cracks. No one checked to see if Jenny's records were requested by a new school—no one realized the girls were alone.

They might've succeeded in hiding even longer if Carrie, then aged five, hadn't gotten so sick she was struggling to breathe. After searching the nearby streets and failing to find her mother, a terrified Jenny called 911. That call led to hospitalization for pneumonia for Carrie and eventual placement for all three girls with one of the over fifty certified foster families in Plainston.

I decided to keep an eye on the girls; I'd come back to North again.

The next item was congratulations to the science teacher who was expecting her first baby towards the end of the year. Her announcement that she'd be a stay-at-home mom for a couple of years was met with smiles.

Then as the lunch hour was coming to an end, head-teacher, Erin McGregory—an Scotch-Irish beauty with ivory skin, deep blue eyes, and sparkling straight black hair worn in a simple bob—added a few words.

"Welcome, Kiki. You'll have unlimited access to all the information you can get out of—"

She paused and turned to the group, who responded in unison, "The kids!"

Grinning, she said, "When you 'dig' the kids, you must be prepared for them to 'dig' back. You've undoubtedly already observed that our students ask questions. We tell you this so you won't misinterpret their responding to your questions with questions as impudence or as a way to dodge the issues. Happy digging!"

*   *   *

What follows is my attempt to condense my copious notes and recordings to let you share my experiences. But first, you must forget most of what we associate with traditional schools—the age-based classrooms in elementary school with promotion or retention at the end of each year, a teacher's desk in front and student desks in rows or groups, bells ringing throughout the day, students filing from classroom to the gym or the cafeteria or the music or art rooms, security at the entrances, noisy hallways with banging locker doors between classes in high school, papers evaluated with letter grades, competition with peers for a class rank and a GPA good enough for the college of one's choice, trips to the principal or dean's office for punishment, hands raised to get called on, bodies slumped down to avoid being called on, closed-up buildings soon after the fleets of yellow buses pull away, teachers wielding red pens for hours at night . . . . I witnessed none of that in the Plainston schools.

I'm unsure I can explain adequately all that I did witness. Ideally, the school experience needs to be lived, but since that isn't possible for everyone interested, I will describe what I observed, hopefully with enough flesh, nerves, and blood to endow it with believable life.

A Brief History of Plainston Schools

All six Plainston schools have the same basic physical layout even though they were built years apart as the community grew and the population increased from the five thousand at the end of World War II to the forty thousand plus full-time residents of today. Southeast was first, replacing Oak Hill, the first school in town to implement the new style of education way back in the 1920s. Even though the Oak Hill building wasn't that old, its four square traditional classrooms with two grades per room didn't lend itself well to the new concept—to be explained later—which had actually started at Ten Maples, a one-room school.

Thus, Oak Hill was replaced with a large rectangular brick building with a pitched roof to reduce the leakage problems most mid-1900s school buildings with the less-expensive, flat roofs have. Some years later, a full-sized gym and the Music and Art Centers were added. And years after that came the Child Development Center first and finally the Alumni Center, both added as separate buildings connected to the original structure—what the students had begun to call the Big School—with covered walkways.

I knew from having read *Plainston Chronicles* that Southeast was located in the first part of Plainston to grow rapidly after World War II, an area with a housing boom due to increased employment opportunities in several factories. The original Oak Hill district had a population of both older "elite" families and blue-collar families who were about 20 percent black.

The other grade school in post-World War II Plainston was Jefferson. For many years after Oak Hill began to offer a totally different type of education called "family style," Jefferson kept its very traditional educational style. The controversy over which way was the best way to educate children raged—and I mean raged—for years. Eventually, the positive results and the strong parental support at Southeast simply wore down the opposition. More and more parents demanded that their kids be placed at Southeast—an impossibility due to the limited space—so that in the end, about ten years after Southeast was built, the old, drafty two-story Jefferson building was demolished and replaced with Plainston South, which had the same floor plan that had been working well at Southeast. A handful of families who were totally dissatisfied with the educational changes packed up their kids and left; however, they were soon replaced by families who'd heard of the good job market and the new educational system—usually from family members already living in Plainston.

Then when the community faced the problem of what to do with an aging, over-crowded high school building, the decision was made—after many months of debates and informational meetings—to make the existing two buildings into combined high school-grade school buildings and to erect a third such building to house the added numbers of students.

Therefore, during the next year and a half, the existing two buildings were remodeled to accommodate high school level students. At Southeast, the Science Center was enlarged to include a lab for chemistry and physics. A large theater area for the dramatic arts and musical performances for the school district was added at South, and the school under construction, Southwest, included auto mechanics and woodworking shops.

About this time, the Plainston community had reached about twenty thousand. Life was good—very good. Adults worked but had time for play, worship, and community service. Kids liked school and progressed remarkably well. The small community college had grown into a university with its graduates in great demand in the "outside world."

For years, people had talked, mostly in jest, about walling up their city to keep trouble out and contentment in. As the anti-war protests, the assassinations during the 60s, and racial strife dominated the national news, more and more citizens in Plainston said, "Why not?"

After a couple of years of serious discussions in many town meetings, the people decided to literally enclose themselves and plan their city's growth.

After the wall was completed, the city continued to grow-up rather than out—with bikes and electric vehicles replacing cars and pick-up trucks. As more families came, the school population eventually doubled. North, Northeast, and finally Northwest were built over a twenty-year period—ending in the new millennium.

A Bird's-eye View

An architect's drawing of a Plainston school—or what you'd see if you could remove the roofs and fly like a bird over the structures below—would look something like this.

A lobby runs across part of the front of the building with student-maintained flower beds flanking each side—welcoming each spring with yellow daffodils and a rainbow array of tulips. The lobby has office space on one side for record keeping personnel—but no space for a principal or a dean—and space for a nurse and a social worker on the other. Beyond the lobby is a long, wide hallway.

On the left side of the hallway are the Language Arts Center and the Social Studies Center, which share restroom, closet, and storage space between them. The third center on the left is the Basic Education Center, which has its own restroom and closet space. On the right side of the hallway are the Science Center and the Math Center, which also share restroom, closet, and storage space. The last room on the right is the library. At the end, the All Purpose Center is on both sides of the hallway with a kitchen-cafeteria area and space for all sorts of other activities.

The hallway ends at the gym, which has a fitness center and a play space for the little kids separated on one side. A stage is at one end. The Music Center is left of the gym—a bird can't see it since it is the bottom story of two. There is a large room for music groups as well as a dozen sound-proof practice rooms. Above the music room is the Art Center, nicknamed the Loft by the kids.

Child Development Centers first and Alumni Centers later were added to the first three schools as separate buildings when Plainston's population reached about twenty thousand. The Child Development Center is connected to the Basic Education Center with one covered walkway and to the gym and the Music and Art Centers with another. The Alumni Center, which is located farther back from the school complex, is also connected with a covered walkway, all lined with flower beds and shrubbery of all kinds.

Sidewalks and bike racks line the building on the right and left sides. Each center has an outside door so that kids can enter either from the outside or through the lobby. On the left are ball fields and a playground. A sizeable vegetable garden and a hoop greenhouse are on the right down by the All Purpose Center. A shed for gardening tools and mowers is attached to the gym wall.

Even though all six Plainston schools contain the same elements, they aren't cookie-cutter copies of each other. Adaptions have been made as needs have arisen. But more about that later.

A Ground Level View

One of my first "diggings" with the kids occurred at North a few days after I started my investigation. I discovered how these buildings were being cared for. A student crew of four was clearing and cleaning the All Purpose Center after the last of the lunch crowd had left a little after one.

I fired a series of questions: "Did you volunteer for this job, or is it punishment for misbehavior? Do you get paid? What does learning to mop floors and move furniture have to do with preparing you for your life's work?"

I got a unanimous "no" to the questions about punishment and pay along with several comments.

"Everyone takes turns learning how to keep our school neat and clean," said one teen-aged boy.

"Nobody does work as punishment," said another boy, who seemed genuinely puzzled by such a question. "Any work that has to be done is worth doing. Why should you associate work with punishment?"

I had no answer for that.

"Our life's work includes taking care of ourselves and where we live. What better way to learn something than to actually do it while supervised by people who are really good at the job?" he added.

In a jesting tone, I asked a final question. "So if you kids do all the work, what do the supervisors get paid for?"

They laughed. Then the youngest one in the group, a girl who looked to be about ten, answered quite seriously, "They teach us how to take care of our school just like our other teachers help us learn other stuff."

As I continued touring throughout the buildings, I noticed groups of kids doing cleaning tasks in almost every room—dusting here, sweeping there, wiping down tables and chairs. A few even handled laundry chores, washing towels and rags from the cafeteria and blankets and clothing from the Child Development Center.

A few days later, after the snow melted—and Lydia had been right since it had melted quickly once the April sun had appeared—some kids were carefully raking leaves away from the building where they'd collected over the winter, preparing for the spring flowers that promised to come soon from the green leaves poking up through the ground. Other kids picked up limbs and twigs that littered the ground beneath the deciduous trees all around the school campus.

I saw a maintenance man showing a group of kids who looked to be about eight how to clean the finger prints off a window; I saw a cook supervising a group of teenagers who were chopping vegetables for the soups that were made daily during much of the year; I saw a librarian teaching two boys how to shelve books according to their Dewey decimal numbers. I saw a nurse teaching a large group in the Basic Education Center how to wash their hands thoroughly.

Everywhere, there was teaching and learning—but none of it was in a classroom with rows of desks facing a teacher's desk in the front. The activities I observed at North those first few days were echoed in the other five buildings I visited in the ensuing weeks.

Chapter 17

The Learning Centers

When "family style" learning had begun in the 1920s, first at Ten Maples, the one-room school just outside Plainston, and later at Oak Hill in town, the terms "first grade, second grade, third grade" and so on had been dropped by the teachers since what those terms signified no longer existed. Instead, students were classified as "first year, second year" and so forth, which identified their time at the school rather than their levels of learning. Thus a second-year seven-year-old might still be mastering first grade math skills but reading in a third grade text.

The kids at Oak Hill, however, didn't keep track of other kids' years in the school, where kids of all ages were grouped in subject-based rooms. Instead, they developed four descriptive categories—a fifth was added when the Child Development Centers became part of the schools. The use of those labels became so popular that the faculty and staff began to use them as well. Now, years later, both adults and kids in the Plainston schools use the terminology, which is quite simple.

The very youngest are called Babes. Once a child is walking well, potty trained, and talking, he or she becomes a Little One, pronounced Little 'Un. These children are what the "outside world" calls preschoolers, but since they are already in school, that label doesn't seem appropriate.

Next are the Beavers—the term coming from the expression "eager beavers," which aptly describes the kids in the Basic Education Center. They are eager to learn the three R's that the big kids know—reading, writing, and 'rithmetic. Sponges are independent learners who are ready to soak up everything, and Seniors are those working to complete high school graduation requirements as determined by the state and, in most cases, to prepare for entrance into college.

A unique feature of the Plainston schools is that these groups aren't separated from each other—a Senior may be found rocking a Babe to sleep in the Child Development Center; a Beaver may be rolling a ball back and forth with a Little 'Un in the gym; a Sponge may be planting seeds in the vegetable garden with Beavers and Seniors. The combinations are endless. And the ages don't matter much either. A group of six Seniors studying algebra together can range in age from twelve to sixteen; Beavers learning phonics may be ages four to seven; a kitchen crew may have members aged eight to eighteen; a beginning orchestra may have players with a five-year age range, depending on when each student got interested in learning to play an instrument.

As the words *grade* and *year* were replaced so was the word *classroom* since the rooms in Plainston schools aren't like any classrooms most of us ever attended. The rooms are called centers.

My original plan was to spend one day in each school to observe the layout of the learning centers. As with most of my original plans for this project, that plan quickly evaporated. What happened instead was that I ended up spending two or three or four days at each school since I was unable to separate the physical layout of the centers from the activity within—and I was rarely just a quiet observer on the sidelines. I kept getting involved in activities: "Do you want to read with us, Mr. Kiki?" "Come help us plant flowers." "You can be on my side when we play badminton." "Want to eat lunch with us?"

The Child Development Center

It seemed logical for me to start at the bottom, so to speak, with the tiniest kids. I spent two full days at Northeast in the Child Development Center, which is, as stated before, in a separate but nearby building which is attached to the Big School by two enclosed walkways. The flow of kids I witnessed all during each day included older kids going to and from the center as well as tiny tots, holding hands with an older child or adult, going to and from the Big School and the Alumni Center.

The Child Development Center is actually several rooms—one very large one and a couple of smaller ones—as well as the glassed-off teacher space similar to what I'd seen in the Big School centers.

One of the smaller rooms contains four cribs, a changing table, and a rocking chair. As I learned later, most Plainston couples arrange for one parent to stay at home with their children for the first couple of years of their lives, gradually introducing them to school when they are two or three years old—and then usually for only part of the day. Actually, parents make the decision about when their children enter school as full-time students. As a result, a few come as infants, more as toddlers, even more as four-year-olds, most by age five, and a final few at age six. Two families in Plainston were home-schooling their children that spring and three others sent their combined broods of ten to a Catholic school in Prairie Grove, using the bus that runs regularly there and back.

The first morning, I observed two infants sleeping in the cribs. One came full-time because his father had been killed in a farming accident two months before his birth and his mother was working full-time in Prairie Grove. The other was there because her mother was spending extra time with her own mother, who was in failing health in the Alumni Center.

The other smaller room is for the babies when awake and the youngest toddlers. It is a busy place with tiny tots crawling and pulling themselves up to stand for a matter of seconds before plopping back down on well-diapered bottoms. There are all sorts of colorful things to play with. Several rocking chairs line the edges, closed off by a low wall to keep tiny fingers and toes from getting pinched beneath the rockers. There older kids as well as adults rock with toddlers snuggling beneath special blankets or cuddling special toys. Some little ones hold small books as someone reads to them.

In the bigger room, there are low shelves filled with materials of all sorts on three walls. The center of the room is dotted with small tables and chairs and many little colorful rugs, each about two feet by four. Children who look to be as young as two and as old as five are everywhere—some sitting at the little tables, some on their rugs—some working alone, some with a partner. Several adults are present as well as older students from the Big School. The kids move freely from place to place, replacing something on the shelves, getting something else.

One afternoon, I watched a small girl in a bright green jumper approach a red-haired boy who was working alone on his rug. Apparently, he said yes to her request to join him as soon both were intently arranging blocks on the rug.

My first question was addressed to a young man, Dustin Ray, who was helping a very young child learn to button and unbutton two cloth pieces in a foot-square frame. Both the teaching device and the presence of a male in such an environment were novel features.

"What's the whole idea of this program?" I asked.

The sweep of the question didn't bother him.

"We operate pretty much on the principles that Maria Montessori developed in the Italian slums a hundred years ago. They've worked in every culture at every level of society for generations. We think Dr. Montessori knew more about early child development than other educators."

This sounded like a canned response prepared for such a question from a visitor. But as we continued the conversation I became convinced that the young man—a sixteen-year-old—fully understood the program. In summary, the theory is that young children need most of all to develop a sense of autonomy, of self-reliance. This translates into helping them learn what Montessori called "lessons of practical life"—dressing themselves, cleaning up their spills, and putting things neatly away on uncluttered shelves.

Children are given all the time and space they need to work by themselves. They aren't forced to work in groups. Their little individual work tables or their rugs are their inviolate territory, at or on which they can work as long as they please with a piece of "didactic apparatus" of their own choosing, alone or with another child if they so choose.

"We have found that when children learn their own rights, they also learn to respect those same rights in others. So they don't force themselves on others; they walk around kids working on the rugs. They learn to wait to get a piece of equipment to work with or to choose something else similar," my young mentor explained.

Later that morning, Miss Joanie, a smiling aide, wearing huge round glasses, filled in some information I needed. She explained that the kids also learn to sing, dance, draw, and play little instruments. Older students read stories to them, take them on tours of the Big School, and sit with them in musical and drama programs in the All Purpose Center. The older kids accompany the little ones to visits in the Alumni Center nearby and gradually introduced them to the adult world.

"Don't their parents do any of this?" I asked, somewhat suspicious of an institution which threatens to replace the home.

"Of course," Miss Joanie said. "We supplement all the home does. But the home can't do all we can do here. Many parents of the youngest kids work only half a day, so they usually send their children for either the morning or the afternoon. But children can stay as long as parents wish—from 7 a.m. to 6 p.m. Very few children are here that long, but if parents are ill or have to be away from home all day, their children are quite comfortable here."

When I asked a girl who was rocking a sleepy three-year-old why older students of all ages spend time throughout their school years working with these small children, I was counter-questioned, as head-teacher Miss Erin had warned I would be.

"What is more important to learn than to understand how little kids develop?" she said. "We don't all have little brothers and sisters, and even if we do, we can't be with them like we are here. Where else can we get expert advice about what we should and shouldn't do to help them. Why wait until we have kids to learn about kids?"

I thought about how little Marie and I'd known about kids—how frightening it was to bring home that first little bundle so totally dependent on us.

The girl's response was totally logical.

I'd planned to spend just one day in Northeast's Child Development Center, but I ended up spending a second day there, mostly just to rock Babes and Little 'Uns while I read the Dr. Seuss stories I'd read to my own son and daughter years ago and the Sandra Boynton ones that I'd read more recently to my grandkids while we cuddled in the huge rocker Marie had inherited from her grandmother.

The Alumni Center

I decided to spend a day at Alumni Center Northwest before going to the Big School. I'd already seen Alumni Center South when I'd visited LL there. The one at Northwest was basically the same. There was the same flow of kids and adults in the walkway that I'd witnessed before. Some of the elderly were walking, and some were in wheelchairs. Some went to the Big School, others to the Child Development Center.

Most of the elderly in Plainston stay in their own homes or apartments until they can't handle their own daily care and meal preparation. Some have family or others close by who can help, but many choose to come to the Alumni Center rather than have help at home. All residents have a private room, but only the very weak or very ill spend much time in their rooms. Most spend their days—when they aren't in the Big School or the Child Development Center—in the large commons area that doubles as the dining room.

I spent the day there, playing Scrabble and gin rummy, working on a jigsaw puzzle of brightly colored fish, watching four women and two men help youngsters with knitting, crocheting, and embroidery projects. Several kids were carving soap while their older instructor, sitting nearby, carved the whimsical little wooden animals I'd seen for sale in a shop in Plainston.

After a hearty lunch of tuna sandwiches on rye, cottage cheese, and tomato bisque soup, a group made up of both elders and school kids gathered around a piano and sang pop songs. Later that afternoon, two fifteen-year-old girls played several flute-oboe duets—a preview of what they were practicing for the spring concert.

Overall, the Alumni Center is a busy place. I learned that most of the residents spend some time volunteering as long as they are able. For example, one married couple helps out two mornings a week in the cafeteria. They'd worked in one of the city's restaurants before moving to the center. Five are math tutors in the Basic Education Center for two hours every day. Several are "rockers" in the Child Development Center. Three work with a special phonics program. Many go to the Art Center to work on their own projects and to help kids as needed. Half a dozen help kids learning to play instruments in the practice rooms. The rest who choose to volunteer are one-on-one tutors for specific kids. How one spends his or her time is a matter of choice.

By the time I'd visited all six Alumni Centers, I realized that the vast majority of the elderly choose to be involved in some way with kids. It wasn't long before I figured out why.

The Big School

The Big Schools contain seven content learning centers, each with the floor space of about three single-grade primary classrooms: language arts, social studies, science, math, art, music, and basic education. The other areas in the Big School are the gym, the library, and the All Purpose Center. Using my basic math skills—six hundred kids divided by ten rooms plus the Child Development Center—I figured that each area needs to hold just under sixty kids.

Each learning area center is different, depending on its specific use. For example, the **Language Arts Centers** have many study carrels on one wall. Some carrels have computers with earphones; some don't. The opposite wall has glassed in office space for two teachers and lots of file cabinets for teaching materials and portfolios. High windows cover the end wall with bookshelves underneath. One area of slanted shelves holds booklets written by the students themselves. There are tables for groups of six or eight, some with little chairs, some with big ones. There are also comfortable chairs of all sorts and lots of colorful beanbags scattered around for those just reading.

I decided to count the number of students in the Language Arts Center one morning when I was at Northwest—a task tantamount to trying to count birds flying to and from the feeders Marie and I had at one house where we'd lived. There were kids moving around and going in and out. When I first arrived, I counted forty-two—give or take a couple—but when I recounted a few hours later, there were fifty-eight.

Before the number could change again, I quickly jotted down what the fifty-eight were doing. The study carrels were filled with one or two students at each, mostly Seniors or older Sponges, it appeared—a total of sixteen there.

Seven younger kids were sitting in the beanbag chairs, reading silently or aloud—some with an older student beside them—for a total of eleven more. One little girl was curled up in a bright yellow beanbag chair, sound asleep. The ten easy chairs were also filled with kids reading—some sitting upright, some draped over the arms in stereotypical teenaged style. About half of the tables were being used with those writing and the other half had students in groups of two to four either reading aloud, round-robin style, or working on group projects—fourteen there. Two were diagramming sentences on whiteboard easels, and four Sponges were sprawled on the floor making book jackets for their favorite books with a picture on the front and a synopsis on the back. A large bulletin board was covered with jackets already completed by other Sponges. After lunch, I saw two kids remove jackets from the bulletin board, read the backs, and then replace them. They were apparently looking for a good peer-reviewed book because, soon afterwards, they signed out to go to the library.

And the adults, what were they doing? One teacher was in her office with a group of four older Seniors, whom I'd failed to notice when I'd made my initial count. I learned later that they were going over the first drafts of their final papers for the combined three-unit American literature, American history, and American geography unit required for all Plainston graduates. The other teacher was helping the two at the easels with sentence diagramming. I noticed that after he left, two other students wandered over to the easels and asked what they were doing—and soon all four were diagramming on easels they'd moved close together. An aide was at one table with a young group reading aloud. A volunteer from the Alumni Center sat with four young Sponges at a table, going over comma rules on worksheets they were completing.

A peaceful hum predominated, punctuated by occasional giggles from one of the tables. I wandered over to see what they were reading. It was one of my son's favorite books—one I'd recently sent to my nine-year-old grandson—*Soup and Me* by Robert Newton Peck. As I stood listening, one boy asked, "Would you like to read with us?" And I did.

The **Social Studies Centers** resemble the Language Arts Centers with a similar arrangement of carrels and easy chairs but with more tables and chairs and no beanbags. Pull-down maps and historic time lines cover the walls. The shelving beneath the windows is full of displays created by the kids—especially dioramas. The traffic between the Language Arts and Social Studies Centers is heavy since most of the students, especially the older ones, do combined work units as described above.

My count for that room during one afternoon ranged from a low of forty-two to a high of fifty-five. About half the carrels were filled with one or two students watching a video—one about geographical regions of the United States, one about the importance of letter-writing during the Civil War, one about the various activities of First Ladies since 1900, and one about the Louisiana Purchase. In the other half, students were either reading or writing.

Four Sponges were drilling each other on the names of states—each taking a turn at pointing at a state on an outline map with the other three identifying that state in turn. I thought back to when I'd learned the names of the states in fourth grade. Then it was one teacher in front with one map and a pointer, and each of us got called on to name two states of the fifty—actually, two of us got called on only once since there were twenty-seven in the class. I eventually learned to name the states, but I don't remember enjoying the lesson as these kids seemed to.

Another group of young Sponges was working at a flip chart of maps with different illustrations but no words. A Senior was helping them learn geographical terminology by asking lots of questions. For example, he pointed to one area and asked, "What are these?" The answer was mountains. Then he followed with a series of related questions: "What is a mountain? How is it different from a hill? Does anyone know the name of this group? Or this one? What makes these look white on top? Why does it snow so much there?" I was impressed with the youngsters' responses to the more complex questions like "Why aren't there big cities on the tops of mountains?"

When I visited the Social Studies Center again the next morning, I was surprised to see that almost all the Seniors were absent. When I asked one of the teachers, Drew Madison, he explained that all the Seniors had to complete the government course, which required them to periodically do out-of-school work. For two days, they were going to Prairie City on the bus to observe real courtroom proceedings. Another out-of-school project was conducting a survey they'd written to assess Plainston adults' knowledge of the political system. All in all, this center was also a hub of activity.

The **Math Centers** contain more tables of varying heights, some for groups and some for individuals. Two long walls are covered with white boards where many kids work problems—usually a bigger kid with a smaller one. Beneath the windows are shelves with Cuisenaire rods, all sorts of containers for measuring, and lots of yardsticks, meter sticks, and rulers. There are tubs with compasses and protractors, stacks of graph paper, boxes of flash cards, and containers of geometric shapes.

One far corner of the room contains individual tables where a number of students sit with headsets on to muffle the sound in the room. The students there take quizzes to see if a specific step in their sequential math program has been mastered so that they can move on to the next one.

The **Science Centers** are actually divided into two separate areas—one a lab for chemistry and physics and the other for biological sciences. Huge storage cabinets line two walls. All sorts of posters related to the plant and animal kingdoms, the atomic numbers, and such cover all available wall space. Most of the computers are used for programs on DVDs with two or three students watching at the same time.

In the biology lab, there are banks of lights above rows of growing plants on one side and several aquariums, terrariums, and cages for live critters on the other. Almost all the activity I witnessed is of the hands-on variety. In this center, no one sits in a chair, reading a book. Instead, books and papers are strewn about, books open to whatever information is needed for whatever the students are doing. At Southwest, the largest group I observed working together was one of eight older Sponges—all huddled around a large piece of white butcher paper, drawing and labeling carnivores and herbivores found on the American Plains with the food they need to survive.

The ratio of adults to kids is higher in the Science Centers. There are three teachers, three adult aides, and generally about four volunteers present, probably because of the hands-on nature of the instruction. The adults are scattered around the labs—talking, demonstrating, and listening to kids' questions.

The **gym**, which is supposed to be called the Activity Center but which both kids and adults call the gym because it looks like a typical school gym, also contains a fitness center. The gym is one of the places where kids often show up at specific times for specific activities. For example, in the winter, girls play basketball at three different hours, depending on skill levels; the same is true of the boys. Volleyball is on alternate days for both girls and boys. One week, there is basketball on Monday, Wednesday, and Friday with volleyball on Tuesday and Thursday. The next week, the schedule is reversed. Other indoor activities include badminton, basic tennis, dodge ball, rope climbing, and ball throwing. The goal is to expose kids to as many different activities as possible with skill building and conditioning as important as playing competitively. All the kids need to be physically active a minimum of half an hour a day. When the weather permits, kids are outside with some physical activity planned but also with lots of free-play time, especially for the little ones.

Music is also a scheduled activity with three levels of band, chorus, and orchestra—beginning, intermediate, and advanced. These activities alternate the same way basketball and volleyball do. That spring, 76 percent of the Seniors were in either band, orchestra, or chorus, and 42 percent were in two of those musical groups. With participation like that, I could readily understand the high quality of music I'd been enjoying at the Temple and the Beanery. Music is a life-long love for most Plainstans.

Aware of my new interest in physical fitness, I climbed the stairs to the second-floor **Art Center** at North, called the Loft, rather than opt for the elevator. The Loft is a huge open room with a high sloping ceiling and high windows to let in morning and afternoon light.

In elementary schools attended by both my children and grandchildren, both art and music are sort of assembly-line affairs with the teachers having whole classes trooping in and out all day long for little lessons of about half an hour. However, much of the time available is spent getting art materials out for one group, for instance, and clearing them away before the next group arrives. The Art Centers in Plainston schools are organized not for classes but for small groups working on similar projects.

For example, that day one group of twelve Sponges was working on learning the color wheel, painting in the primary colors, then mixing blue and yellow to make green, red and yellow to make orange, and red and blue to make purple. Then they went a step farther to make the tertiary colors—blue green, yellow green, and so forth. The paints were there every day; their papers were in cupboards. The teacher had gotten them started. Then the kids came in whenever they wished and worked to finish the wheel. They would take little quizzes periodically to be sure the material was learned—with additional help if it wasn't. Later they would use the tempera paints for other types of painting to show their ability to mix colors.

Some students were working on black and white drawings; another group was learning to use watercolors; there were collages and mobiles being created. Six kids were carving and making clay figures. Another group was embroidering samplers they'd designed themselves on graph paper. An older lady sat with them, stopping work on her own piece to answer questions from the young stitchers.

As in the other rooms, there were two teachers and other adults as well as older kids moving around, stopping here and there to help and comment. Soft classical music and the buzz of voices filled the air. It was a wonderful atmosphere.

The **All Purpose Centers** are just that. Lunch is available from about 11 a.m. to 1 p.m. with kids and adults coming in whenever they wish. Tables for four are set up by the kids before lunch is served, most are taken down after everyone finishes about 1:30. Some tables are up all the time for kids wanting snacks which are available all day long—granola bars, sacks of nuts, cheese sticks, fruit, milk, and juices.

The All Purpose Center doubles as a dance studio for an hour or two after the lunch period with lessons for different types of dances—all ages included. Sometimes, community members from different ethnic backgrounds teach folk dancing. For a month, for example, one might hear a local man calling square dances; during the next month it might be Celtic line dancing or the 50s jitterbug. Kids can use dancing to replace their physical education activity.

Morning activities are of all sorts. Sometimes kids just need more floor space than a center has for large poster drawing, for example. Small group performances are common—plays kids have written. Every week, in each learning center, there is a list of any activities that will take place in the All Purpose Center. Kids are free to attend. Sometimes, lots of the Alumni residents come, or maybe the activity appeals to the Little 'Uns. Overall, something special is happening there often.

The cooks manage the kids on both the cooking and the kitchen clean-up crews. By the time a Senior leaves a Plainston school, he or she has likely logged at least an hour a week gardening, cleaning, cooking, shelving books, doing laundry, caring for Babes, scooping snow, or raking leaves—beginning when he was a young Beaver. Those activities are as much a part of the school day as working an algebra problem or reading a biography.

The **Library** looks about like you'd expect a school library to look with books of all kinds on shelves; racks of videos, magazines, and newspapers; tables and chairs; and computers. The back third of the large room is walled off—the only totally quiet place in a Plainston school. There, older Seniors type papers, read, and take on-line classes from the University of Plainston.

The **Basic Education Center** perhaps most represents what we in the "outside world" think of as an elementary classroom. This center is designed to teach the 3 R's. It is here that the Little 'Uns from the Child Development Center come when they enter the Big School. But even here, there aren't individual desks in rows or a teacher's desk in front. Instead, there are groupings of little tables and chairs everywhere. Small white-board easels are scattered around the area, used by the youngest students who are just learning to write.

Instruction, for the most part, is done in small groups. For example, about every two months a group of anywhere from six to twelve kids starts a special phonics program called YAK. Some learn the sounds in one time through the program; some repeat the session one or even two more times.

There are no same-age groups of kids, all working on the same levels of reading or math. Instead, there are groups of varying ages working on similar things. Most of the kids there are Beavers; however, some of the kids are there only part of the day—Little 'Uns, not quite Beavers, still spending some time in the Child Development Center and older ones, not quite Sponges, starting to spend some time in the other centers.

The level of skills mastered by kids in the Basic Education Center is equivalent to grades K-2 in a traditional program. In other words, once kids can read independently, do basic math calculations, and respond to questions with clearly constructed sentences, they are ready to move to the other learning centers where they will continue to learn at their own pace.

The Basic Education Center has even more older students helping there during the day than the other centers. Besides the little groups working at tables all around the large spacious room, there are pairs sitting around everywhere—on easy chairs, beanbag chairs, and floor rugs.

The ones in the Basic Education Center are also flowing in and out for art, music, and physical activity. At the end of the day, all pitch in to tidy up the room; to feed the critters—a menagerie of goldfish, three rats, and a dozen baby chicks just hatched at South, for example; and to water a variety of plants—their first experience in taking care of their school.

*   *   *

As I watched the movement of kids all around the Big School and in the Child Development Center, the Alumni Center, and even outside, playing or working, I wondered how on earth kids didn't get lost—accidentally or on purpose! I soon learned the answer—computers. When the kids arrive each day, they check into their homerooms by using the computers by the entrances. As they go from place to place during the day, they type in codes—every location has a one or two-letter code—identifying their destination. Even the youngest Beavers can find their names and type in G for gym, AP for lunch in the All Purpose Center, MC for music, M for math, and A for art. At any given time, anyone can locate any student in the school.

When I asked Erin McGregory if she is certain the kids can be trusted, she laughed before answering. "We know kids are kids, and we all can tell you stories about various escapees, but they are the rare exceptions—certainly, not a reason to pitch a system that has such benefits for the kids—and the community as a whole."

"So how do you know most kids are where they say they are?"

Erin laughed again. "Can you keep a secret?"

I nodded.

"We have volunteers who do checks that the kids don't know about. For example, a person who regularly works in the Science Center will print out where all kids claim they are, and then he or she will go all over the building and grounds, looking to see if the kids are actually there. These checks are totally random, and we do them in all the schools often enough to be convinced that the kids can be trusted."

"And what about the ones who aren't where they're supposed to be?"

"We simply talk to them. Usually, it's an 'Oops, sorry, I forgot to sign out.' When it's a matter of wanting to avoid something or a matter of run-of-the-mill orneriness, the intervention of teachers and the kids' Big Brothers or Sisters generally does the trick."

"And if that isn't enough?"

"We call in parents if the problem seems to be more deeply seated. Remember, we have a lot of foster kids in Plainston as well as kids who've been adopted from other countries. It can take time and a lot of attention to get some of those kids acclimated to the freedom our kids have here. But our "veteran" kids are well trained on how to help newcomers. Just look around, Kiki. Doesn't the system seem to be working?"

I had to agree that it was.

*   *   *

Though I was most interested in recording the activities of the kids in the learning centers, I also spent time in each building talking with the adult personnel. And, as you might expect, the Plainston schools are different in their treatment of the adults as well.

First, there is no separate designation for faculty and staff. All working members in the school are faculty because all have responsibilities in instructing kids. All the usual people are there: secretaries, teachers, aides, maintenance workers, cooks, nurses, social workers, and coaches—all faculty. But there are no deans, principals, or superintendents. Instead, each school has a head-teacher who is responsible mostly for communication among the faculty of his or her building and with the other buildings. The job moves among faculty members with one person's tenure as head-teacher lasting just two years. The weekly meetings, like the one I'd attended at North that first day, keep the schools running smoothly.

There is not a huge differentiation in pay among the faculty members. All are considered critical to the running of the schools. Some work is done for regular salary and some counts toward hours to be used for goods and services in the city. Nowadays, in the "outside world," the pay of administrators is often triple or more that of teachers, whose salaries may triple the pay of aides or cooks, some of whom make just minimum wage. In Plainston, there is a widespread belief that all work which contributes to the common good is valuable; therefore, all workers deserve a fair wage for their time. Wages and salaries do vary based on levels of education, experience, and degree of responsibility, but the extreme differences found in the "outside world" don't exist in Plainston.

Another difference faculty members talked about is scheduling. Plainston schools are open forty-eight weeks a year—closed for two weeks around Christmas and New Year's Day and another two weeks in late June through the July 4th holiday. There are four-day weekends for Easter, Memorial Day, Labor Day, and Thanksgiving. That adds up to a school year of about 230 days, much more than what the state requires students to attend. Therefore, both students—with parental involvement, of course—and teachers have some choices about both when and how many days they will attend.

Faculty positions are very flexible. For example, faculty members can choose to work between twenty and forty hours a week and between nine and eleven months a year. Since the school day is from 7 a.m. to 6 p.m., the faculty members can also choose early or later starting times. The workers in each center make the decisions about work hours to make sure the centers are staffed fully all day. Compromises are made; people cover for each other when some want vacation time or are sick. For example, when a teacher who usually worked year-round in the Math Center at Southwest wanted to go to Europe for a month while her son was stationed in Germany, one of her colleagues increased his schedule from nine months to ten to cover for her. I found that kind of helping attitude in every school.

A central record keeping staff, housed at Southeast, keeps the schools fully manned with a cadre of experienced Plainston teachers who work whenever and wherever they are needed—the "floaters," they're called. Since the kids are so used to being independent, having a different person—a "floater"—in a center doesn't disrupt at all—not like having a substitute did when I attended public school.

The system seems too good to be true—and too complicated to be workable—but as I visited the buildings and talked to teachers, I found a system that does work, partly because of the type of individuals I met. In response to my often asked questions about job satisfaction, I consistently got very positive answers. People like—most actually said "love"—working in the Plainston school system.

I thought of the articles I'd read in the popular media as well as educational publications about burnout, the need for police in some schools, the added security in most schools, the failure to recruit enough of the best and the brightest into the profession, cases of post-traumatic stress disorder among veteran teachers—the list of problems goes on. The degree of dissatisfaction with the profession, both within its ranks as well as with some in the public, doesn't exist in Plainston.

The more I talked to teachers in Plainston, the more I wondered if any of my teachers had loved their jobs as much as those in Plainston seem to love theirs.

Chapter 18

The "Solids" Curriculum

Traditional school systems operate for the most part like car assembly lines. Kids at a certain age are brought together at the same time to learn the same things in essentially the same way with teachers acting as the foremen, moving the kids along, year after year, with new things added in each grade until after thirteen years of public education the product emerges—a nice new shiny graduate ready to tackle more education or to learn a trade or to enter the work force.

Only not all of them get the right parts added at the right time and some come out with missing headlights—can't do math well enough to balance a check book—or missing bumpers—can't read well enough to handle college work—or a missing ignition—can't find work he or she is capable of doing.

Not only that but many kids are convinced that they're dumb because they've failed at one time or another. Or they've given up since school is stressful and unpleasant. They try but fail anyway. No one at school has time to repeat what's been told to the whole class to just one person again. We're all familiar with the scene—some of us lived it.

Lack of reading skills seems to be behind most of the failure noted in schools—kids who never master phonics, who never read well independently, who avoid reading as much as possible, who then struggle with all other subject matter from solving "story" problems in math in fourth grade to understanding anatomy and physiology, American history, psychology, and Shakespeare as older teens. There's not much one can do in the modern world without good reading skills.

For all the elaborate changes that a succession of "education Presidents" has promised and which school people proudly claim to have instituted, the majority of public school graduates are still far below the level of literacy needed both to get and to hold good jobs and to continue to develop their minds.

On the other hand, Plainston students, I discovered, were almost 100 percent literate, starting at an early age, not just technically, but at the higher level of enjoying reading and writing. How is this accomplished?

Addie, a fifteen-year-old with dark skin and shining black eyes, was in the Child Development Center at North when I was observing there one day. She was puzzled at my question about literacy and typically answered with questions.

"What is hard about learning to read? Did you ever hear of a kid who was read to who didn't want to learn to read? And to write? These kids can't wait to learn all the stuff we older kids know."

"But why do Plainston kids learn so much better than kids in most public and even private schools?"

"Haven't you noticed a difference in the way we do things around here?"

Thinking of my week with the economics group and the time I'd been spending in the schools, I said, "Kids get a lot of individual help."

"Couldn't that make all the difference?" she replied. "If every time you wanted to learn something, somebody was there to help you, wouldn't you learn a lot and not waste time or lose interest?"

These were rhetorical questions, intended to show me that I already had the answer.

She continued. "From the time a kid shows the slightest interest in reading and writing and anything else, some older kid is there to give whatever help the kid needs. Teachers, of course, help decide what's the best way to help the kids learn, and they supervise the tutoring."

She went on to explain that kids fail because they don't get the help they need when they need it, so they get discouraged and lose interest and faith in themselves.

We talked a while longer. It was no surprise that she planned to become a teacher. Actually, she already was one, in my book. I wished she were my grandchildren's teacher—in a Plainston school.

The Early Years: The Babes and Little 'Uns

As explained before, many years ago, the Oak Hill students in Plainston developed a series of labels for kids who were at various levels at the school. However, the labels were quite flexible, not like the ones my granddaughter experienced in pre-school when she turned four. One day she was a yellow duck; the day after her birthday, she was a green frog in a brand new room with new classmates. The problem was that she was a tiny mite for age four, not at all ready to handle the rough and tumble of a class of sixteen boys and only four girls, aged four and five. She'd changed categories on a rigid criterion, calendar age. A child aged four-plus-one-day could no longer be a yellow duck. She was a miserably unhappy green frog for weeks.

Plainston schools have totally abandoned such lock-step progression through the system. Babes gradually become Little 'Uns, and the Little 'Uns generally stay in the Child Development Center until age four or five, depending on mental and social maturity.

As mentioned before, the Child Development Center is run basically on Montessori principles of developing both independence and respect for others. Everyone working in the center learns Montessori's admonition: "Never do for a child what the child can do for himself." Following that principle leads kids to develop independence and to remove their self-doubt about their own ability. Thus, everything in the center is designed toward furthering the goals of independence and self-confidence.

The room is full of educational toys. The Little 'Uns learn to count to at least 20, to name basic colors and shapes, to recognize the letters of the alphabet. They all do this at different times, not as a group all sitting together. Because there is a constant flow of adult volunteers and older kids from the Big School into the Center, the Little 'Uns frequently have someone there to help with all learning tasks. The teachers check off the mastered skills as reported by the tutors—not just once but several times. Just because a three-year old knows how to count to 20 on one day doesn't mean he or she remembers how to do that three weeks later. But there is never an atmosphere of failure. It is simply a matter of learning it again—and again—and again until knowing the difference between red and pink and a rectangle and a triangle will be remembered forever.

As we all know, kids learn at completely different rates. In the typical kindergarten, the age range will be almost a year since the youngest ones will have birthdays in late August, if the cut-off is September first, and the oldest with birthdays in September will be almost a year older. Any parent will tell you that even a few months of maturity of young children makes a huge difference—whether it is potty training or picking up toys or saying please and thank you. At Plainston schools, age isn't a determining factor, especially since kids enter the schools when parents decide to send them. And since the school is open year round, there is no starting date when a whole new bunch of students enter. Instead, new kids are absorbed gradually into a program, rather like cars merging onto an interstate—going slowly as first, then getting up to speed and sliding into the flow of traffic.

The move to the Big School is also gradual. The Little 'Uns are taken to the Big School by older students regularly—maybe to see newly hatched chicks in the Basic Education Center or a movie about butterflies in the Science Center or a music program after lunch in the All Purpose Center. They go to the Music and Art Centers and the gym.

When the Child Development teachers think a Little 'Un is ready to move on, he or she goes to the Basic Education Center, usually for half a day in the beginning. Sometimes, a group of half a dozen or so begin going to the Basic Education Center together. If a child seems overwhelmed or fearful, he or she may return to the Child Development Center for a few more months until he or she is emotionally ready to handle the learning environment there.

I remembered my son's reaction to leaving first grade years ago. That spring Marie and I noticed a marked change in his behavior. He was regressing in using manners. He cried often for no apparent reason. Finally one evening after a particularly difficult time at supper, I left with our daughter so that Marie could talk to him. In bits and pieces, along with lots of tears, the story came out. He was afraid to go to second grade and therefore had decided to act like a baby so that he'd be kept in first grade. The cause of his fears was having seen second grade work on the school bus—and he knew he couldn't do it. He didn't understand that second grade work at the beginning of the year would be something he could do. Our story had a happy ending. Marie talked to his first grade teacher, who took our son to the second grade classroom at a time when that teacher made sure the class was doing something our son—and other first graders—could do. That's all it took. He went back to acting like a seven-year-old and survived second grade.

His experience would never have happened at Plainston.

Basic Education: the Beavers

The term "eager Beavers" aptly describes the kids in the Basic Education Center. The room is a beehive of activity.

A group of anywhere from six to twelve start the phonics program every couple of months. The program is an update of the first method developed after World War I at Ten Maples by a student named B.V. Colby, who was asked by his friend Walter to teach him to read. Walter had simply been passed on year after year, despite his inability to read. B.V. had agreed without having any idea what to do. On his own, he figured out pictures that looked like letters and had sounds related to those pictures. The whole story of B.V.'s method and Walter's reason for finally wanting to read is told in *Plainston Chronicles*.

Many years later, a phonics program called YAK, which is based on the same principle, was developed. The Beavers learn a story with lots of shapes in it, such as a horse, a curve in the road, a wagon, a bat and ball, and a dipper. They associate the initial sound with the object—dipper is "duh." Then the object is reduced to a black and white drawing—an ideograph—and finally to the letter.

Once a Beaver has phonics well in hand, he or she is ready to begin sounding out words, learning sight words, learning some basic rules related to the spelling of many English words, and so on. Except for the YAK Phonics program, the kinds of materials used are about the same as what you'd expect to see in any primary classroom. The huge difference is the lack of a lock-step system for age-based groups. A YAK group has four, five, and six-year-olds in it. Some may be repeating and thus even helping some first-timers with parts the repeaters have already learned.

Around the room are various pairs or small groups working with a teacher or an aide or a volunteer or an older tutor, perhaps, sounding out word families—*rat, bat, cat, fat, hat, mat*—or learning some common sight words or reading the very first readers. In each case, someone is there to help. At no time is there a student who is failing to learn to read because there is no set timetable for students. No one is passed from first grade to second with minimal skills. Instead, a child begins a second level reader only when he or she has mastered the first level—and no one cares exactly how long that takes.

The same is true for math. A carefully outlined sequence of skills is covered in the Basic Education Center, and a Beaver doesn't move on to the Math Center for more difficult work until those skills are in place.

Writing is learned along with reading. As soon as letters are recognized, students are encouraged to print them. When the issue of learning handwriting first came to the forefront in education, Plainston teachers decided that handwriting is also worth the effort it takes to learn it—believing it a mistake to count on technology for writing and recording everything. Students are encouraged to write letters and booklets and articles from their earliest days, beginning with stories they dictate to their tutors, who show them how to write them down, explaining periods to end sentences and capital letters for special words and the beginnings of sentences. Long before kids can write themselves, they can record their thoughts with their tutors and then add the all-important pictures.

Because mastery is the goal of basic skills, the line between Beavers and Sponges—the next and largest group in the schools—is blurred for most kids. Just as a Little 'Un may spend part of his or her day learning YAK Phonics in the Big School, a Beaver may spend most of his or her day in the Basic Education Center for reading and writing skills but be ready for more advanced math in the Math Center, where he or she will also have a tutor. It can take a year or so before a Beaver fully becomes a Sponge. It isn't unusual to have a seven or eight-year-old say, "I'm a Beaver-Sponge," with a feeling of pride even though it means that all basic skills haven't yet been learned.

Such a statement is so much more positive than the kid in a traditional school saying, "I'm passing reading with a B, but I get F's in math." And the saddest part of the statement is the fact that he or she may be saying the same thing years later since remediation is unlikely in the lock step system which determines that a student either passes a grade or fails it regardless of his or her strengths or weaknesses.

The Solids for Sponges and Seniors

The four centers for math, language arts, science, and social studies are populated with Sponges, who soak up information, and Seniors, who are working to complete high school graduation and to meet college entrance requirements.

Sponges work in math, for instance, in a carefully outlined sequence of skills—always with a tutor available for help. The other element that makes the math program unique is the emphasis on practical application. For example, Sponges are often required to write "story" problems to fit calculations. For example, 8 x 6 = 48 can become "If eight students each need six sheets of graph paper for a project, how many sheets of paper are needed for that project?"

Students are encouraged to weigh and measure, to count money and make change, to figure averages, to chart data, and so on. Calculators are used only after students have memorized the addition and multiplication tables and are very proficient with pencil and paper calculations. Sponges are expected to ask if an answer to a story problem is logical. For instance, if you have 13 apples and you use 7 in a pie, would it make sense to have 20 apples left?

I had to laugh when I learned about this feature of the math work. Years before, while waiting for an airplane flight, I'd been sitting beside a young teacher who was diligently marking a stack of sixth-grade math papers. At one point, she said aloud with a sigh as she checked an answer wrong, "Another 50-pound kitten."

Most Sponges spend about an hour a day in the Math Center, mostly working alone since all units are self-corrected. The need for a tutor comes when the answer is incorrect and the Sponge doesn't know why. That means that even though an older student may be a math tutor for an hour a day, he or she may actually be tutoring only part of that time. The tutor will be completing his or her own work during that hour as well.

One day when I was in the Math Center at Southeast, I questioned the wisdom of having all ages working together in the centers.

Typically, my respondent got me to answer my own questions first by asking what I found wrong with it.

"Do you find anyone wasting time or interfering with others?" he asked.

"I don't, but what good is it for you when you're deep into advanced algebra to stop and help a seven-year-old learn how to use the Cuisenaire rods?" I asked the young man whom I'd seen doing just that.

"What do you waste when you help somebody? What did the girl waste who helped me learn how to use the Cuisenaire rods? She went on and got a scholarship to MIT."

Such questions, asked by children barely into their teens and directed to a man of some national reputation, may sound like impertinence as Erin McGregory had warned I might so regard them. But once you hear the students' voices and see the concern on their faces as they ask them—almost pleading with me to rethink the matter from a less egocentric point of view—you completely dismiss the idea of impertinence. These kids care.

One might ask how older students have time to help at all. The answer became quite clear after I spent a couple of days in the Math Centers. Most of us remember times when we were bored in school because we were still doing math sheets related to multiplication when we'd already learned how to do it or when adding fractions made sense even though the majority of the class still didn't get common denominators. When the lock-step of a class disappears, material can be covered much faster and more efficiently. Once I know how to find the area of a rectangle, I can move on to the area of a triangle without waiting for the whole class to move on to that. If I get stuck, there is someone readily available to help, and when I have to explain those concepts to someone else later, I relearn material that will stay with me even longer. Tutoring helps both the tutor and the tutee.

I witnessed an example of Plainston's method when observing a fifteen-year-old who'd entered Northeast just a month before. His tutor was a twelve-year-old girl named Kayla. Miss Shelby, an aide, filled me in. The boy, Michael, was listed as a Senior at Plainston with a record of A's and B's in all his previous middle school and high school classes, except math—C's in middle school, a D for high school algebra. As a result, he'd been given a battery of math tests when he first arrived. Now he was working to fill in the gaps—long division, the concept of place value, and anything related to fractions, for example. Once the basic math he'd failed to learn before was mastered, he'd repeat algebra and then take at least two more years of math.

"But won't getting three years of math done after this remediation keep him from graduating from high school on time?" I asked.

"Maybe or maybe not. Generally one of two things happens with students who have major difficulties with a subject matter area. Take Michael, for example. In the better case, the tutoring will help him move quickly through the missing skills, and he'll eventually end up able to finish the requirements in about the same time as most Seniors, especially if he chooses to go to school year round. In the other case, Michael will continue to take the math classes needed at Northeast while starting some college level courses at the university—a dual enrollment program offered for high school students. He won't technically have graduated from high school until he's completed the math requirements, but by then, he'll have finished a semester or two of college work before he actually enrolls as a college student. Either way, he will graduate with solid math skills, and he won't have to say again what he said when he first came here, 'I've never been any good at math.'"

I received good grades in math in school, but when I watched a fourteen-year-old girl explain not just the how but also the why of long division, I was amazed. I'd learned the steps by rote without ever thinking about why I would subtract and then bring down the next number, for instance. I'd also never thought about why the number is bigger when you multiply whole numbers—6 x 6 = 36—but smaller when you multiply fractions—1/6 x1/6 = 1/36. But I discovered that a fifteen-year-old tutor could explain the concept.

So my conclusions about the Math Centers include the following: Students really learn math concepts. Material is covered much more efficiently and quickly by many because they can move from unit to unit as each is mastered. No one fails math, even though some move at a snail's pace through the units. Math is made to be a part of life. No one asks, "Why do I need to know this?" or "When will I ever use this?"

Overall, I wished my math-challenged daughter, who'd struggled to bring home C's all through grade school and high school, had had the opportunity to learn math the Plainston way. Then she wouldn't have said to Marie, as they were shopping one day for clothes for college, "Don't yell at me, Mom, but how do you figure what 30 percent off is?"

*   *   *

The Language Arts Centers and the Social Studies Centers have a lot of overlap in the work students do. The Language Arts Centers are full of Sponges who are still working to become strong readers and writers. Experience has taught teachers that kids like to read and write in small groups, so much of the reading being done by the younger Sponges is in pairs or groups of three or four. I spent one day at Southeast observing in that center.

There were several groups reading specific books—one of three boys was reading one of my son's favorites—*Hatchet.* A group of two boys and two girls was reading the first book in the *Little House on the Prairie* series. Eight young teens were working on mythology. They'd already read a book of Greek myths and studied material about ancient and modern Greece. Now they were creating a dictionary of words related to Greek mythology as well as Greek and Latin root words. For example, they now knew what it meant for a job to be Herculean and why someone might say that a day was as hot as Hades and why a huge ship had been named the *Titanic.* They made long word lists using prefixes like *tele-* and *photo-*, figuring out why words like *telephone* and *telemetry, photography* and *photosynthesis* begin the same way. They discovered what an octopus, an octagon, an octave, and an octogenarian all have in common.

The teacher there explained that those particularly interested in mythology may choose to move on to other myths from other cultures. Others in the group can move on to other sorts of units. Each unit is designed to develop vocabulary, to stimulate discussions, to encourage meaningful written responses, and to achieve a high level of comprehension of the material read—all the goals of a traditional curriculum. The primary difference is that not every student has to complete all the same units. Some are core. All older Sponges complete the basic mythology unit, for example. All have to complete a unit related to cultural differences. At one time or another, before becoming Seniors, the Sponges have to read and write poetry, read biographies and historical fiction, recognize different genre, and learn how to do research related to whatever they are studying. However, much of what they do is of their own choosing.

The ties among the disciplines are also very important. For example, all Sponges are expected to learn the names of all fifty states and their capitals, the continents, the oceans, and the major mountain ranges, seas, and rivers. But when those are learned can vary. The students reading the Little House books will learn the states and geography of the regions where the Ingalls family lived. Periodically, Sponges are tested to see how much of the required material has been learned and how much needs to be filled in with a tutor. A student interested in baseball may read a biography of Jackie Robinson for language arts while learning about life for African-Americans before the Civil Rights movement for social studies and then identifying each city and state where current major league teams are located for geography. He or she may even learn how to keep baseball stats. At the end of the extended unit, there will be suggestions about related materials. For example, the student who wants to know more about race relations may read *Roll of Thunder, Hear My Cry* or *The Cay* or move on to another biography. Regardless of the choice, there will be work to increase vocabulary, comprehension, and writing skills.

Speech and drama are considered to be as important as other subjects, but rather than separate classes for speech or acting, drama and speech are integrated throughout the curriculum—the course in economics I took is a prime example. Most kids are natural hams. Developing this natural tendency to notice how people act is an important way to sensitize students to others' individuality. As they mature, students enjoy writing, producing, and acting out their own dramas, which are then enjoyed often in the All Purpose Center.

* * *

To recap, students in what are the elementary grades in the "outside world" don't fail in Plainston. Their time during the school day is productive since time isn't wasted doing what's already known or being unable to do what they aren't ready for. Students like school because, being naturally social creatures, they are able to work with and share ideas with other kids all during the day—or to work alone when they so desire. They are constantly exposed to new ideas.

So how can the basics be covered if kids can choose so much of their own material? We already know that we forget much of the content that we have learned at earlier times in our lives. Plainston educators have developed a basic core curriculum of what all kids should learn and remember always. For example, concepts about how plants grow and reproduce should be always known. Therefore, material about photosynthesis, the need for water, plant fertilization, seed distribution, and so forth are part of all units Sponges can choose—and all have to choose some that involve plants. All units related to animals also involve learning about the various systems in the body. All do some work related to the relationship of plants and animals in various biotas. All do some work about our solar system. All learn why we have seasons of the year and why Christmas is in the middle of the summer in Australia. Most of all, a major goal of the Beaver and Sponge years is to produce kids who not only learn and relearn the basics—and thus remember them better—but also enjoy social studies and science and math. They are avid readers, good researchers, and competent writers.

And how are competent writers produced without the often neglected or more frequently disliked emphasis on grammar and mechanics so prevalent in language arts text books? Again, the Plainston educators have developed a sequence for basic writing skills so that by the time Sponges are ready to become Seniors, they are writing almost error-free. As stated before, when Little 'Uns and Beavers dictate their stories, the student scribe explains such things as capital letters and periods as he or she writes the story. YAK Phonics works with both lower and upper case letters. The Beaver learning how to write also learns right away what words need upper case letters. From then on, writing done is expected to have capitals used correctly. Commas are taught as soon as students' sentence structure moves beyond the simplistic subject-verb pattern. For instance, as soon as a student wants to start sentences with *If* or *When* or *Before* or *Because*, the rule about using a comma after an introductory clause is introduced and practiced. So rather than a student having a grammar text, many short units are covered as the skills are needed.

The vocabulary for grammar is learned gradually as well. Young Beavers soon picked up the difference between nouns and verbs. Adding adjectives is next. Most learned the basic prepositions with a song sung to the tune of "Yankee Doodle Dandy." Early grammar is taught with the idea of sentence building. For instance, a sentence like "Kittens are playing" can be expanded with phrases and descriptive words to "The four tiny black kittens are playing in the kitchen with a ball of blue yarn."

All students keep individual notebooks which they fill with journal entries, lists of new words learned, words to practice for spelling, and ideas they want to explore in the future. Thick portfolios of students' written work are kept. Students don't get A's or B's or F's on written work. Finished work is expected to be high quality; material with weaknesses is worked on until its quality is acceptable—mostly in the students' eyes—because that's what is desired—work that reflects the best students can do.

When visiting the Basic Education Centers, I never saw the dull, glazed, frightened, or hostile looks so common in so many children's eyes in schools I'd visited before coming to Plainston. Neither did I ever sense that fragile armistice that successful teachers somehow maintain with their thirty or so troops, so often on the verge of mutiny. Nor did I sense any competitiveness among students on a personal basis; instead, they're all dedicated to doing their very best—not to be better than someone else or to meet a teacher's standard or even to please that teacher. The students are working for themselves.

As I kept seeing the goal of personal best in the schools, I remembered a story that had made the rounds of faculty lounges at the university where I'd taught early in my career. A student turned a major paper into a professor, only to have it returned with a note: "Are you sure you have done enough research?" When the student resubmitted the paper after another week of working on it, the professor wrote, "Reading this paper in this condition will be a waste of my time." Again, the student worked feverishly to rewrite and reorganize. When the student finally presented the third draft of the paper to the professor, this time in person, the professor asked, "Is this your best work?" When the student hesitantly replied that it was, the professor said, "Then I'll read it now."

*　　*　　*

The curriculum does change for those pursuing high school graduation. Now there is a core curriculum that all follow to meet state requirements and university entrance prerequisites. However, the method used to reach those milestones is uniquely Plainston. For example, all graduating Seniors have to pass the usual course requirements: three years of math to graduate but four years to enter most universities, three years of social studies, four years of English, three years of science, and so forth. Since the early 80s, Spanish has been a part of the curriculum, beginning with the Beavers learning some basic vocabulary and everyday phrases. Sponges learn about verb tenses and basic grammar differences between English and Spanish. All listen to tapes and practice speaking. Seniors can continue Spanish to meet the two-year foreign language requirements or they can begin intensive study of another language since that instruction is individual.

What makes the pursuit of a diploma different is again the emphasis on individual instruction with help from older Senior tutors, teachers, and volunteer tutors. Often times, a small group of three or four work on a unit together. Because basic writing skills are mastered before a student becomes a Senior, there is no need for English grammar to be taught for high school credit. Instead, the emphasis is on literature, speech, and drama with writing being an integral part of all work in all disciplines. Research skills are important as is learning to develop ideas and write persuasive argument. One particular unit all take is a combined American history, literature, and geography course that students work on for a year or more. Even though all take the basic class, there is flexibility that allows for a student to further pursue either or both the history or literature of a particular time period. For example, the relationship between Native Americans and settlers is a part of the course. But a student can go beyond the basic part of the course and read more about that aspect of our history—both fiction and non-fiction. There are expansive mini-units related to all phases of our history. Some students take two years instead of one to finish the requirements if history and literature are particular interests of theirs.

The same is true with science. All take what is a basic high school biology class, but there are side units related to camouflage, migration, plants and animals of certain climes, the effect of climate change on certain species, plant genetics, and so on. There are units related to certain plants and animals, such as birds, fish, amphibians, insects, deciduous trees, garden vegetables, and noxious plants. Math continues with carefully constructed sequential units on through algebra and geometry and beyond.

In summary, the high school level curriculum is about what you'd expect to see, but the way the learning is achieved and the overall expectations for Seniors is different. Remember—there are no bells, no lock-step classes. Instead, there are lots of Seniors helping others and being helped themselves.

Chapter 19

The Extras

In some school districts, art and music are considered to be "frills"—and are thus expendable. In some parts of the country, free-play recesses are being omitted to allow more time for the basics—and the need to meet testing requirements. Even worse, some schools have deleted physical education from their daily offerings. And in many districts, huge expenditures are made to put a computer into each child's hands, beginning with some in elementary schools.

Those scenarios aren't happening at Plainston.

Computers

I haven't yet mentioned computers beyond saying that they are part of each center in the Big Schools except the Basic Education Centers. The Plainston faculty decided when technology first burst onto the scene to compromise, rejecting both the all or the nothing approach. The kids use pencils and later pens for years before touching a keyboard or a calculator, for example. They learn both to print and to write in cursive. They read print books, use paper dictionaries and thesauruses, look up information in books and periodicals, using indexes. They take notes by hand.

When they're ready to write multi-paragraphed papers, they learn keyboarding and basic computer skills in the library. All Sponges are required to take a class related to using the internet safely. All Seniors take one related to using the internet effectively and to judging the reliability of material found.

Art and Music

Since art and music aren't "frills" in Plainston, they are part of everyone's schedule for years. Early on, the kids are exposed to lots of different forms of art and music. Later, each child is dealt with on an individual basis. Teachers and older students observe what a child seems most interested in and arranges for individual help to nurture that talent.

"We haven't found a child yet without some artistic ability or at least an interest in doing something artistic," one young artist at South claimed one day. "Don't you feel you have some artistic ability that wasn't developed?"

He assumed I'd been culturally deprived in that area—as I certainly was. I remembered lots of purple outlined dittos to color and short classes later with the special art teacher who saw us for thirty minutes once a week.

It is the same in music. The Little 'Uns and Beavers learn songs in group singing, and they play in little rhythm bands, using Carl Orff's *Schulwerk* method to develop the sense of rhythm and harmony. Most children are able to read music by the time they're Sponges. Most begin playing an instrument or singing in a chorus or both by the time they are ten. As stated before, participation in music among Seniors remains high all through their years in school.

Physical Education

One of the ironies I've been seeing the past decade or so has been the reduction of physical activity in the schools at the same time the number of unhealthy, overweight kids has been increasing. Physical education is an essential part of kids' education, at least in Plainston. However, there are no gym classes as such and no sudden stop in the middle of the morning for a whole class to erupt onto the playground for a noisy twenty-minute recess when too many kids have too little time to play a game. Instead, the goal is to provide exercise, conditioning, skills, and enjoyment for all—the latter component often missing in many school programs.

Miss Brittany, an attractive young teacher at Southeast said, "Every person is physically different, so every person needs to know a lot about his or her own body and especially about diet and rest and exercise. That's what we teach in physical education, starting with the little tots. We brainwash them against junk food and drugs and in favor of enough sleep and keeping clean and being happy—all things our Health Services doctors tell us we need to be healthy."

The younger kids are introduced to both individual exercises and then team sports. They learn the basic rules and skills needed for basketball, volleyball, softball, and soccer, for example. They play tennis and badminton. When they get older, they can choose the physical activities they wish to participate in as long as they are active for a minimum of thirty minutes a day.

I talked to a fourteen-year-old Senior girl in the gym at Southwest one day. She'd just finished being on the Plainston track team, earning a third place in the county in high jump. She was currently using the fitness center while waiting for a dance class of 60s dances to start in mid-July. Last winter she'd played both volleyball and basketball. This coming fall, she was thinking about trying cross-country running since she'd really enjoyed track. I doubt if it ever occurred to her that kids in traditional schools don't choose their own activity program.

Physical education is integrated with biology as kids study the body and nutrition. Sex education is covered as an interdisciplinary unit as well—a natural progression since reproduction is a part of all botany and zoology units.

"In fact, all student work is interdisciplinary," said Chase Young, a forty-something science teacher at North. "That's one of our teachers' main interests and responsibilities—helping kids plan their units of work so there's some connection among them. We have these different departments, but the teachers are constantly helping kids see how knowledge crosses those boundaries. Fascinating how it all comes together, one way or another."

Special Education

One day in late April, I watched some Little 'Uns and Beavers in the gym at South. A pale thin girl, about eight or nine I'd say, was sitting in a wheelchair while tossing a whole variety of things onto the gym floor as a boy who looked to be about four or five called for them. She tossed stuffed animals—a monkey, a pig, a frog, a turtle, a bear—a comb, a key, a small book, a ball, a box of tissues, and a plastic spoon. When all were strewn about on the floor, the little boy picked them up one by one, saying the name of each before putting it into a tub beside her chair. Then she tossed a dozen plastic rings of all different colors onto the floor, again one at a time as he called out the colors.

I felt certain that the activity had some purpose, but I sure couldn't discern what it was. Feeling somewhat sheepish, I asked a Senior boy, Phillip, who was helping with the group.

He grinned. "Well, she needs the upper body exercise of throwing things to move her arms, but even more important, she needs to sometimes be the helper, not just the one needing help. Actually, this activity is my brainchild."

"But the little boy? How does he fit in?"

Phillip laughed. "I guess it wouldn't make sense to you, just watching. That's Ivan from the Ukraine—recently adopted by a family here. He doesn't speak much English. This is vocabulary building. He's learning the names of common objects and colors. Yesterday, he counted what she threw."

I was witnessing special education, Plainston style. Though I did observe some more conventional practices in teaching English as a second language later, I always liked best what I saw in the gym that day.

And Mary Beth, the little girl, had been mainstreamed at South since she was two. And even though she was likely never to walk, she was learning more than had been predicted she ever could, most likely because she'd had helpers of all ages nearby for years.

One idea came through loud and clear when I asked several teachers about special education at Plainston, and that was the objection to the word "special" in front of education. As one said, "Every kid is an individual here. Every kid has some degree of weakness as well as strengths. Since we work to provide ways for all to learn, it seems irrelevant to label just certain kids as 'special.' We provide help for everyone."

And that's precisely what I observed. I suddenly realized that for weeks I'd been watching what most schools refer to as special education kids without especially noticing that they were in the centers—two kids sitting in chairs reading aloud, one in a wheelchair; two small Beavers writing numbers on an easel, one with Downs Syndrome; two Seniors working on a lab project, both using sign language.

I remembered that it'd been the third day in our economics course before I'd realized that the oldest member, a sixteen-year-old boy, was blind. He was doing so well, with subtle help from others, that I hadn't notice anything different, despite his dark glasses.

It was a sixteen-year-old girl at North who explained the attitude about handicapped kids best, I thought. Ed Grossman had recommended I talk to her. Alicia had already been accepted at the University of Plainston and was planning to major in special education. We met for a snack in the All Purpose Center.

After some small talk about what I'd been doing for the past month or so in the schools, she told me some of what she'd learned about special education. She said, "Plainston started mainstreaming kids with all kinds of handicaps—putting them with other kids as regular students—back about 1940 or so. That was when it was common for a child with Downs Syndrome, for instance, to be institutionalized or kept sort of hidden away at home, but not at Plainston. These kids do need a lot of individual help, but it's help that other kids can give—help which a teacher alone can't give from sheer lack of time."

I'd learned by then not ask "selfish" questions such as "What good does it do you to learn sign language or lead a blind child around or help a spastic learn to catch a ball?" I had received too many pained expressions from youngsters who could hardly understand how anyone could be so "un-understanding," as one little girl with two missing front teeth had said one day.

So instead I said, "Giving these handicapped children help is a part of your general human relations curriculum, I suppose, helping you become more sensitive to and understanding of people who are different from yourself."

I sounded more formal than I'd really intended.

She frowned slightly, then smiled. "We don't call it a curriculum," she said, gently correcting me. "It's just that whoever needs help of whatever kind gets it, and we can't get it if we don't give it. Mostly, it just makes you feel good to help someone. And the more help a person needs, the better you feel about giving it. That's why a lot of kids like to learn sign language and how to help the blind and how to work with all kinds of kids who have some sort of learning or behavior problem out of the ordinary. We like a challenge.

"You got time to go meet someone special?" she asked, rising from the table.

When I said that I did, we headed for the Math Center. As soon as we walked in, a child with the short stature and facial features of a child with Downs grinned broadly and beckoned to Alicia to join him at a small table.

"My name is Sam," he said in a halting manner. "Alicia is my friend."

For the next half an hour, I watched the eight-year-old identify the value of coins and make change for items costing less than a dollar. Sam's educational program was to learn to be as self-sufficient as possible. But his love was plants. He was becoming quite a proficient helper in the greenhouse. He also cleaned tables in the lunch room twice a week and helped the Little 'Uns, who adored him, roll balls back and forth in the gym.

Alicia said as I was leaving North that day, "Sam needs lots of help. We started working with coins over a month ago. But he is also a giver of help. He gets to feel that joy as well."

Alicia had just summed up the tone, the flavor, the atmosphere, the ambience, the pervading morale of Plainston schools—the caring, the joy of learning, the cooperation, the creativity, and the laughter.

The Family

One thing I didn't understand when I was first visiting the schools was how an individual child could have all these contacts, go to all these different departments for specialized and individualized instruction, and be in constantly changing groups with different tutors for different subjects, and not get lost in the shuffle of about six hundred or more kids per school. Where did a kid belong? It sure wasn't like being in a traditional school with your own room, your own teacher, and your own desk.

When I ran into Manette, our economics guide, one day at North, I asked her about this. In response, she invited me to join her for the family meeting the next morning at 8 a.m. I'd been observing the little tots, thereby missing a major feature designed to solve that problem of alienation.

"You're right," she said. "The school is too big for any of us to feel we really belong to it as our main group. And our little study groups and units of work with various teachers change so often that we don't feel we really belong permanently in any of the centers. What we do belong to is our family."

Manette explained that every center has sixty or so kids in the family—from the youngest Beavers to the oldest Seniors—who usually stay together for their whole school life. The teachers and the aides organize and plan the students' academic program, making sure that requirements are met along the way, and keep in touch with the parents.

"We're a real close-knit group. I've always had a Big Brother, but he's graduating in a few weeks, and I'm a Big Sister to two smaller girls—one who's ten now and a new six-year-old Beaver. My ten-year-old brother is in this family, too, so our parents have known the teachers in the Social Studies Center and the other kids' parents for over ten years. The main thing with the family is building relationships that go on and on."

I asked what they do in the family meetings.

"It's really loosely organized, I guess you'd say. There are always announcements about things happening that day, and anyone can share any ideas they may have. The youngest ones can bring in a special item—kind of like the Show and Tell my grandma talks about when she was a teacher in Iowa. Sometimes we sing songs or celebrate a birthday or watch a video a kid may have made during a vacation—really anything. We start at eight and end in twenty or thirty minutes.

"Since not everyone comes to school at the same time, not everyone is necessarily there. Sometimes, someone will come in during the meeting, which is okay, and sometimes kids will leave early if they have a group activity like orchestra or volleyball which meets at a specific time. My Big Brother isn't coming at all now since he's taking both advanced chemistry and physics at Southeast. He doesn't bike over here until around eleven.

"I don't know what's on for tomorrow but come and take potluck."

I did exactly that. "Pot luck" was group singing of "The Erie Canal," which several kids were studying for a unit related to transportation. Then two children showed a short video from their skiing vacation in Colorado—some wonderful scenery along with some very funny shots of the beginning skiers' spills. The main event was a fifteen-minute skit some students had put together on the life of George Washington. It spoofed the myths about his boyhood—the cherry tree fable, of course—then dramatized some actual events with a narrator setting the scene. It was both well produced and well acted.

I made a point of attending family meetings in the other five buildings—always surprised at the variety of activities that took place—but the esprit de corps was always the same.

Speech Patterns

Something I'd noticed about Plainston students, almost from my very first encounter with them when I'd visited LL at South many months ago, was their very adult speech patterns. I was alternately impressed and amused by the youngest ones who often sounded pedantic in trying to explain "big ideas." Sometimes ending up hopelessly enmeshed in convoluted syntax, they'd stop, grin sheepishly, and conclude in a kid's more normal sounding tone, "Or something like that."

I discovered the reason for their delightful speech habits while listening in on tutoring sessions, during which great effort is made to say things clearly and precisely. A dictionary and a thesaurus are always at hand and consulted quite frequently. The gravest conversational boo-boo is to fumble and throw in a "You know." The tutor, or even friends in informal talk, will purse lips, frown slightly, and hold up a hand until the miscreant finds words to express adequately what he or she wants to say. Writing and acting in plays also contribute mightily to their speech.

I thought of my schooling. In a traditional middle or high school, a kid may be silent during a whole class period since much of the time, the teacher talks and kids raise their hands to participate. We all remember the kids whose hands were waving frantically a lot and who dominated the class participation time. We also remember the ones who faded into the background and participated rarely or not at all. In a Plainston school, however, kids are often in pairs or small groups, making it next to impossible to be reticent. From the time they are Little 'Uns, they are expected to ask and answer questions all the time.

Another big plus is Plainstans' general rejection of the "new" ways to communicate—short twitters, abbreviated text messages, social networking, and such. Conversation is valued. People talk to each other, real back and forth exchange of ideas. Kids don't have cell phones, or if they do, they don't bring them to school.

All in all, something is going really right in Plainston.

Extras for Seniors

The curriculum for Seniors is enriched with on-line courses from the university—a system called dual enrollment. Students earn both high school and college credit for courses completed. As a result, most Plainston students meet high school graduation requirements when they are sixteen or seventeen. Those going on to college are readily accepted at colleges and universities all around the country since Plainston has gained a reputation for producing highly motivated, well-prepared graduates.

Specialized classes are generally located in one building. For example, Southwest has large well-equipped woodworking and auto mechanic shops. South has a large auditorium for musical and dramatic performances. The Loft at North has a kiln so students doing advanced art work go there. The Science Center at Southeast is larger to accommodate advanced chemistry and physics courses. A home economics room has been added at Northeast and a full-sized greenhouse at Northwest.

Many Seniors bike each day to these schools for the special courses offered, or they can choose to transfer to that school to finish all their work towards graduation—which leads to another feature of Plainston schools.

Students are free to choose the school they wish to attend. Most do go to the one closest to their homes, but as their interests develop more specifically, they may go to a different one. Even though each school is designed for about six hundred students, the addition of more doesn't cause a hardship, especially with the cadre of floating teachers in the district who can work anywhere they're needed. As noted before, the number of students in a particular center varies all during the day, so what does a few more or less matter—that was the attitude I found among the teachers.

Those students who're going into the work force after high school also have a "leg up" on graduates from many other schools since preparation for jobs is an integral part of the Senior curriculum. Seniors who wish to do so can become apprentices in restaurants, at Health Services, in small businesses, on some farms, and in the Alumni Centers.

What I discovered was that kids who graduate from Plainston schools leave with confidence in what the next step will be. No one seems to be fearful of failing to become a productive adult.

I found no Senior like Jeffrey, the son of our dear neighbors in Washington. Marie and I attended a backyard barbecue to celebrate Jeffrey's graduation, but he was quiet and morose while the rest of us ate hotdogs, danced on the patio, and visited. I went to talk to Jeffrey later in the afternoon after he'd been sitting in the same place for a couple of hours. When I bluntly asked him why he had such a long face, I didn't expect to hear this handsome, six-foot eighteen-year-old say, barely holding back the tears, "I'm not ready to be an adult. I don't know how to do anything."

What a sad commentary on a "good" American elementary-high school education that had produced a graduate with so-so grades. And Jeffery was right. He wasn't prepared. He later dropped out after one semester in college because he had no idea what he wanted to do. Then he completed two years in the army, hating every minute of it, he admitted later. He went from job to job for two more years before finally finding work he liked in a music store, which led him to learning to tune pianos and do basic repair of musical instruments. Within a few years, he was a technician who made the rounds of schools in the area, tuning pianos and fixing instruments.

If Jeffrey had gone to a Plainston school, he'd have graduated when he felt prepared—not because he'd been there a set number of years. He'd have explored lots of different jobs, maybe finding his talent for fixing things early on. Maybe he'd have gotten to know the violin maker in Plainston or worked in the piano factory part-time. He wouldn't have left the school feeling like he was already a failure as an adult.

Extra-curricular Activities

When Plainstans first began to plan the growth of their town and thus their school system, it was decided not to make the buildings separate entities and thus competitive foes for each other. Instead, the name of the school district is Plainston, and each building has the name of its geographic location within the city. Because each building houses all grades, the actual number of students at each age level is fairly small.

What to do about competitive activities and sports was a problem, especially when the middle school and high school populations were spread among six different buildings. The cost of and the space needed to have a track and a swimming pool as well as baseball, softball, and soccer fields at each of the six buildings wasn't a reasonable expenditure of money or use of space. Therefore, it was decided that competitive sports would be located at different buildings. Thus, the track is at Southwest, swimming pools at both Northwest and the University, baseball at North, softball at South, and soccer at Northeast. Long distance running trails are at Southeast, which is the building closest to a wooded area. Indoor sports like volleyball and basketball are learned by all students in the gyms at each school with the competing teams meeting at a specific building during that sport's season. Outside sports are available for kids late in the afternoons.

For kids who want to take sports to the level of competition beyond their classmates, the district fields teams to compete in tennis, soccer, volleyball, track, softball, basketball, baseball, swimming, golf, and cross-country. Plainstans had decided early on that the expenditures for football weren't worth the benefits to students—and as the years passed, that early decision seemed to be wiser and wiser as research about the often debilitating long-term effects of the hits on the head became known.

All kids are involved in music in one form or another during all or almost all of their school years. Those who wish to be more involved join the all-Plainston bands, orchestras, or choruses. These go to annual contests and perform regularly for the community. Music students also prepare for the annual solo and ensemble contests. There are debate teams and a drama club, a scholastic bowl team, a yearbook for the whole district as well as chess, gardening, and photography clubs—basically all that is offered at any modern school—just not all in the same building.

All year long in all sorts of weather, the exodus begins around 2:15 in each building with lots of kids hopping on bikes and heading for other places—sometimes for an extra-curricular activity or a specialized class or a job or an internship. Seasonal athletic practices are generally from 2:30 to 4:15 to make use of daylight. Music and other non-athletic activities are scheduled to begin around 4:30. There is a concerted effort to arrange schedules so that kids don't have to choose orchestra over soccer or baseball over drama or chorus over the debate club or swing band over cross-country.

I'm used to seeing gigantic parking lots around schools, especially colleges and high schools, but in Plainston there are rows and rows of bike racks. Kids learned to ride bikes in Plainston not just for recreation but for transportation all around the city.

Chapter 20

Meeting Some Kids . . .

After I wrote the first drafts for the four preceding chapters about the Plainston schools, I felt that something was missing. I'd promised to try to provide enough flesh and blood to the descriptions of the schools to give my experience meaning for those of you who hadn't spent weeks there. But when I finished, I didn't feel that I'd quite done so—and neither did Lydia, who'd faithfully critiqued my writing to that point.

Finally, one evening when I was feeling particularly discouraged, she said, "Do you realize that when you tell me about your experiences at the schools, you most often give examples about specific kids? You've done that only briefly so far."

And from that brief comment came the idea for this chapter and the next one—the ones I hope finally give the Plainston schools full life for you readers.

During my time in the schools, I'd observed hundreds of kids and adults in all six buildings. I'd talked to many of them as well. My notes were full of what they'd told me and what I'd observed. But I decided to spend a little more time at the schools in order to complete this last part of the story of Plainston's schools.

*   *   *

The following Monday, I arrived at North where I talked to head teacher Erin McGregory about my new plan. She gave me an enthusiastic go-ahead and then produced a class list. I asked a nearby student to choose two numbers between 1 and 63—the number of Seniors on the roster. She picked 12 and 37.

Number 12 was Jake Alexander, a short, stocky sixteen-year-old with lots of freckles and sandy hair, the youngest of three boys. The older two had already earned bachelor's degrees. One brother was in dental school, studying to become an orthodontist, and the other was a police officer in a small city in Indiana. Both of his parents taught at the University of Plainston.

Jake said, when I asked to "shadow" him the next day, "Sure, but I'm not very interesting."

When Jake arrived the next morning at 8:10, he proceeded to his homeroom in the gym, where the family meeting was already in progress. Jason checked himself in on the computer by the door and then took a seat on the floor. I chose to stand. A very small little boy, a new Sponge, was sitting next to one of the gym teachers, holding her hand, as he tearfully told everyone that his fourteen-year-old cat, Rascal, had died over the weekend. After some questions about the cat's burial in the backyard, the teacher asked if anyone else had news. And several did—a tall, thin girl had just gotten back from a trip with her parents to see her cousins in Dayton; a boy who looked to be about fifteen proudly announced that he'd gotten an after-school job helping an elderly man in his neighborhood; another little tyke named Joey asked for help naming three new fish he'd gotten for his aquarium.

During this family meeting, several more kids came in, and a few left before it ended. One of the gym teachers pointed to a large white board on the wall and went over several items. Mary Sue was absent so Victor wouldn't be tutoring her in math that morning. A pair of trumpet players would be performing duets in the All Purpose Center at 1:00. Baseball practice would be cancelled if the predicted rain came, but anyone wanting to practice throwing and catching could go to the gym at the usual time. Everyone was to remember that the advanced orchestra would be performing in the Temple three times over the coming weekend.

When Jake rose to leave, I asked him about his North family. He said he's been with the group since he was seven—the same family his older brothers had been part of. His parents know the teachers as well as the other kids and their parents. His mom has been volunteering two afternoons a week in the Music Center for fifteen years—mostly playing piano accompaniment for kids learning musical instruments. The family teachers keep track of academic progress and advise Seniors about colleges and job opportunities.

"I'm the Big Brother for Joey, the fish kid. He's not quite eight, and he already wants to save coral reefs. Don't get him started on that subject! He'll convince you in minutes that your life depends on protecting the oceans and the reefs and the many ocean creatures we haven't yet discovered."

"So are you his tutor?"

"No, not really. I'm just his friend—someone he can relate to."

During this conversation, Jake and I walked upstairs to the Art Center where he was working on precision drawing—a sort of design unit. I sat quietly while he worked for about forty-five minutes. Then we headed back downstairs to the gym where he played half-court basketball with seven other guys about his age. A team of girls used the other end of the court. A little after ten, we headed for the Language Arts Center, stopping briefly in the All Purpose Center for a granola bar and a bottle of grape-pomegranate juice.

Jake's language arts work was a combined project about the Depression, involving both historical material and the novel *No Promises in the Wind*. With a language arts teacher, he reviewed a short paper he'd written, based on an interview he'd had with his ninety-two-year-old great-grandmother about her experiences during the 30s. Then he went to a study carrel to revise the paper, deciding to use more of his grandmother's exact words and fewer generalizations. He also pulled a booklet on comma use from the file cabinets.

Half an hour later, he went to another carrel where a girl was working. There was a green emblem hanging on a string on her back, a sign which I'd learned means that the person is available for anyone needing help—a red emblem acts as a do-not-disturb message. Teachers use the same signs to indicate when they are free for questions.

Jake and the girl talked a while before he went back to his carrel to work for another ten minutes or so. Then he printed the interview and put it in his folder in one of the many file cabinets, explaining to me that he had one more part to finish for the unit—an evaluation of the novel as history based on his other readings.

"Are you hungry?" Jake asked as he closed the file cabinet. "I usually meet Joey for lunch about noon."

We three enjoyed a lunch of beef stew, rye bread, and fresh fruit. Joey was excited about a song Mr. Tyler, the music teacher, had sung to him—after he'd told the teacher about his fish-naming problem.

"It's a really old song called 'Three Little Fishies.' It tells a story about them disobeying their mama and swimming over the dam and out into the ocean where they meet a shark, so they decide to swim back to the pool. The song has all these funny words in it. Mr. Tyler is going to teach it to all of us next week."

"So what did you name your fish?" Jake asked.

Joey thumped himself on the forehead and said, "Duh!" Then he grinned and added, "The song has another title, 'Itty Bitty Pool,' so that's their names—Itty, Bitty, and Pool."

Jake talked about his morning's work, which seemed to interest Joey, especially the interview with someone who was "really, really old," Joey said. His only grandma was in her mid-forties.

I sat quietly, enjoying the exchange between the two boys. All in all, it was a relaxing, friendly lunch time.

After lunch, Jake headed to the Math Center where he worked on advanced algebra problems—checking his work as he finished each problem. Twice Jake asked a boy nearby for help; twice Jake stopped his work to help a girl with fractions—there were a lot of green emblems around kids' necks in the Math Center.

At two o'clock, Jake went to the Music Center for chorus which meets twice a week. He was also in the advanced all-Plainston chorus, which would be going to contest the following week. He biked to South for that practice two evenings a week.

On the non-chorus days, he spent more time in the Science Center, working on a botany unit related to vegetable gardening in cities—using backyard space or even containers on apartment terraces. Most of his science time was spent in the greenhouse from three to four o'clock.

As he worked in there, Jake said to me, "I know my parents are disappointed that I'm not automatically heading to the University of Plainston like my brothers did. But I really like to work with my hands. I've got a job with a local nursery, working weekends from April to July. I met a landscaper there who's interested in teaching me the trade—after I get an associate's degree in horticulture from the community college in Prairie Grove. I can get my high school diploma next December if I stay on the year-round program. So that's my plan right now, and my parents are beginning to come around to that plan.

"Last week, Mom said, 'Well, you can always get a bachelor's degree later.' And when I said, 'Don't hold your breath,' she laughed instead of frowning."

At 4:15, he checked out on the computer for the day.

As we left the greenhouse, I asked, "Who decides when you leave?"

He laughed. "I do. I go year round, so I pretty much come and go as I want since it's easy to meet state attendance requirements. I just know that my goal is to start college in January, so I have to get my classes done here before then. My family teacher is checking my progress with the other centers, and he thinks I'm doing fine."

"It sure seems that way to me—and by the way—I think you're very interesting, Jake. Thanks for a great day!"

He grinned as he got on his bike, and with a wave of one arm, he was off.

*   *   *

The next day, I met Sui Lee Carpenter, number 37 on the Senior roster, at 7:45 in the Language Arts Center, where she'd start her day. We talked a while before the family meeting.

Her background was totally different from Jake's. She'd been adopted when she was about three from a Chinese orphanage—coming without much experience beyond the bare interior of that institution. She'd been slow to both walk and talk, her new parents were told. Since she'd literally been found, a sickly infant on the doorstep, no one knew her real name or her exact age or anything about her biological parentage.

According to her parents, for about four months, she'd sat motionless and silent for hours on end, staring at all that was going on about her—and that was a lot since she had two older siblings and one younger—ages seven, four, and one. Her father referred to the home as the "House of Chaos" with the four kids and a huge Great Dane named Claude.

One evening, Sui Lee had stood up suddenly and walked from person to person and object to object, naming each one in her tiny voice—"dog, cat, chair, Tommy, Annie, Katie, Mommy, Daddy, bed, table, dish, bathtub . . ." She'd developed a vocabulary of about thirty words, and within weeks, she was creating little sentences: "I tired now. I like pancakes. Tommy break dish. Katie cry."

"That's a wonderful story," I said as Sui Lee smiled at me.

Family time was short that day. Besides announcements, only Sui Lee participated—introducing me, though most had seen me around during the preceding weeks.

By 8:15, Sui Lee was immersed in her classwork. She'd been a Senior for about a year—one of the younger ones. She'd likely graduate when she was sixteen, her family teacher told me.

Sui Lee had been working with a group of three others on the American history-literature-geography unit. The four girls, all close friends since they were young Beavers, had decided to follow the same units so they could work together to finish the course. Right now they were studying race relations after the Civil War and before the Civil Rights movement—studying how many freed slaves continued for generations to be "enslaved" by white laws and practices. The girls had decided to study the era from the African-American point-of-view. That day they were reading *Roll of Thunder, Hear My Cry* by Mildred Taylor. I listened in on the discussion of what they'd assigned themselves to read the day before. Then they read aloud for a while before answering some questions in writing individually. After about an hour, the girls talked about how much to read for the next day since two of them had advanced band practice that evening. Finally, they decided to read only one chapter instead of the usual two or three.

About 9:30, Sui Lee went to the Basic Education Center. "My favorite part of the day," she said.

She went to the computer to check on her assignment for the day. Each volunteer was listed with approximate times and possible kids needing help.

"Sometimes, I'm just a 'floater,'" she said. "That means that I wear my green tag to show that I'm available for anyone wanting help."

That day, however, she was helping a group of three kids review YAK phonics—matching first the fanciful, colored drawing of an element from the story with the ideograph card, saying all the while the name of the object and stressing the first sound heard. A curve in the road is "kuh," a bat and ball positioned side by side is "buh," and a horse with its head down and its tail up is "huh," and so on. Sui Lee was so excited to be helping them with the first stages of becoming readers.

At 9:45, she said good-bye to her little group and headed for the Math Center.

"Math isn't my thing," she said on the way to the center, "but I know I have to have the credits to get into college. And I guess I see how math is related to my life because I keep having to write and solve practical problems."

Once there, she plugged away at the sequential, individualized math program all Sponges have to complete before starting algebra. Sui Lee was close to the end. Even though she was listed as a Senior, technically she was still a Sponge in the math program.

Her tutor arrived at 10:00, and they worked together for another half an hour. Then Sui Lee moved to the back tables, put on a headset, and took a quiz.

When she returned, she was beaming. She hugged her tutor and said, "Wow! I did that one in less than two weeks, and I have only one more big unit to finish before I start algebra. Maybe this math stuff isn't so bad after all."

We had a quick banana and milk snack in the All Purpose Center before heading to the Music Center where she was working on a clarinet duet for contest. She practiced her part for a few minutes before her partner showed up. After they went through the piece several times, Sui Lee went to get one of the music teachers to listen to it. Mr. Joe pronounced it contest ready.

Glancing at the clock, Sui Lee said, "I think I'll get my walk in before lunch today since I'm running a bit early."

Since it was raining, we headed for the gym where she and I found treadmills not in use. She checked in on the computer and identified what she was going to do for her daily activity. As we paced on the treadmills, she explained that she was between activities right now since her favorite, tennis, hadn't started yet. She'd first played tennis when she was nine as a part of the school's introduction to all kinds of activities. Two years later, she'd joined the all-Plainston team, and now she was good enough to compete with students in schools outside Plainston.

Half an hour later, we headed for lunch—she looking refreshed, me feeling a bit beat.

Sui Lee's afternoon started with an hour of science. She was working with a group of six other new Seniors on the required unit of classification of animals—the different phyla, the naming of species, the basic systems all creatures have, the criteria used to place animals on the various branches of the animal kingdom tree, and so on. That afternoon their job was to tack cards of various creatures onto the appropriate branches of a bare animal kingdom tree. They worked quickly, studying the information about the creature on the back of each card and then deciding where it should be placed and why. One boy, acting as scribe—a job which rotated daily—jotted down on a chart the reasons given for the choices. On the table near the chart lay several reference books, which the kids consulted often.

A volunteer father stopped by the table several times during the hour to check their progress. He told me that the next step will be independent study. Sui Lee will choose a representative of each phylum and study it in depth, analyzing it to understand the reasons for its classification. The kids had already learned about the various body systems.

I'd always loved biological sciences—two years in high school and eight hours required for my liberal arts bachelor's in college. I wished I could jump right in and finish the unit with them.

After science, Sui Lee went to the library where she worked at a computer with a headset for a basic Spanish class. Later, she'd join others to practice conversational Spanish with people from the community whose first language is Spanish.

As we left the library, Sui Lee said that she likes to end the day in the Art Center, which she described as relaxing.

"I'm not much good at the drawing and painting stuff, but I like crafts a lot. I've designed a wall hanging with the YAK ideographs on it for the Basic Education Center."

She showed me a piece of monk's cloth about three feet by two with about half the ideographs completed in bright colors of yarn. A woman from the Alumni Center was going to help her apply a backing and figure out how to hang it when she got done. As I watched, Sui Lee finished the "y" shaped horns, eyes, and long face of the yak in dark brown.

A little before 3:00, she said, "I need to meet Tommy in the Math Center. When I'm not heading for some practice after school, I walk home with him."

She put her embroidery work into one of the huge cabinets that lined one wall of the Loft. Then she went to the large sink at the back of the room, where she retrieved a sponge, a small pail of water, and some towels. Ten minutes later, all the table tops were cleaned of paint spills, glue droplets, and such. Two boys were sweeping the floor and putting chairs back neatly around the tables.

"I usually help clean up since I most often end the day here and most of the other kids have cleared out by now."

We headed back to the Language Arts Center where she picked up a copy of *Roll of Thunder, Hear My Cry* and her umbrella from the coat room. After checking out for the day, she went to the Math Center and got Tommy, waiting first for him to finish some math problems he was working on with a volunteer. He also checked out for the day and retrieved his umbrella.

I stood outside in the warm May rain and watched them walking away, umbrellas dancing side by side. They turned around at the end of the front walk and waved good-bye.

*   *   *

Next I shadowed a Sponge. An aide in the Science Center at Northwest closed her eyes and touched a class list. Mario Gomez said he thought it would be fun to be shadowed by Mr. Kiki. Mario was actually still a Beaver-Sponge, he told me. He was a round-faced little guy, not quite eight, shorter than most his age with snapping dark eyes and several missing teeth. He started his day in the Science Center, as he had since he'd left the Child Development Center at age five, with his Northwest family, including two real older brothers.

Lydia knew Mario's father, Luis, since he'd grown up in Plainston just a few doors down from where she and Don had lived while raising their children. Lydia told me the family background. After Luis graduated from high school, he left Plainston to join the military. Then after his wife and his infant daughter died during childbirth—Mario was just four—Luis received a hardship discharge to raise his three young sons. He'd returned to Plainston where he knew he'd have the kind of support he needed.

Mario is one of those kids who are academically "unbalanced." His talent and interests lie in math and science, but he still needs more work in the Basic Education Center for reading and writing. Thus his academic day is split between the Beaver and Sponge levels—without any labeling of "failure."

After the family meeting adjourned, we headed to the Basic Education Center where Mario worked for the next hour and a half. That particular day, he read aloud to his older tutor, answering comprehension questions posed by the tutor. Mario wrote down several new words in his own notebook—taking time to look them up in the dictionary. His tutor helped him figure out how to use them in sentences of his own. Later, Mario read silently some skill building exercises, writing sentence answers to questions. Finally, he and a partner pronounced spelling words to each other—a list of twelve words ending in—*ion*. They checked each other's papers.

"I'm done," he announced, holding out several papers. "I've just got to give these to Miss Anna."

He walked over to the aide, showed her his work, and then filed it in a folder.

"Now I can do math!" he said with a grin.

And that he did, working on long division and multiplication problems. As all Plainston kids do, he had to write story problems to fit some of the calculations.

"Let's see," he said to me. "Why would I ever divide 176 by 5?"

He frowned a bit, then brightened. "I know. A group of five Sponges is reading a book together. For their written work, they've decided to write questions about the book. They will each be responsible for an equal number of pages—but one will have to have an extra one since there is one page left over."

Within minutes, Mario had the problem written out. He took it to a nearby tutor with a green tag to see if the tutor could work his story problem. He could. Mario returned with a grin on his face and wrote three more story problems.

"I'll be taking the test for this soon," he said. "Then I can start fractions!"

I hid a grin. I hadn't met too many kids in my lifetime who were excited to start fractions.

We headed down to the All Purpose Center for an early lunch before going to the Science Center a little after twelve. There Mario was working on a beginning unit about the solar system with a group of three other young Sponges and a volunteer from the Alumni Center. They were figuring out the relative size of the planets and their distances from the sun.

Mario ended his day with the "frills." He went to the gym at 1:00 to play dodge ball with other Sponges. At 2:00, he went to the Music Center to sing in a beginning chorus. That day they were working on singing two-part harmony. He'd been able to read music since he was six. And finally, we walked up to the Loft at 2:50 where he worked on illustrating a story he'd written in the Basic Education Center about frogs. Each page had a different pond creature on it—the bass was already done as was a turtle and a water snake. That day he worked on a dragonfly, looking at a book he'd checked out of the library. An aide came by to sit with him for a while, asking him about his choice of colors, showing him how to use his pencils to blend some colors.

About 3:30 we headed back to the Basic Education Room where he helped clean up for about fifteen minutes. We parted with a fist bump, which I'd discovered had replaced the more familiar high-five.

I walked over to Lydia's apartment, feeling so right-with-the-world after another day in a Plainston school.

*   *   *

Two days later, I went back to North to follow up on the kids that had been discussed at the April 1st meeting I'd attended. I went to observe the four-year-old twins in the Child Development Center first. The boys were a study in contrasts—each resembling one parent in both physical features and personality, I was told. Davy was a stocky round-faced, freckled little boy with rusty-colored hair and round wire-rim glasses—the spitting image of his dad and named after his paternal grandpa. Darren had a narrow face, dark eyes and hair, and a slender build like his mother. He was named after his mother's brother. The original concern of the teachers was how to separate the boys so that each could pursue his learning at his own rate without upsetting the closeness they'd had since birth.

As it turned out, the solution proposed had worked well. Darren already knew his letters and numbers; he liked quiet play for which he had great concentration for one so young. Davy was active and gregarious. At home, both had pursued their own interests, but they had done it in the same basic locale—the family room or the backyard or their shared bedroom.

Since Darren was clearly ready for some time in the Basic Education Center as a part-time Beaver, at the end of their first week at North, both boys were taken there by the Big Brothers they'd been assigned. Darren immediately gravitated to the book shelves under the windows. Davy, however, began to investigate the animals in the room. Soon his Big Brother suggested they go to the Science Center to see some more. And that led to their first separation. Each day their time apart became a little longer until Darren was able to begin YAK phonics and some basic math work while Davy remained in the Child Development Center.

As kids so often do, the boys shared their experiences, and soon Davy was interested in the letters his brother was learning about. As Davy learned to recognize them in the Child Development Center, Darren was teaching him the sounds he was learning in the Basic Education Center. As a result, Davy was scheduled to begin the YAK phonics program with a group after the July 4th break—and it seemed that he'd sail right through it with Darren's help. Even so, Davy was likely to spend afternoons in the Child Development Center since he needed more time to expend his energy with free play. He was also going to the Science Center regularly to help with the animals and to look at short videos about them.

With a smile, Mr. George in the Science Center told me that one day, Davy had said, "Someday I'll be able to read about the animals, too."

"That's a real important statement," Mr. George said. "Once a kid gets interested in learning, all we have to do is provide the help and the atmosphere!"

Darren would likely be a full-time Beaver a year or so before his brother—and in a Plainston school that wasn't labeled as failure for Davy or precociousness for Darren; it was simply the recognition that kids mature at different rates and in different ways.

*   *   *

The three little girls who'd been abandoned by their mother and who were now in a foster home in Plainston were also making progress—but slowly. Jenny, now nine, was still hanging on to her parenting role for Carrie, now five, and Ellie, now four. It had taken two weeks to get Jenny to leave the Child Development Center at all. And that had finally been for her to work in the cafeteria to help prepare the lunches for the Little 'Uns. Jenny was proud that she'd kept her little sisters fed during the year their mother was mostly absent from the apartment. Jenny had also figured out how to run the washing machines and the dryers in the basement of their apartment building, so she was helping with the kitchen laundry two days a week.

Thorough physical exams had shown no major physical problems. The girls simply needed fresh air, good food, and exercise, which they were getting now both at home and at school. Jenny was very good with the Little 'Uns in the gym or outside. She ran around herself, pushing this one in a swing, chasing a ball for that one, and playing tag.

Jenny's academic progress was slower. Her math skills were about third grade level, but she was basically a non-reader. For weeks, she'd pretended to know the sounds of letters—guessing mostly, watching her tutor's face for clues, saying often when she was wrong, "I knew that. I was just fooling you."

What finally broke through Jenny's barrier was Carrie, who, with a book in hand, asked anyone around to read to her. She was highly motivated to learn to read. An ingenious aide decided to make Jenny Carrie's tutor. It worked like this. The aide would help Jenny learn what she needed to help Carrie learn, so in reality, the girls were learning together. Very quickly, Carrie learned to recognize the names of the letters of the alphabet, to count to twenty, to recognize colors and shapes, and lots of other things—as Jenny strengthened her own skills.

Finally, Jenny was willing to go to the Basic Education Center with Carrie to learn YAK phonics—again under the guise of her going in order to help Carrie. And Jenny decided it was all right to leave Ellie during that time since Ellie napped each afternoon after lunch.

Now Jenny was also beginning to cooperate with a Sponge named Heather who was her tutor for basic math. They were still working together mostly in the Child Development Center so that Jenny could keep an eye on her sisters, but at least they were working.

The most rewarding part of the story, I thought, was an unplanned bonus—Carrie was teaching what she was learning to Ellie. As a result, the teachers in the Child Development Center were hoping for Jenny and Carrie to be in the Basic Education Room full time by fall with Ellie going there at least part of the day. Even though Jenny was both older and taller than most other Beavers, there were so many Sponges and Seniors in and out, acting as tutors, that the older Beavers neither looked nor felt out of place.

*   *   *

That evening, I talked with Lydia about what likely would've happened to the twins and the girls in a traditional school system. We figured that Davy and Darren would be compared—with Davy the loser since his readiness for school wasn't as developed as Darren's. He'd likely feel inferior when Darren brought home report cards with checks in the right places, and he brought ones home with "needs improvement" marked more often than not. The differences in their academic abilities at school would likely overshadow other differences that could end up mattering a lot when they got older—like Davy's friendly nature and enthusiasm for getting things done. Traditional schools so often value only certain personality traits. In other words, both would be expected to fit into a mold that fit Darren so much better than it fit Davy.

The girls would be split up upon entering school with Jenny being placed in third grade where she'd immediately feel like a failure since her skills were barely passing for first grade. Maybe she'd be put into a "special" classroom for "slow" kids—even though her progress at Plainston showed that she was anything but slow. Her anguish at being separated from her sisters might be considered a personality problem rather than a real feeling of grief. She could well become the victim of teasing for acting like a baby. For sure, there wouldn't be a Big Sister or a math tutor or several teachers and aides and adult volunteers monitoring her progress every day. She could very likely get "lost" in a system with a ratio of one adult to a classroom of twenty or so.

Carrie would be placed in kindergarten, suddenly separated from her sisters, suddenly expected to be prepared for learning the same way others kids her age were learning. There wouldn't be someone there to read to her for hours on end. She'd have no opportunity to be the "teacher" for Ellie. The girls wouldn't likely get the extra exercise they needed or high quality fresh food at school.

Lydia listened quietly. When I finally stopped talking, she said, "So now you understand. It's not just that our kids learn better because of all the help they get. It's that our kids learn to care for each other."

*   *   *

The next day, I headed to Southwest to follow up on three others I'd met before, the Prairie Grove gate crashers—Rick, Hank, and Rosie. It'd been just over a year since they'd started to work off their fines. When I entered the auto mechanics shop, I looked around for Hank and Rick but saw neither one. I was just about to ask a teacher when a young man approached.

"I know you," he said, his hand extended in greeting.

"Hank?" I said, eyebrows raised.

I was looking at a well-groomed, smiling young man, dressed in jeans and a dark blue polo shirt.

"Good memory, Mr. Kornhauer. I heard that you've been visiting the schools. Great places, aren't they?"

Then Hank briefly filled me in on the past year. Two months after he started working in the auto shop on Saturdays to pay his fine, Mr. Guy, his counselor, asked if he was interested in getting his high school diploma. Hank had jumped at the chance. His Prairie Grove transcript showed what classes he'd passed with a C or better—no D credit allowed in Plainston. Then he took a battery of tests to show his strengths—math and history—and his weaknesses—literature and science.

"I have to pay for my classes here since I'm not a resident and I'm older, but Mr. Guy got me this job on a farm just three miles from Plainston. It's mostly a grain farm, but they have a menagerie of about every creature you'd find on a farm—kinda like Old MacDonald." Hank grinned. "I take care of the animals seven days a week since they eat seven days a week. And now I'm working some overtime in their gigantic garden."

"You sound very busy."

"I am, but it's working out. I come here to school for four hours every morning. I need five full credits to graduate—a combined literature-writing class for two credits, a music class—I'm learning guitar with Rick, a government class all their Seniors have to take, and advanced biology. I've got great tutors—kids a whole lot younger than I am—they call me the 'old man' and I call them the 'young squirts.' I'd never be able to learn all of this without their help.

"I eat lunch here then work in the shop for about an hour—my fine will be paid up in about two weeks. Then I bike out to the farm for three hours, bike back here around 6:00, and catch the bus to Prairie Grove.

"Judge Gray stops by to see me every couple of weeks. She thought I'd like auto mechanics—working on these electric cars—and I do some, but what I really like is the farm work. If I don't mess up, she thinks I can get into the university here to study agriculture. Then I can live in the dorms and keep my farm job."

It was hard to believe that I was talking to the same young man who'd had no direction and not much of a future to look forward to a year and a half ago. I asked about Rick.

Hank laughed. "If Rick was here, he'd greet you with '185 days clean and sober.' That's what he tells everyone. It was 184 days when I saw him yesterday. He ended up in the woodworking shop. His fines are paid up, but he has stayed to learn more advanced carpentry since his cousin is going to hire him to work on his crew in Indy. They specialize in restoring old houses.

"Rick had a rough six months when we first came here—trying and failing twice to get clean. But now it looks like he's on the right track."

"And Rosie?"

"She's doing great, too. Actually, she's a Senior here like me, just not so old. Turned out she didn't care much for working with the little kids, so she ended up working off her fine in the cafeteria. Now she's in class all day and works after school in the kitchen in the Alumni Center to pay her school costs here. We usually take the same bus back to Prairie Grove each evening.

"You know, Mr. Kornhauer, we owe a lot to Judge Gray. Give her a hug for me next time you see her."

Chapter 21

And Some Adults

Before I leave the subject of the Plainston schools, I'll include here a few stories about some of adults I met on my daily visits: an Alumni Center volunteer, a parent new to Plainston, and a teacher who'd first taught in a traditional school.

Miss Agnes was a seventy-seven-year-old daily volunteer from the Alumni Center at South. She was a native Plainstan, educated at South. She'd left Plainston for college when Plainston was still a fairly small city without a wall. In college, she met her husband, who became a career army officer. As they traveled from base to base, she worked as a registered nurse while raising two sons and a daughter. Three years after her husband died, she returned to Plainston at age seventy-two and eventually got involved with the kids at South.

"In the beginning, they gave me a reason to get up every day," she said. "I'd totally lost my way when Al died. My days had no structure or purpose. But once back here, I sort of naturally followed others from the Alumni Center to the Big School. At first, I helped with the kids in the kitchen. Later, I was on greenhouse duty, helping kids select and prepare anything ripe and ready for salad or soup. I was there from about 10:00 to noon, when I stopped to eat lunch.

"After a month or so, I started going to the Science Center after lunch. Now I work with small groups of Sponges each afternoon. Mostly, I record their progress on whatever project they're pursuing. The units are well-structured, so the kids know what to do in sequence. When they decide, as they sometimes do, to branch out on their own, I'm the one who helps them outline their plan in writing so it can be presented to a teacher for approval. I had one group of older Sponges who, after they completed the basic unit on ornithology, wanted to pursue adaptations of birds' beaks and feet to their ability to get food."

Miss Agnes laughed. "I will never again be able to see a bird without noting the shape of its bill and knowing it's related to its preferred choice of food!"

When I asked her why she and others volunteer so much, she gave the answer I found echoed by others from the Alumni Centers. "In a world that is full of bad news, these kids provide us old people with hope. Besides, the kids are just plain fun! What better way to spend my time than being here?"

*   *   *

I found that parents who volunteered felt the same way—the kids were a joy to help. And parents also recognized that the continuation of the overall good life in Plainston rested on the shoulders of these kids.

I met one parent, Barbara Godfrey, whose two boys were new to Plainston. She fairly gushed with her enthusiasm for Northwest.

"Isn't this all too, too unbelievably beautiful?"

She didn't strike me as the congenitally gushing sort. She was truly overwhelmed by the schooling her two boys were getting. The family had been on the Plainston waiting list and had moved in after the flu epidemic.

"What they've done with our two boys in only three months is unbelievable. Stevie, who's only ten, hated school and was becoming a behavior problem there and real rotter at home. He'd been labeled dyslexic. He couldn't do his homework because he couldn't read the directions and he couldn't write answers.

"But he's not dyslexic at all! He'd never learned basic decoding, so he and his tutor, a boy named Chuck, went through some program called YAK. Suddenly, the letter shapes and their sounds became related, putting sounds together made sense, and he was off and running! He reads to us every night while we do dishes after supper."

She continued to explain that the plan for Stevie outlined by his family teacher is for him to stay in the Basic Education Center for a few more months. Even though he is ten and most Beavers in that center are younger, he, like Jenny, fits in because of the older kids who are there to help.

When he goes to the other centers later, he'll be dealing with easy-reading materials. Therefore, his reading competency will be strengthened while he learns content like other Sponges. He'll have different student tutors nearby in all centers until he is reading and writing totally independently. Since Stevie also loves sports, he is involved in soccer as both a player on a team of his peers and a helper for Beavers just learning the rules.

"Our older boy, Jon—he's thirteen—and totally different from Stevie. Jon is a bookworm. He does great in all his classes, but he's overweight and shy. He hated gym classes in his old school, but here the teachers have developed an individual exercise program for him, which means he isn't with a bunch of other kids who make fun of him. They also worked out an eating plan for him—with his input—not just a diet that some doctor would dictate to him and Jon wouldn't follow.

"Last week, he started swimming after school here with a group of seven other overweight boys. They do some swimming, but mostly they play a game of keep-away with a beach ball. I watched once. It was a real workout as they battled over the ball, but what I liked most was all the laughter and sputtering as they dunked each other. Jon has never been a part of something like that with kids his own age. He actually said the other day that he doesn't mind going to school. That's a first!"

Barbara Godfrey had become a volunteer for coordinating afterschool activities. The school buildings in Plainston are open for community activities until about 10 p.m. She keeps track of scheduled activities at Northwest. There is this huge chart with dates running down one side and all the spaces inside and outside the building listed across the top. She pencils into a grid square when the gym is being used for men's or women's basketball games or when the Art Center is being used for the Art League's monthly meeting or when the music practice rooms are open for adults or kids wanting to use them during the evenings or when the stage is available for play practice. Plainston's schools are community centers for many adults as well as the kids.

*   *   *

Finally, I asked to shadow a teacher. I chose Amos Allan Jones because he wasn't a Plainston native, and he'd taught in a traditional school system before coming to Southeast.

Amos Allan was a tall, thirty-eight-year-old, black man—a language arts teacher. He was a relative newcomer to Plainston after having taught in a middle school for eleven years. Since I taped our conversations, I'll use his own words for much of what he told me.

But first some background. He'd met his wife, a Plainston native, seven years ago at O'Hare Airport in Chicago while both were waiting for a long-delayed flight. That meeting had led to lots of long-distance phone calls and then visits as he got to know her then six-year-old twin daughters—her husband had left when the girls were infants, and she'd returned to Plainston. Amos Allan had gotten a job at Southeast after they were married.

"I had an intensive four-month internship here first. Though I liked what I was seeing, I have to admit that I wasn't convinced that kids were capable of so much freedom or could be trained to be tutors when they were just barely old enough to go to school at all. It was a culture shock! I'd been teaching in a good middle school in Indiana—the faculty and staff were dedicated, our kids tested well, we had no need for police in our hallways, parents generally came to conferences. Even so, I wasn't prepared for Southeast. I had to totally change my concept of what I should be doing each day—I would not stand in front of a group and direct the learning from my well-prepared lesson plans; I would not patrol a study period to keep kids on task; I would not place a number or letter grade on hundreds and hundreds of papers and calculate a letter grade for quarterly report cards; I would not call parents to report discipline problems."

Amos Allan shrugged his shoulders and paused.

"Frankly, I had no clue at first what I should do, and it became clear that no one was going to tell me. So I started to study the center. I literally looked at everything: the woods beyond the playground, the books on shelves under the windows, the booklets kids had written, the restrooms, the coat rooms, the student portfolios and the work units in the file cabinets, the computers by the door where kids checked themselves in and out, the tables and chairs, beanbags, easy chairs, computers in study carrels, easels, and bulletin boards, and the teachers' office spaces. I looked at it all.

"Once I figured out what teachers in Plainston schools don't do, I sat down in an easy chair to observe what they do do. They work with individual students or small groups all day long, sometimes in the center, sometimes in their offices. They wear red and green tags around their necks just like the student tutors do, and they have a big board by the office with time slots for students needing extended time.

"That first day when I observed, one teacher was working individually with some Sponges, going over their portfolios of completed units and discussing what each student would tackle next. I saw another teacher working with a small group of Senior tutors who then worked with small groups of Sponges. Using flash cards, an aide was going over irregular verb forms with a group of young Sponges. When the aide left, the kids continued to drill each other in the same way. That afternoon, I saw several lengthy conferences in the glassed office—Seniors discussing projects with a teacher. Another aide recorded completed projects on student records.

"Everyone was busy, but no one seemed pressured. No bells rang. No roll was taken. The system had evolved into a smoothly oiled machine."

Amos Allen stopped and shook his head as if he were still in disbelief. Then he grinned and said, "I thought I was in paradise."

After a week of observing, his training began. First, he sat in on the formal tutor training sessions all kids go through, including the refresher courses offered twice yearly to the kids. The key is the ability to question—to get a kid to see the right answer or figure out a logical conclusion on his or her own. The tutoring classes stress that the kids should be learning for themselves, not to please their tutors. Even though a high-five, a fist bump, or a hug often accompanies a break through, the students are working to do their best. When work is being checked, a math paper, for example, the wording is "Let's do this one again" not "This one is wrong." And tutors are trained to recognize frustration levels and to know what to do when a student reaches that level.

After the tutoring class, Amos Allan began to shadow the aides and the teachers, taking over an activity when he felt comfortable that he knew how to proceed.

"I've now been at Plainston for five years. I work year round, and I don't miss the summer vacation I used to need to recuperate. After the two-week breaks we have, I never dread coming back like I used to dread the beginning of a year in late August—knowing that for the next nine months I'd teach all day and do lesson plans and grade papers for two or three hours every evening. I literally was tired all the time. I loved the kids—"

He stopped and grinned, then said, "Let's be honest—I loved most of the kids—but I knew I wasn't reaching all of them no matter what I tried. I kept detailed notes about what worked and what didn't. Then every summer, I rewrote units and chose new material. But I always knew that some of the kids weren't succeeding no matter what I did.

"Back at my old school, there was a *Peanuts* cartoon on the bulletin board in the teachers' lounge. One little girl says, 'I'm afraid to look at my report card.' So she hands it back to the girl behind her who looks and exclaims, 'AAUGHH!!' The first little girl then says to the teacher, 'You should maybe write horror stories, ma'am.'"

We both laughed.

Then Amos Allan became serious. "You know. That's what returned papers and report cards were like for lots of kids—horror stories, reminders of failures, confirmations that they were dumb, maybe even reasons for their parents to punish them. I never felt then like I do now when I know that every kid is making it. Every kid has help from me or someone else whenever he or she needs it. And no one fails. That's the greatest thing for a teacher!"

There is absolutely nothing else to add to Amos Allan's description of what it means to be a teacher in Plainston.

*　　*　　*

That night when I told Lydia about my day with Amos Allan, I said, "The real key to why the schools work is the kids helping each other, isn't it? The 'family style' learning."

"It has a different name now," she said.

"What?"

"I'll let you find that out," she said with a grin.

* * *

So there I was the next day, back at North where I'd started six weeks before, ready to get my last answer.

To complete my study, I needed a name for the system. I looked up Manette and, as usual, got questions instead of answers—no surprise at this point.

"What's a three-syllable word for benefit to both parties?" she asked.

After searching my mental thesaurus, I said, "Mutual?"

Manette nodded then said, "What's a three-syllable word for teaching and learning?"

I said, "Pedagogy," then corrected myself. "No, that's four syllables."

I rejected *education* for the same reason. I thought a bit more before saying, "Instruction?"

There was that usual silence while my questioner waited for me to answer my own unasked question: Does "mutual instruction" fit what I'd been observing for the past six weeks?

I smiled. "Mutual instruction," I said, "which is a benefit to both parties, intellectually and emotionally—head and heart mutually reinforcing facts and feelings."

Manette grinned. Then she delivered me to Ed Grossman.

"Mr. Kiki got the magic words. He's ready for initiation," she reported.

Ed took me to the noon hour staff meeting. "We have a little ritual we like to perform for those who pay sufficient attention to understand us and to identify our name. Are you familiar with the Jewish legend about what Rabbi Hillel said when he was asked to summarize the Torah while standing on one leg?"

"I am. The rabbi said, 'What is hateful to thee, do not unto thy fellowman; this is the whole Law. The rest is but commentary.'"

The lunch group applauded.

Ed continued, "Can you, while standing on one leg, similarly summarize the education you have experienced and witnessed—which, by the way, we shorten to MI and pronounce as two letters, 'em eye'?"

I paused to gather my thoughts, bent up my weak leg, stood unsteadily one-legged, and intoned in a ministerial manner I thought appropriate for this serio-comic little ceremony, "Mutual Instruction benefits the helpers—the tutors—by reviewing what they've learned when they help the tutees. Those being helped—the tutees—get the individualized attention every learner needs and deserves. That's a mutual exchange."

Thus far I was mostly plagiarizing ideas I'd gotten from students although their views had become my firm convictions. I added a thought of my own.

"The most precious mutuality is to learn that we love those we serve even more than we love those who serve us."

My leg gave way as the group broke into applause again.

As I left North that beautiful afternoon in mid-May, surrounded by the new spring green of trees and grass, I felt that all was right with the world.

*　　*　　*

That evening as Lydia and I walked through a neighborhood park, I told her about what I'd said to define Mutual Instruction.

"It's the root for everything that's right in Plainston, isn't it? Kids don't just learn better here; they learn to care about the really important things, especially each other. That has carried over into every part of life here."

"You're right, Kiki. Doesn't our wall make sense now?"

It was a question that needed no answer. We walked on in silence, hand in hand.

Finally, I said, "There was this one tiny little girl, probably three years old—I don't even remember which school I was in—but she made quite an impression on me—maybe because she represents the spirit of the schools though I didn't know that at the time.

"Anyway, all the little tykes are neat and orderly, Montessori-style, in the Child Development Centers. But this little lady seemed so to enjoy neatening. She stopped to look at a bouquet of flowers on a table. She touched the petals gently and turned the vase this way and that to get the best effect. She picked up several scraps of paper and straightened some books on a shelf. Then she got a wet rag and a small blue towel and did a thorough job of scrubbing several messy little tables. After she'd finished, she primly straightened her yellow apron and stood smiling at the shining tables she'd restored to beauty.

I asked her, "Why do you like to keep everything so neat and clean?"

She looked up at me with her big brown eyes, and then, with a little frown, she shook her head and said, "Can't stand ugly!"

Lydia laughed. "She sounds delightful!"

"She was. She already recognizes beauty. She is eager to help—to do her share—and she will flower as she is nurtured by Mutual Instruction."

"She will," said Lydia as she hugged me.

Chapter 22

Exploring the City

For several days after I finished my "digging" at the schools, I mused. I didn't read. I didn't write. I only thought. I thought about how beautiful it was inside Plainston's walls and how ugly it was so often outside them. I thought about kids and schools and change.

In all societies, the real forces of change are mostly well-hidden, unidentifiable, and largely uncontrollable. Most people don't know why they change their minds and feelings—if they change at all. Although I had no firm conviction as to why people change, I'd dedicated my life to trying to change them—by top-down appeal of adult to adult through writing and speaking.

The goal of public schooling is to prepare young folks to accept and fit into the society they inherit. If their world has severe problems, how have their schools prepared them to solve those problems? I'd never pondered that question in depth.

I'd accepted the school system that had prepared me as adequate though certainly improvable. I'd never thought of it as basically flawed although both professional educators and laymen were continually calling for a major overhaul. And we were certainly facing many problems that weren't being solved—the continuing overall moral decay of our society, escalating violent crime associated with drug abuse, rampant greed, lack of stable families, glorification of sex out of all proportion to its basic importance in life, the pervasive violence on television which still dominated people's leisure time, especially that of children and youth—the list is long. In the terms of Plainston's Temple, America and the world were falling farther and farther "below the line."

For generations, a long parade of educational changes, some no more than fads, have been implemented: mainstream or don't mainstream, test more or test less, put more emphasis on the basics or allow more freedom for kids to explore their interests, grade more rigorously or use more smiley faces for effort—this list is also long. Changes have been implemented but, for the most part, without making kids smarter, teachers happier, parents more pleased, or taxpayers and employers more satisfied.

But as I mused, my usual pessimism over the state of the world was replaced by a feeling that was almost euphoric—and not just because I was spending more and more time with Lydia. I was living in a humane community, designed on a human scale, which had been successful for several generations—long enough to prove its viability. Six weeks with several thousand kids had converted a skeptical Pagan. Those students' understanding of and devotion to the values of their life style were broad and deep, based on intensive and extensive firsthand experience, not verbal indoctrination. My firm belief in Mutual Instruction was generating confidence that Plainstans would find a way to spread the good news.

* * *

The next morning, my phone rang a little before seven.

"Good morning, Plainstan," said Lydia in a cheery voice. "It's a beautiful late May morning. If you'd like to come for breakfast, I'll be more than happy to be cook, waitress, and conversationalist."

No Plainstan in his or her right mind would decline an invitation from Lydia Colby Gray. Being in my right mind, I said I'd be there in half an hour.

As we drank mint tea, I said, "Do you realize that in the eighteen months I've been "living" Plainston, I've actually been here only about half that time, and I was too sick to do much for some of that time. If I'm to fulfill my mission to write an outsider's story of this place, I need to "dig" Plainston more. Would you be my guide?"

And so after breakfast, we began my exploration of Plainston itself. We started at the university library where I was given several books about Plainston's past. I decided first to reread *Plainston Chronicles,* the collection of documents describing MI's origins and development, edited by B.V. Colby, Lydia's father. Now that I was positive that MI was the source of all that was right with Plainston, reading about it would be more meaningful.

"Can we visit Ten Maples tomorrow?" I asked after we left the library about noon.

"How about a three-mile tandem bike ride to the school right after you have breakfast with me again?"

The invitation was accepted.

*   *   *

Ten Maples was a lovely little one-room country schoolhouse outside the city wall. It was set on an acre of land, still shaded by a collection of huge old trees, mostly maples. During World War II, when school district consolidation was started, a second one-room school was attached to it. However, the original Ten Maples building had been preserved by the Historical Society as it had been when a young World War I widow, with an infant daughter, taught there.

B.V Colby's fascinating collection of letters and diaries and his own anecdotal comments in *Plainston Chronicles* had already given me the story. B.V. himself was a major actor in the drama, having been dragged reluctantly into teaching his best friend, Walter Hazlitt, to read. Their success had more or less accidentally launched MI.

That day Ten Maples was in full session as a real school. It had a fireplace, hand-woven rugs on the beautifully polished oak floor, colorful curtains on the windows, small study tables, a cozy library corner with overstuffed chairs, and old-fashioned kerosene lamps. In one corner of the room were some old one-piece seat-desks. A few students were working there alone, but everywhere else, students were working together as they did in Plainston's modern learning centers. The teacher was in conference at his desk on a raised platform which stretched across the front of the room.

"This is part of our students' Living History unit," Lydia explained. "The kids come here for a few weeks to have school like some of the early Plainstans did. Only this school isn't really typical of most one-room country schools of the time. Let's go next door to see what most of those looked like."

The adjoining one-room school had been preserved in its original condition with oiled floors, no curtains at the windows, a big pot-bellied stove at the back of the room, much carved seat-desks firmly bolted to the floor in rows from smallest to largest, and the teacher's desk in the center of the front with a blackboard behind it—a dismal, dreary room. Here about twenty students dutifully worked silently at their desks, using steel pens and ink from inkwells, laboriously practicing Palmer Method penmanship while a lady teacher, dressed in an 1890s long skirt and blouse, patrolled the rows, feigning severity while dispensing both restrained praise and criticism.

She got out of character long enough to explain to us with a smile, "The kids can't take more than two or three days of the old-fashioned three Rs here. Even this small dose of the 'good old days' is enough to make them appreciate MI."

We spent the rest of the day going back and forth between the two rooms. The MI students helped prepare a soup and salad lunch in the kitchen in the clean, cool basement. They ate on cloth-covered tables in their classroom. The kids next door ate cold lunches from lunch pails, sitting on wooden benches outside. The MI school had toilets in the basement; the other school had two old privies outside.

Lydia explained why Ten Maples had been so much better than most one-room schools, even before MI evolved there. "The Colbys were strong for education. My Uncle Will, whose grandfather gave the land for Ten Maples, really ran the school board. He hired some young Progressive teachers, John Dewey disciples, who were responsible for the physical improvements. Then when "family style" learning happened, the teacher, Grace Muenster, got moral support and encouragement from Uncle Will and the board. When the country schools finally closed, Grace was instrumental in establishing "family style" learning at Oak Hill, one of the two elementary schools in Plainston. The idea grew from there—but not without lots of growing pains."

Lydia explained that the Historical Society also maintains two mostly self-sufficient, animal and man-powered family farms that are being run as they had been run a century ago—before electricity, tractors, high-potency fertilizers and chemical pest controls, and assembly line production of meat, eggs, and dairy. "Uncle Will's farm is one of them. Students can choose to spend several weeks on these farms. They go to school at Ten Maples, except the older kids, who walk or ride horses into town like country kids used to do."

"Appreciation," I said. "That's what kids gain from experiences like this—appreciation for the competence of people before modern technology, to which we should give credit for much of our comfort and leisure."

*   *   *

Our first stop the next day was the Indian village. I'd thought that the Indian teepees and bark wigwams painted on the mural in my room were just empty structures erected for historical purposes. But I was wrong. For several months each year, kids as well as adults can study the culture with the descendants of the Native Americans who'd once lived in the area. The visitors can learn to paddle genuine canoes on Mill Pond and Sugar Creek, and they can catch and smoke fish, Indian style, for instance.

A number of Native American families are permanent residents of Plainston. Others come as exchange students and teachers from reservation schools where MI is being implemented.

Later, Lydia insisted that we take a horseback tour of the city. Since I was a city boy without equestrian experience, the stable owner provided me with a gentle mare with no interest in either trotting or galloping. We followed Plainston's bridle paths, which crisscrossed the city following the original prairie right-of-ways of the two railroads which had been rerouted around Plainston many years ago. The path also went through the forty acres of woods near Southeast.

We also rode on the paved road that served the city's "manufactories" and laboratories.

"Manufactories?" I asked, catching Lydia's mispronunciation.

"That's what I said. It literally means 'made by hand.' Plainstans specialize in labor-intensive, highly-skilled work. We get contracts from all over the world, which are an important source of our dollar credit."

She mentioned two such manufactories—ones making pianos and musical instruments.

"Plainston also does a large mail-order business. We make handy little gadgets that solve nuisance problems. We also create a lot of very artistic items in ceramics, glass, metal, wood, and leather. And of course, there are the sculptures and woven goods."

* * *

We also walked the city for a couple of days. The original Plainston is in the area around Mill Pond. When the city planners began to redesign the city with the idea of limiting the population to 40,000 permanent residents, they first decided to preserve the old homes in Old Plainston, many of which were built of field stone, oak, hickory, and walnut in the middle and late 1800s. Many of the fine old carriage barns were turned into artists' studios, workshops, or smaller residences. Separate garages were similarly converted or torn down. Smaller houses were sometimes built behind the larger homes to house visitors—many from other countries—or to be homes for aging parents or young couples with no children.

Plainston doesn't seem to be crowded, yet 50,000 people live in four square miles. Most cities with that population are at least four or five times larger than that. Building up rather than out had been the answer.

When we had lunch one day with Pete Hammill, he said, "Do you realize how much space cars take up—parking lots, street-side parking, wide streets, multi-laned highways, and garages, not to mention gas stations, repairs places, and dealerships? Bikes don't take up much space at all in comparison."

"But what about people who need cars?"

I should've guessed that Plainstans had solved that problem as well. Lydia told us about her neighbor, who travels a lot throughout the Midwest for his job as a small business consultant. He keeps his car in the garage just outside the walls, using his bike or an electric car to get to and from the garage. Others who need cars periodically, like Lydia and I had for the airport trips, simply rent a car or van or truck, most of which are hybrid or totally electric, from the fleet kept in the city garage just outside the gates.

Then Lydia explained about the little electric cars used inside the city—Plainston's answer to yellow cabs. I'd already used one several times.

"Have you noticed the bikes on racks on the back?" she asked.

I said that I had.

"Our college kids mostly run the business. It's simple. You call for a car. A kid delivers it quickly, collects the rent for however long you say you need the car, removes the bike from the rack, and pedals off. You call when you're done with the car, identifying its location. A kid pedals back, puts his bike on the rack, and takes the car back to its base—one base in each of the six sections of Plainston. An extremely simple system and great part-time employment for college kids."

And I didn't need to ask if people cheated when paying in advance—maybe using the car for all day instead of the half day paid for. I already knew the answer—a Pagan might try that, but the native Plainstans wouldn't.

"But back to the fact that the majority of Plainston residents live in apartments," I said. "What about people who want their own green space?"

"There are single-family homes with yards and garden space to buy or rent, but most apartment residents are happy to work in the public flower and vegetable gardens is they so choose. The parks department personnel are mainly professional horticulturists who supervise the green-thumb volunteer workers. And then there are those who love having no responsibilities of maintaining a house and yard—the truly contented apartment dweller."

The next day, the *Gazette*'s science editor told us about Plainston's goal to be energy efficient, using both solar power from panels on almost all rooftops and wind power from a "wind farm" just outside the wall. Multi-story residences have less outside wall and roof space, thus reducing both heating and cooling costs. Escalators and elevators are cheaper energy-wise than one-story structures with exposed walls and roofs.

After two weeks of touring the city and talking to lots of people as well as Lydia, I was convinced that Plainston had almost all the advantages of a big city—all the opportunities and facilities that the human mind and spirit need for fulfillment—minus a large museum, an aquarium, a zoo, and a large sports arena.

*   *   *

The last question was about the wall. Why the wall?

Actually, the wall was mostly invisible except when exiting or entering the city through the gates. Much of the wall was hidden behind the manufactories and the many trees throughout the city. Even so, it was much in people's thoughts, I discovered, since I heard expressions like, "I live near where the east and north walls meet" or a certain place would be "about three blocks from the center of the south wall."

Lydia took me to meet Susan's grandparents, Grandpa Frank and Grandma Sarah Hazlitt, both in their mid-70s, who eagerly told us the story of the wall.

It had begun in the town of Gyor, Hungary, Mihaly's hometown. It was where Walter Hazlitt, Frank's father, had taken a bunch of his Ag Club boys with livestock, seed, and some tools to get the farmers there going again after World War II. Gyor had been a sort of distribution point for American aid. A number of Plainstans visited the city and some Hungarians from there visited Plainston. Then when the Cold War started, some settled in Plainston.

Grandma Sarah said, "I visited Gyor. It had a little river running through it, something like Sugar Creek, and it was the center of a farming community like Plainston. But none of us had ever seen a city with walls."

"They specialized in farming horses," Grandpa said.

"Frank, they've come to hear about the wall, not horses."

She took over the story again. "Peasants had helped build it way back when there was a lot of warfare in the countryside. With the wall, peasants would have a safe place to take their grain for storage."

"So when it got so bad in this country, we thought about a wall here," Grandpa said. "Not that it would protect us from bombs or anything, but it could keep our good stuff in and keep some bad stuff out. Then Reverend Gordon said that building a wall would be like Noah building the ark to start the world all over again after the flood. He said that the wall could be our earth ark.

"Selling the idea was much easier after that. The owners of the quarry offered all the limestone for the cement free. Lots of people donated money for the mixers, the trucks, and the forms that had to be built."

The Hazlitts continued the story. The whole community pitched in. Lots of the men had concrete experience. Volunteer teams were organized with each team building a two-mile section.

Frank said, "I worked on the south wall. Crews were working around the clock. Our shop fellows built movable forms that ran on rails we'd build. We jacked those forms along about two inches a minute, well over two hundred feet per day. With Sundays off, we were done in less than two months that summer. I never worked so hard before or since, but we had such a good time."

Sarah told us that the women helped as well, mostly with cooking meals and providing lemonade and cookies and barrels of water between meals. Then when the men took staggered breaks, the girls would step in for a while, jacking the forms along, shoveling sand and gravel, and pouring water.

"I even drove a truck a couple of times," Sarah said proudly.

"You sure did, Sarah girl. That's when I decided you were the girl for me."

Sarah leaned over to give him a kiss.

*   *   *

When I reviewed all of this later with Pete Hammill, he said, "I was too young to work much, but I hung around, trying to help as a water boy or a gofer. People almost got in each other's way, trying to help. It was the beginning of our community working together—you know, the conspiracy."

He paused, with a faraway look in his eyes, then continued.

"We'd been through almost forty years of often bitter arguing over the schools—the 'family style' learning. Integrating our black students was all tied up in that issue as well. But when we built the wall, black and whites worked side by side, men and women. I don't think I ever heard the n-word again in Plainston after that summer. By then, we had a couple of generations of MI schooled adults in the city, people who continued to work together as they'd done all through their school years. Once the community spirit was established, everything else seemed naturally to follow."

When I left Pete's office, I was fully convinced that I was home.

Chapter 23

Heading West

For the next several weeks, I read and reread my notes and listened to my tapes. I made lists of material to put into the various chapters of a book. I made lists of topics for individual columns and articles. I would go to bed satisfied with what I'd done that day only to cross out lots on one page and add more to another the next morning. It was a writer's angst I was familiar with. Only this time, I felt like the weight of the world rested on my shoulders—to use a common cliché. I desperately wanted to get this right. The story I had to tell was too important not to be perfect. The world needed to know about Plainston.

Lydia was a wonderful distraction for a few hours every day. We'd meet for a meal or a walk or a swim in the university pool. Just as I could no longer imagine leaving Plainston, I could no longer imagine the rest of my life without Lydia.

One very warm evening in mid-June, as we were walking around Mill Pond, enjoying the slight cooling that a northerly breeze had brought, Lydia said, "Kiki, I'm going to make a swing around the country. We're negotiating with the FINs to include some of our issues in their platform for the next election. Would you like to come? The trip would give you a chance to see our political clout firsthand and some other MI schools."

I couldn't turn down that triple invitation—to be with Lydia, to get an inside look into FIN politics, and to see how well MI takes root in less fertile soil outside Plainston.

Without hesitation or much thought, I blurted out, "Could we make it a honeymoon?"

Lydia gasped. She turned to me, wide-eyed. Then she burst into laughter, hardly the response I expected—or wanted.

"Kiki," she said, after getting her laughter under control, "that has to be the most unromantic proposal I've ever heard of!"

"How can I improve it?"

"You don't need to," she said softly. "I've been hoping to hear it in any words."

*   *   *

I think we had one of the shortest engagements on record. In short order, we decided that I would give up my room at the Tower and move into Lydia's apartment which was big enough for both of us since I had few possessions with me in Plainston. After the cross-country trip, we'd discuss whether or not to move to a house or stay in the apartment. In order to keep the wedding simple, we also decided to tell our families after the fact. We'd stop to visit our children and grandchildren on the trip.

There was one concern that was nagging at me—a concern that I needed to get resolved.

At lunch the day before the wedding, I said, "Lydia, we've got to clear up this conspiracy business. I don't feel comfortable being involved in something that's so secret, even if it's conspiring to save the world. So exactly what is the conspiracy everyone bandies about so publicly without letting on what it is?"

Taking on her school-teacherish tone, Lydia said, "What do you think the word *conspiracy* means?"

"Well, it means a plot. To conspire is to plot against something."

"Check the etymology," she said, handing me an Oxford college dictionary. "Check the root word, *conspire*."

I did. *Con*—is a form of *com*—meaning with, together, jointly. *Spire* means to breathe. *Conspire* in its basic form means to breathe together as *convene* means to come together; *connect* means to bind together . . . .

When I laid the dictionary down, Lydia said, "We Plainstans do things literally. We are breathing together. Is there anything wrong with that?"

"So that's what it means, that Plainstans think alike, have the same values—the kind of diverse unity that MI produces."

Lydia nodded. "It wasn't long after the wall was built that someone on the outside referred to Plainston as being full of conspirators. Soon the term *conspiracy* was almost synonymous with Plainston—that was even before the likes of Wilber Bickersley came on the scene. The group we now call the Consensus as well as citizens in the regular city meetings talked about responding to the negative label but finally decided to ignore it. A conspiracy can be benign—our plan, which we've been developing for over fifty years, certainly is—but for most people, the connotation is negative. However, since the word arouses people's interest, we don't protest. Leaving some mystery here keeps us in people's minds so that when we want to make our plans public, it'll be easier to get attention in the press. One reason for this trip is to assess when that time should be."

Lydia paused. Then taking my hands in hers, she said, "Dear Kiki, can you breathe with us? Will you join the conspiracy?"

I knew in my heart I already had.

*   *   *

A week after my impromptu proposal, we were married in a small chapel in the Temple in a private ceremony with Pete Hammill and Mihaly as our witnesses. I felt so at peace as I said the simple vows I'd written.

Three days after that, on July 1st, we were on the road, heading west in our rented mini-van packed with clothes, my computer, and a cooler we kept full of cold water, snacks, and light lunches we enjoyed at rest stops and parks.

*   *   *

Our first stop was in Chicago, a short trip from Plainston. I was quite nervous about introducing Lydia as my wife, but it turned out to be easier than I'd expected. My daughter, Joyce, and her husband, Rob, weren't surprised since, as Joyce told me as we did dishes after supper that evening, "Don't you know that about every third sentence you've said over the phone for the past year and a half has included something about Lydia?"

"Really transparent, huh?" I said with a laugh.

One small problem had arisen during the meal when my granddaughter, Jean Marie, said to Lydia, "But what should I call you?"

Lydia realized that the word *grandma* had already been used for Marie and for Rob's mother, so very wisely she said, "I'm sure 'grandma' doesn't fit and I've never been a fan of 'nana' so why don't you just call me Miss Lydia. Will that work? Grandpa Kiki and Miss Lydia?"

Jean Marie smiled and Matt said, "Works for me!"

We had two relaxing days of talking and game playing and piano duets before heading for Kansas to break the news to Will and Vangie and their kids.

It turned out that they were even less surprised than my family had been since they'd been with Lydia and me for a while in Plainston during the epidemic.

Vangie said with a smile, "Maybe you didn't know it yet, but I knew you were in love months ago."

Since the kids had already met me, they quickly adopted just plain Kiki for my title. We had another couple of wonderful days there, including a July 4th picnic and fireworks display. Then it was on to Boulder.

I had traveled extensively during my post-teaching career, but I'd mostly flown from city to city. Seeing the United States from the ground was delightful. I reveled in the open space of the Bread Basket states, the miles and miles of undulating golden wheat fields that would be harvested soon and the dark green corn, already tasseled, standing tall in neat rows. The ground began to rise as we reached eastern Colorado and we saw more and more pasture land with cattle scattered across it.

We reached the home of our host and hostess, John and Margaret Hamilton, about three o'clock in the afternoon. Several Plainston families had formed a cell—one of many cells in the United States.

"Doesn't 'cell' sound conspiratorial?" Lydia said with a laugh.

I was soon to know what this particular cell was doing.

John explained, "We are negotiating with the FINs to help run their campaign if they'll put some of our planks in their platform and agree to run a genuine educational campaign and not just an election campaign."

"What do you mean by an educational campaign?" I asked.

"Our theory is that political parties should be primarily educational. They should devote major effort between elections to educating the public about proposals for change so that when election time rolls around, at least most voters will be well informed—and not be influenced by divisive ads and inflammatory rhetoric."

"It sounds like you are putting out specifications for doing a job and asking for bidders."

"We are, in a sense. Plainston doesn't have the resources to enter national politics directly. We are gambling on the FINs because so far we feel that their third party represents a strong contrast to the two established parties. They're a coalition of special interest groups—ethnic minorities, ecologists, the disarmament movement, human rights groups—groups that most of us in Plainston support. Last election, as you well know, the FINs did campaign without the usual negativity."

That I did know.

* * *

As we headed for the West Coast, we visited a number of other cells, and I learned more about Plainston's conspiracy. Their goals—freedom from exploitation; adequate food, clothing, and shelter; health care; and some leisure time—are basically universal. People everywhere work for these basics for their families. Plainstans have discovered how to achieve them through Mutual Instruction in their schools. They simply want to share the bounty of their lives.

The FINs could help them get the word out, so to speak, and the FINs would benefit from what one woman said was the "largest, best-organized, most dedicated, and best-trained grass rooters ever known."

The figures were impressive. Since the mid-1970s, Plainstans who left home had mostly settled in fairly tightly knit communities in major cities of over 200,000 population around the United States—about a thousand a year, usually older couples who'd already raised their children in the Plainston schools. In some places, they have helped to establish MI schools, usually private or charter. Some have entered local politics; most are activists for any number of causes.

For example, we visited an MI school founded by Lisbeth and Phil almost fifteen years ago in Hillside, a city across the Bay from San Francisco. They'd found a small group of elementary teachers and a principal who were more than willing to try something totally different to "save our kids," they said. A group of seven adults and fifteen kids spent a summer in the Plainston schools. That fall they returned to Hillside with a group of four Plainston teachers and a dozen Plainston students, who spent the fall semester there. More teachers came to Plainston along with more kids the next summer. And that's all it took to get it going.

Over a period of about five years, MI was gradually introduced, beginning with K-2 classrooms where the older little ones helped the younger little ones. Then there were 3-4 combined classrooms and finally 5-8 rooms related to subject matter areas. At the end of five years, the school had become year-round; promotion from grade to grade had ceased with kids moving from level to level in their subjects with lots of help from other kids; report cards simply checked off what was mastered; parents no longer resisted contact with the school since they no longer faced disapproving school personnel, telling them about their children's failures; discipline problems melted away when most kids were aware that they didn't want to mess up a place they enjoyed.

The high school administration resisted a total overhaul of its program even when the kids from the grade school began to enter as ninth graders; however, the quality of the kids from the MI school couldn't be ignored, so a number of concessions were made. One, kids could enter the high school for either the fall or spring semester, depending on when they'd completed the MI school program. As a result, freshmen in the high school had a wider age range than in a traditional school—some as young as twelve, some as old as fifteen. The high school retained its curriculum of specific courses, meeting at specific times with bells and noisy halls and lockers and all that. But students were trained to be tutors in all subjects and peer tutoring was firmly entrenched throughout the building.

The best news was that two other K-8 schools in the area had begun to implement MI, and one would become totally ungraded at the beginning of the next year. The good news was spreading, and part of that was economic. The MI schools had better test scores, much better attendance, and fewer discipline problems than most other schools in the area—including two in affluent neighborhoods. Yet the cost of running the MI school was no more than the cost of running traditional elementary schools. Taxpayers like getting more for less. When the discipline problems had begun to decline, the position of vice-principal was eliminated and two record-keeping aides were hired. No additional teachers were hired.

Lydia and I spent a day at the original MI building in Hillside. The school was in a predominately black neighborhood which had once been home to the usual ills that plague poor areas in cities all over the country—too many kids being raised without fathers, too many drugs, too much crime, too few legitimate jobs, too many boarded-up stores, too many rundown homes—too little hope.

What should've been no surprise to us was that the staff told us to talk to the kids.

Jay, a short, stocky thirteen-year-old black boy, gave MI all the credit for their good school and their good neighborhood.

"Your school got rid of drugs, gangs, early pregnancies, and crime?" I asked.

He laughed, "Mr. Kiki, I never said we didn't have any problems. We just don't live in a place like our parents did. When we start here as little bitty kids and we learn to care for each other and we really want to learn, it makes no sense to wreck our bodies and our brains with drugs. Girls don't seek sex to feel important as often; we respect our bodies. Gangs lost their power when kids had a "family" here to belong to. See what I mean?"

We did.

A girl, a twelve-year-old named Shayne, explained, "You get to teach, you know, help other kids learn what you've learned. We care about the kids we help and that carries over to what we do out of school. School is clean and neat. When parents see how well we're doing in school, they work to make our neighborhood better. People know each other better. We have community events more than we used to. We just had a big barbeque for the Fourth of July."

A handsome, tall young man named Joseph, added, "There's a lot of peer support here for going straight, for doing the right things."

We found out later that Joseph had been an exchange student to Plainston when he was fourteen. He'd already been accepted at the University of Plainston for the spring semester.

"I can hardly wait to go back," he said. "It's a beautiful place, isn't it?"

*   *   *

That evening I asked our hosts about what I'd been thinking about for days. With so much evidence of success, why wasn't change coming faster?

Our host, Trevor, explained it this way: "Americans seem to worship that which is big or rich or famous. So here's this little city tucked away behind a wall in the Midwest—not a place to be taken seriously. Many view Plainston as too different and too good to be true. When problems have been around for ages and haven't yielded to repeated attempts to solve them, people come to believe they are insoluble or not even meant to be solved. And anyone so brazen as to suggest solutions must be a charlatan or a fool."

"So what's the answer?"

"We keep doing what we're doing—getting MI into more and more schools, working to back political candidates who have values we support, making our cells throughout the country bigger and stronger. That's about it. Change will come, but like evolution, it's slow."

*   *   *

Before leaving California, we had one more major stop in Los Angeles. We'd traveled down the beautiful coastal route, taking two days to make the trip so that we could stop often to enjoy the sea air and the scenery. We were again hosted by a sixtyish couple from Plainston. Our purpose was to sit in on a meeting with FINs from both the California branch of the party and representatives from other branches, who were meeting in Los Angeles for a planning session.

When I met the FIN representatives, they didn't strike me as the usual sort of politicians I'd become so familiar with while working with the GBO. First of all, most of this group of men and women weren't lawyers but rather from professions related to education and the social services. Among the twenty-five or so were five teachers and professors, two ministers, two family counselors, three registered nurses, a drug abuse therapist, an accountant, three farmers, and two novelists. They got down to business immediately.

In short order, a consensus was reached on several issues. The FINs wouldn't run a candidate for president in the next election; instead, they would concentrate on Congressional races and state legislators. They would focus totally on issues, refusing to participate in any "dirty" tactics or negative campaigning. The last election proved that the FINs could succeed with a clean educational campaign. Finally, they agreed to include basic goals and methods of MI in the education reform plank of their platform.

Lydia and I left California in great spirits.

*   *   *

Our next stop was a small city near Flagstaff, Arizona, where I met Lydia's youngest son, Christopher Wayne Gray. Chris was a smiling, unmarried twenty-nine-year-old with his mother's blue-eyes. He'd left Plainston after graduating from the university with a master's in education. He'd joined a small cell in Flagstaff where he'd gradually organized a group of thirty parents who wanted the public school where he was teaching fourth grade to implement MI. It'd taken two years for him to convince the school principal and the majority of the teachers to give it a try and another year to get board approval—and that only after he'd arranged for a dozen teachers and board members to visit Plainston during their spring break. They were now in their second year of gradually getting tutors trained, the curriculum more flexible, and more parents on board. Chris felt that within two years the school would be using MI in all eight grades—the elementary school, the middle school, and the high school were all on the same campus.

"Getting changes in the high school will be tougher," he said, "but when all these MI trained kids get there, they may simply insist on a more flexible schedule that will include time for them to help each other. We'll see."

As we talked, Lydia was trying to be a good, non-interfering parent; however, her curiosity was obvious as she glanced around his small apartment, looking for photos or other signs of a female visitor. Finally, when her search became too obvious, Chris laughed.

"Mom, she's coming over for dinner."

"Who's that, Chris?"

"My girlfriend, Elaine. She's agreed to run the gauntlet to get your approval. By the way, she totally has mine."

As it turned out, she had no trouble getting Lydia's. Elaine was delightful—a twenty-six-year-old fourth-generation Arizonan with a wide smile and large blue eyes. She was a registered nurse with the school district.

"She has a huge extended family of aunts, uncles, and cousins whom you'll get to meet in November at the wedding—assuming that you'll come," Chris said with a mischievous grin.

Lydia hugged Elaine and then Chris and then Elaine again.

Chapter 24

Stella Rising Star

After leaving the Flagstaff area, we worked our way eastward, stopping at several Indian reservations, which had flourishing MI schools that were staffed by teachers trained either in Plainston or in other Plainston-sponsored reservation schools. The reservations themselves looked much better than I remembered them to be in the late 80s when they were even more depressing than some inner-city ghettos I'd visited while doing research for a series of articles about poverty in America. I suspected, rightly, that the Plainston-aided MI influence deserved much of the credit.

Lydia filled in some background as we drove. Oklahoma was originally called Indian Territory. It served as a dumping ground for over sixty tribes that had been forced off their lands by land-hungry pioneers who'd encroached on tribal lands.

Eastern Oklahoma was resettled in the 1830s by the Five Civilized Tribes—Creeks, Choctaws, Cherokees, Chickasaws, and Seminoles. These five tribes weren't put onto reservations. Some land was owned by the tribes, some owned privately by individuals. When oil was discovered on Indian land in the early 1900s, many Indians became wealthy, but their wealth was sometimes as destructive to Indian character as was their former poverty.

However, on the whole, the Oklahoma Indians had made a better transition to white society than Indians had on the more than six hundred reservations nationwide. Yet there were many tribes who strove to maintain or recapture their native culture. The Cherokees, who'd managed to preserve some full Cherokee bloodlines, were leaders in this movement.

We drove to Muskogee, a city only a little larger than Plainston, which was in the center of the area settled by the Five Civilized Tribes. Our hosts there lived in a modest home in a middle-class neighborhood. Because Lydia had given me no advanced information about them, I stepped back in surprise when the door opened and I faced a whole tribe of stern-faced, full-blooded Cherokees in native costume, looking to be about ten feet tall!

After holding their forbidding pose a few seconds, their faces broke into grins and all six doubled over in gales of laughter. After they straightened up and shrank to their tall but normal statures, I was introduced all around: the father was Leonard Tall Shoot Mason, very striking at six feet six; the mother was Stella Rising Star, a mere five feet eleven, and their four children ranged from the eldest son at six feet four to little nine-year-old Lily, who was already five feet four. All except Lily towered over my five feet nine and Lydia's five feet two.

Lydia, of course, had put the family up to this surprise. She'd known the Masons most of their lives. Their story unfolded in bits and pieces during a leisurely meal and a long evening visit.

Years before, one of Plainston's most ardent promoters of MI had been the Cherokee wife of a Plainston doctor. After a visit to her hometown of Muskogee, she'd brought a niece back to Plainston to attend the first MI school, Oak Hill, which later became Southeast. After going to Normal to get a teaching degree, the niece had returned to Muskogee, a true believer in MI. With the help of wealthy patrons, both Native American and white, she'd established a private MI school. Over the years, the concept had taken hold and more reservation schools had begun to use the Plainston model. For years, there had been a regular stream of both kids and teachers going between Plainston and Muskogee in an exchange program.

Stella Rising Star had first attended that school in Muskogee. Then she'd gone to Plainston for her last two years of public schooling and had finally gotten a teaching degree from the University of Plainston. She'd returned to

Muskogee to establish an MI teacher-training program for teachers in Indian schools, using the original MI school as the model.

Leonard had attended the same private school in Muskogee, where he and Stella had been childhood sweethearts. He'd also gone to the University of Plainston, majoring in physical education.

After years of working to train MI teachers and to establish a Plainston-style outreach network in reservations and Indian communities nationwide, Stella Rising Star had turned her persuasive power to politics. Due to her influence, a plank related to the Native American movement had been adopted as part of the FINs' platform.

Stella had a fascinating approach to the politics of reform, a mixture of lofty idealism and down-to-earth practicality. She believed that Mutual Instruction was the ideal way to recapture the essence of democracy—the rule of caring, informed people who vote for ideas not images.

Over the past forty years, I'd spend thousands of dreary hours listening to professional politicians trying to put together a platform. What so often came out were weasel-worded Mom-and-apple-pie planks that neither the politicians nor the voters took seriously. However, no one hearing Stella Rising Star Mason expound her version of American democracy and the MI system could possibly ignore her ideas.

"The FINs have a leader," I said to Lydia when we were getting ready for bed.

"That they do," she said as she kissed me good night.

*   *   *

We headed north to Duluth where delegates to a national conference of FINs would discuss launching the type of pre-election educational campaign that Plainston had proposed. There we again met the Mason tribe.

About one thousand FIN delegates were attending the conference. If the grassroots educational campaign idea was accepted, as recommended by the steering committee, the push for FIN victories would begin immediately. The delegates heard well-prepared proposals for planks on pollution control and related ecological problems, on more research on alternative energy sources, on closer regulation of financial institutions, on speeding up of disarmament, on reducing the national debt, and on investing in the ever-deteriorating infra-structure. The proposals were all people-centered, quality-of-life oriented.

At 10:30, Stella Rising Star Mason was introduced to present a proposal for the education plank. She was already well-known by many at the convention due to her work in the Native American rights movement. She received an enthusiastic round of applause.

Wearing a lavaliere microphone, she stood beside the lectern. Her Cherokee ceremonial dress added to her regal appearance. As was her wont, she raised her arms and recited a simple prayer to the Great Spirit for guidance. Then she began her presentation, speaking without notes. I'll quote some highlights.

"A political platform is intended to support society," she said. "We are gathered here because our society is collapsing. Too many of the individuals who compose it are weak. All human problems, save those caused by natural disasters, are the result of ignorance and/or ill will. The solutions to all such problems are intelligence and good will, which must be nurtured. The education of head and heart must, therefore, become the primary concern of society.

"For centuries, mankind has been struggling to build societies ruled by free people—democracies. However, democracy has two conflicting roots. One comes through the Greek philosophical tradition that contains the concept of the ruler and the ruled. Plato's Republic was modeled more on the repressive, rigid, caste society of Sparta than on the relatively free society of Athens. Democracy on this model calls for rulers, persons with more power than those they rule. The democratic element is the freedom to elect those rulers—representative government.

"Centuries before your ancestors arrived on our shores"—she paused for a ripple of laughter that followed her emphasis on the word *our*—"our ancestors had developed and practiced a different form of democracy, both within the small villages and among the larger tribes.

"Our concept of democracy is genuine equality among all persons. The individuals then grant superior wisdom to certain members of the tribe, the chiefs. Americans, with their ideas of rulers, have never understood our concept of 'chief.' Our chiefs have no power other than that of persuasion. In the past, most tribes had several chiefs, equivalent to respected elders in any society. These chiefs would be sent to meetings, such as the annual conference of the Iroquois Federation.

"The critical difference was that then the individuals took personal responsibility to live by the recommendations of their councils. Tribal law became a moral force, not a legally imposed tyranny. Indian society did punish those who failed to live by the codes, but Indians didn't live under the fear of secret police or threatening bureaucracies or distant administrators with powers to mess up their lives. Democracy was the personal responsibility to live by customs that the wisest found were good.

"These ideals of individual freedom and equality and responsibility—for every Native American contributed his or her full share to the community welfare—came back to America in the writings of European philosophers, who'd heard of Rousseau's 'noble savages.' Thomas Jefferson's assertion that we're all born free and equal may've come from us in this roundabout way."

Stella Rising Star paused and walked to the other side of the podium. Her voice dropped.

"Now we must consider the missing keystone in the arch of civilization— what we must have to make democracy strong again. That, ladies and gentlemen, is Mutual Instruction, which educates both the heart and the head. We are born bundles of potentiality, not pre-programmed organisms like the lower animals which are ruled primarily by instinct. Only man has the powerful desire—instinct, perhaps—to learn and the special ability to share that learning through the powers of speech and writing.

"We've never before devised an educational system that integrates the learning with both head and heart. Schools have always had adult teachers in the role of rulers, who aren't elected by either their pupils or the parents. The traditional school is undemocratic. It stresses obedience to authority. How can youngsters learn self-reliance and responsibility when they are always under adult control and having to fit into a group that isn't of their own choosing? How can children learn to make decisions when most are being made for them—when to read and when to write and when to go to lunch or music or art class—and what to read and what to write and what to sing and what to draw and what to do in p.e. class?

"Traditional school is almost exclusively for the head—facts, concepts, theories—most of them memorized. Such schooling teaches students almost nothing about making decisions and communicating their knowledge."

Stella Rising Start continued to outline the problems with traditional schools: the emphasis on competition rather than cooperation; the age-graded, lockstep classroom instruction; the emphasis on testing and grading; the fear of failure felt by many kids.

Then after another pause, she began to talk about Mutual Instruction. "We can offer a wholly democratic system—a system in which kids aren't ruled but a system in which they become responsible for their own learning and behavior, one in which they understand that their own welfare is bound up with the welfare of others—the kids they see every day and know by name. Later, that concept can extend to their community and the world beyond it."

She sketched two main features of MI—the individualized instruction and the lack of failure since, with help, the students work until the skills are learned. She stressed the latter point with the example that students don't pass from the first grade to the second because they have gotten a year older and it's June and the time for promotion has come. Instead, a student passes to a new level in any subject matter only when he or she is ready to change levels.

"And most precious of all, kids get lots of experience in learning not only to understand others but also to care for them. They learn to care and to love right along with the ABCs. Caring and love implies responsibility. Responsibility requires competence. Competence requires individualized nurturing of each person's unique interests and abilities.

"Tailor-made instruction *cannot* be given by a single teacher in charge of a group of twenty or thirty same-age children, covering the same lessons, expecting them all to progress at the same rate and achieve the same level of competency in the same time frame. That system has never worked well for all kids simply because, as common sense tells us, it is unworkable. Generations of many good, talented teachers have dedicated their lives to trying to help all kids learn—while knowing they've failed many. But the teachers have *not* failed—the system has failed because it's terribly flawed.

"We must state frankly that children must learn to love learning, to love themselves, to love beauty, and to love others. We are our brothers' keepers. Let our FIN platform propose that our schools move as rapidly as possible to the Mutual Instruction model that unites efficient teaching of head and heart."

Stella Rising Star raised her arms and looked upward, saying nothing.

The audience rose in a quiet wave with arms held high in silent tribute. When Stella Rising Star looked down at us, she smiled in surprise, then lowered her arms and gave the gesture for us to be seated, but we remained standing as we applauded for a full two minutes.

*   *   *

Stella Rising Star's speech to the convention made the national news. She was on TV in full regalia, arms uplifted in silence. The cameras then panned the audience standing in a similar pose with tears streaming down many cheeks.

Her speech, unfortunately, was neither excerpted nor summarized, just mentioned in tones barely disguising humor or contempt, a speech by a "full-blooded descendant of Cherokee chieftains." It was treated as a novelty, not as a speech of substance and importance.

The next day, she was followed by a flood of stringers with shoulder-mounted cameras. She didn't wear her traditional garb, but she wore her hair in the traditional long braids. Leonard and the "Four Little Indians," as the media dubbed the Mason children, were also dogged. They granted interviews, which showed them to be a delightful, if not somewhat exotic, American family.

The editor of a Duluth paper wrote, "If the unconventional but allegedly successful Mutual Instruction system of education turns out children as intelligent and warm-hearted as this Cherokee sample, then our school people should give respectful attention to the FINs' school plank."

Other big media guns soon started booming. Wilber Bickersley mounted a triple attack: on the FINs, on Plainston, and on me.

After reporting the "hand-in-glove FIN association with the well-known, notorious Plainston conspiracy," he ended his piece with what he intended would "finish FINism." In a paragraph, outlined in gray rather than the black reserved for the truly departed, Wilber printed a tongue-in-cheek obituary:

> We regret to report the passing of our highly respected fellow commentator, Karl 'Kiki' Kornhauer. In July of this year, he departed the world of responsible political analysis and

commentary to enter the realm of the dead, dying, and destructive. He is no longer on active assignment with the Global Betterment Organization, whose executive director, Max Baum, is on the same downward slide since his marriage to the twin sister of one of Plainston's most insidious plotters. Kiki was well-launched on his own investigation of the Plainston conspiracy, in cooperation with this commentator, when he contracted the flu. During the treatment directed by the unconventional Health Services, he was probably given a mind-altering drug, for he has completely abandoned independent judgment of Plainston, especially of its educational system. Now he is touring the country to visit schools and FIN centers with his new wife, who has totally taken over his reasoning. Anything we hear from Kornhauer from now on will be a voice from the grave in that Paradise-posing Hell, Plainston. True American values have been buried with him. I send this heartfelt plea across the River Styx: 'Kiki, come back to us. We need you. Lydia, you sorceress, let him go!'

Chapter 25

Heading East—Then Home

It was hard to leave Duluth and not drive southward toward home, but we headed easterly instead. Our next stop was in Michigan to visit my son, Ross, his wife, Jennifer, and my youngest two grandchildren, Eddie and Cameron, ages five and seven. The boys, who hardly remembered Marie, were delighted to have a "new" grandmother. Lydia was instantly taken on a tour of their room to see all their treasures, including a recently captured garter snake now living in an old aquarium.

That night we four adults talked well into the wee morning hours about Plainston. Jennifer was home schooling the boys since she and Ross felt that the public grade school was too overcrowded to give the students the attention they needed. Both boys were very bright but strong willed. Jennifer was allowing them to follow their many interests in a way the public school wouldn't have. Both had learned to read quickly because they wanted to know what the books said. But, so far, the boys were resisting reading anything Jennifer chose, so instead, they scoured the public library for books they wanted to read.

Lydia and I gave our full support to what Jennifer was doing, but she was concerned about how she'd handle a balanced curriculum when they boys got older. She and Ross were intrigued with my description of Plainston schools.

"Does Plainston have room for us?" Jennifer said with a laugh.

And the seed was planted—maybe Plainston could accommodate four more Kornhauers if Ross's training as an accountant was needed there. It was an idea that warmed my heart. I was almost afraid to hope.

*   *   *

Next on our itinerary, besides several more stops at FIN centers in the Detroit and Cleveland areas, was a visit with the last of our combined brood in eastern Ohio. Lydia's daughter, Susan, had been widowed at twenty-four just before her daughter's first birthday. Her husband had died from a brain tumor only five months after diagnosis. His mother and two sisters had been wonderful support for Susan and Valerie for years. Susan loved her job as the head librarian in the local library, and she had a long-term relationship with a man whom I didn't meet since he was in Sweden on business. Lydia liked him a lot, she said later. Valerie was now married and expecting her first baby in just a couple of months.

"You didn't tell me I was marrying an almost great-grandmother," I said the next day after we headed toward West Virginia.

"Must've slipped my mind," she said with a laugh.

*   *   *

We drove straight through to Max and Lisbeth's house in the Washington, D. C., suburb where they lived in a fine old home near the Plainston headquarters in Coral Hills. After a leisurely dinner of quiche, spinach bisque, and vanilla ice cream covered with Lisbeth's famous homemade chocolate topping, we retired to a lovely second-story guest room.

Much refreshed the next morning, we joined Max and Lisbeth on the outside patio for a breakfast of waffles and fresh fruit. Max hardly waited for us to take a sip of coffee before launching into a description of a grandiose GBO project—a complicated media campaign to arouse world public opinion in support of a new world order.

He said, "It's all the things Plainston has been doing and advocating for over fifty years. The world is crying for this. Our backers are putting up all the money we need to blanket the world with our proposals. We need your reporting skills, Kiki, especially now that you have firsthand experience with Plainston and can speak with your heart as well as your head.

"This will require a lot of international travel since we want to have face-to-face contact with people of influence in every country. You'll get to meet a lot of very important international figures."

Eighteen months ago, this would've elicited an immediate "Let's go" response from me, but when I looked at Lydia, she wasn't shining with her usual glow at the proposal for good works.

"The pay will be very good during the three-year program. It's got to be a global appeal, simultaneously worldwide."

Max continued to talk with downright fervor. He'd gone from competent executive to dedicated reformer, all in less than a year—with the help of an attack of the flu and falling in love, both Plainston related.

Finally, I said, "I'll need to think this over."

"Always the procrastinator," Max growled, sounding much more like my old boss.

I wanted to talk Lydia. Max had said that travel would take up about half my time and that I could make Plainston my home base. Even though I didn't want Lydia to make up my mind for me, I needed her input. I needed to see if she was feeling as I was.

When we were alone that night, I said, "I have questions about the validity of this project and its timeliness—even its basic strategy."

Lydia made no comment.

"If I hadn't been through last year's campaign and with you on this trip, I might be jumping at this chance. I really am an internationalist at heart, and I agree with all that GBO thinks should be done."

"So what's wrong?" Lydia asked quietly.

"It's their process, not their product."

"And what's wrong with the process?"

I didn't answer that right away. Finally, I said, "Basically, it's a top-down approach without roots. They think it's educational, but you don't get real change with leaders dictating what should be done."

I paused, then added, "When a worthy ideal is presented and rejected, it's very hard to resurrect it. People think of it as a dead horse when actually it was a good idea, just born before its time. What the GBO wants is too good to risk death by premature birth. If the plan fails, it will take a full generation to recover enough strength to try again. In the meantime, problems will get worse."

"So you're going to turn Max down?"

I was surprised that I'd made a decision so quickly. I usually suffer from considerable ambivalence in reaching decisions—as I had done before going to Plainston in the first place.

"Max thinks he understands Plainston. He sees it as a remarkable place, and he wants people all over the world to make the changes necessary to achieve what Plainstans have achieved. But what he doesn't get is that Plainston grew from the roots that I found in the educational system. You've raised generations of good people who make Plainston what it is. There is no one at the top dictating what you should or shouldn't do. That's what would be missing in Max's plan—growth from the roots, change coming from the people."

Lydia gave me a long, warm hug. "You really do understand. Let's go home soon."

When I talked to Max the next morning, he was disappointed with my decision, but he wasn't surprised. He attributed it to my marriage to Lydia.

"I, too, would find it hard to be separated from Plainston's main attraction, now that I have a duplicate copy to live with," he said with a laugh as he hugged Lisbeth.

Before we left that afternoon, Lydia and Lisbeth talked. Lisbeth also felt that the GBO plan was premature and too much focused on reaching leaders. She felt that Max would come around to seeing that change from within was the answer—and that would come with more and more Mutual Instruction schools and the FINs grassroots campaign. She'd be quietly urging him to accept that idea.

*   *   *

We'd planned on a leisurely three-day drive back to Plainston, but once we got on the road and headed west on I70, we were like the cattle in old

Westerns that smell a waterhole and stampede. We drove until after nine that night and got up early the next morning to finish the trip home.

When we rolled into Plainston shortly after one that afternoon, I realized, as we guided our quiet little mini-bus down the clean, tree-shaded streets why Plainstans so often and so lovingly refer to their "beloved walls" which so unobtrusively separate their little city from the rest of the world where there is more hustle and bustle than is needed to make a living and a life.

Although we'd spent most of our time with dedicated, intelligent individuals, even they didn't have the relaxed, joyful air of life-long Plainstans. Almost all the "outsiders" we'd met displayed some sense of insecurity about themselves or their own work or the FIN project. Plainstans, even those living beyond the walls, have an inner peace, I feel, based on the belief that the world will move on an upward path to be "above the line."

After stowing our luggage in Lydia's apartment, we went to the Beanery for supper. Even though we sat in the back conversational section, I was quiet as we ate and listened to the music.

Finally Lydia asked, "Are you having second thoughts about turning down Max's job offer? Will it mean financial problems?"

I laughed and took her hand. "I can eke out an existence here in Plainston since two can live more cheaply than one, they claim."

Then getting more serious, I added, "When we drove through the gates and got inside the walls, when I looked at the Temple, when I saw the sun shining through the trees onto Sugar Creek, I knew beyond all doubt that I was home. This is where I want to spend the rest of my life.

"I will write, Lydia—I'll write about the schools and the Temple and the people. I will tell about the wall and how it came to be. I will explain that Plainston needn't be cloned in all its unique features as a total society. There doesn't have to be a wall or even a Temple. Only the MI rootstock is essential. I will explain Plainston's conspiracy."

*   *   *

And so I began to write. Lydia almost instinctively seemed to know when I needed to talk and when I needed silence. During the day, she was often gone, busy as she'd always been with Plainston matters. In the evening as the sun was setting, we took long walks. She was my sounding board.

August faded into September. Tall deep purple ironweed bloomed along Sugar Creek as well as asters and chrysanthemums all around the city. The nights began to cool enough to turn off the air conditioner and let the soft breezes in.

Then, amidst the peace and beauty, in walked Wilber Bickersley with a lawsuit for false arrest over a year ago against artist Ruth Condin, the three arresting officers, and Lydia, who'd been the hearing officer. He claimed the arrest had caused him "loss of professional prestige and loss of income resulting therefrom as well as psychological suffering from unwarranted public censure."

The Plainston individuals involved wouldn't settle out of court since they considered their actions to be appropriate and legal. As it turned out, Wilber also didn't want an out-of-court settlement since he planned to use the case to put Plainston on trial nationally. He'd waited until the Plainston-FIN connection was in the news before filing the suit.

The trial, however, turned into a fiasco. First, Wilber's intention to expose Plainston was quashed by the judge who ruled to allow only testimony related to the questions of entrapment and false arrest. The false arrest charge was soon disproved with the taped evidence from Ruth's studio which clearly showed Wilber to be both drunk and aggressive. He'd pulled the cover from the canvas of the almost nude painting of Ruth—which she testified was being done by a sixty-two-year-old woman who was taking art lessons from her. He'd forced Ruth onto the couch, his face distorted with anything but love, his voice threatening. The tape showed Ruth's struggle to convince him to let her get some wine and light some candles to set the tone. She'd called the police from the kitchen. The tape showed him guilty of resisting arrest—first verbally, then physically. Wilber swung at one male officer and then was unceremoniously pinned by a female officer.

The final question was whether Ruth had entrapped Wilber in the first place. Two of her students testified that Wilber had suggested seeing more art work in her studio. But Wilber's attorney asked Ruth why, knowing Wilber's reputation, she'd let him enter her studio-apartment at all.

Ruth answered, "This may sound strange to you, sir, but we Plainstans believe that gentlemen, even under the influence, can and should understand that no means no. Sexual relations in this community are associated with respect and affection, feelings not generated casually. We forget sometimes that such isn't the sexual morality, unfortunately, of some of our visitors."

Wilber's hope for a week-long trial was dashed when the judge excused the jury and threw the case out of court after a day and a half of testimony. He gave Wilber a lecture before bringing down the gavel.

"Under the Bill of Rights, Mr. Bickersley, you have the freedom of the press to try your case against Plainston in the court of public opinion. But you do not have that right in a court of law under a shabby subterfuge only a hair's breadth from perjury. In fact, the defendants in this case would have had a far sounder case in charging you with trying to entrap them with your scurrilous behavior. I only regret that your hearing officer, with agreement from Miss Condin, so generously exercised her discretion in not formally charging you with assault with intent to rape. I can assure you that that case would not have been dismissed in any court."

The judge assessed full costs of the trial against Wilber, who chose not to appeal since he didn't relish the prospect of the video tapes being shown over and over again in the media.

Our hope that the entire sorry affair would silence Wilber's attack on Plainston, however, was for naught. Oddly, some in the media saw Wilber as a victim since the judge was married to a Plainstan native.

One editorial went so far as to attack Ruth as naïve. "Are we to believe that a mature woman is so innocent as to believe that a drunken man who is a relative stranger would ask to go to her studio after ten p.m. to observe art? If Plainston turns out adults so out of touch with reality as that scenario suggests, then truly their educational system is a farce at best, a menace at worst. Either one is dangerous. Their close affiliation with the FINs must be watched closely. Citizens, beware! The trickery perpetrated on Wilber Bickersley may be indicative of what Plainston can do with an entire nation. We are more vulnerable than we think."

Some of Wilber's allies won in the media the battle he'd lost in court.

Chapter 26

The FINs

Though Lydia and I stayed in Plainston that fall, we were closely connected with the FINs' grassroots pre-election campaign, which had started off in high gear after the Duluth planning conference.

Creative individuals soon produced persuasive video discs and study units for all the FIN proposals. The grassroots strategy the FINs adopted was double-barreled: one barrel aimed at the mass media and the other at home meetings.

The mass media campaign kept a steady flow of letters to the editor and essays for the op ed pages. There were also materials for radio and television talk shows and model speeches and video presentations for service clubs. And most important was the information on Mutual Instruction to present to parents, teachers, administrators, and school board members.

The mass media strategy was supported by home meetings. Hosts used CDs to introduce issues with printed material for follow-up discussions. The home meetings grew by cell division—each meeting usually interested at least one attendee in hosting a home meeting, which gained another host, and so on.

With no more to do than to play a CD and to pass out sheets for discussion, almost any interested person felt competent to host a meeting. Hosts were instructed not to be argumentative; instead, they were to encourage free expression on the issues.

Each meeting centered on not more than two closely-related issues. Thus attendees could return to discuss other planks in the FIN platform at later meetings. As the issues were kept alive in the media, people had the opportunity between meetings to read and hear arguments pro and con.

Where did the money come from? Not a dime from special interests. Plainston supplied the CDs and printed materials at cost. Local groups made copies. These modest costs were borne by FIN members and supporters. There were no expensive newspaper, television, or radio ads; no billboards defacing the landscape; no people manning the phones to call strangers. Instead, there were meetings, more and more meetings in people's homes. Such meetings didn't always win over FIN adversaries, but the information provided gave those against the message firsthand.

Though Wilber's reputation had been somewhat tarnished by the trial, he still maintained a steadfast group of conservative supporters. His continuing charge that Plainstans were "pulling the strings that made the FIN puppets dance" appeared again and again in his columns and during his television and radio appearances. He challenged me to answer this charge, but I declined.

When Lydia and I ran into him at a FIN convention in Indianapolis in late September, he said, "Well, Kiki, old man, I see you have enough courage and strength left to show yourself in public with the FINs. Sorry you've lost your voice."

My almost two years in Plainston hadn't sanctified me to the point of loving my enemies. I was churning inside and didn't trust myself to make a reply. I knew that several reporters were within earshot, and a sharp Bickersley-Kornhauer interchange would've made juicy copy.

Lydia saved me. She said, "Now, Wilber, show us your good side and tell us how much you really love Plainston and the FINs. Confess that you're just miffed because we chose Kiki instead of you to join our 'conspiracy.' After all, it is the highest honor that anyone can bestow because, in your own words, we have all the answers. Too bad you're not willing to understand them."

Leaning forward, Lydia gave him a patronizingly motherly hug, which infuriated him as chuckling onlookers enjoyed the scene.

Regaining his composure, Wilber retorted, "All right, smug lady with all the answers, are you willing to put your body on the line? I'll bet that your puppet FINs won't win that third of the House seats you're after. If I'm right, you push me down Pennsylvania Avenue in a wheelbarrow. If I'm wrong, I'll push you."

"I'll take that bet, Wilber, but considering our age and physique differences, would you allow me to pedal you in one of Plainston's plush pedicabs? You'd be much more comfortable, and it would suit your dignity."

"All right, Lydia," Wilber agreed, flashing his most charming smile. "And I'll cushion the wheelbarrow for you and provide a parasol if it's sunny and an umbrella if it's rainy."

That evening, the Bickersley-Gray wager was the liveliest bit of political footage on the evening news. It was rerun throughout the campaign whenever the polls showed the FINs close to their targeted 145 seats. There were even political buttons with either vehicle which identified the wearer's allegiance.

*   *   *

As the weather cooled, the campaigns heated up. The two major parties were somewhat on the defensive since the polls were showing a steady erosion of support for their candidates. Both conservative and liberal voters began taking the FINs seriously. The status quo defenders tried to focus on the political inexperience of most FIN candidates. One of them added "Inc." for incompetent. He said, "If one says 'FIN Inc.' fast enough, the true character of this upstart organization will appear. A dictionary definition of *fink* is a 'contemptible or thoroughly unattractive person.'"

This shot, however, backfired. A syndicated columnist, a FIN supporter, cited the corruption of some allegedly "competent" Congressmen. He suggested that "Inc." should stand for incorruptible. He said, "Please note that they take not a penny from any special interest group."

The "Inc." suffix stuck with the FINs for the duration of the campaign, giving commentators a hook on which to hang either praise or censure.

The polls continued to show steady FIN gains. A week before the election, several polls agreed that the FINs had pretty well locked up 148 seats, three above their projected third of 145, with ten or so more possible if the FIN bandwagon kept rolling.

Then, one of Plainston's "failures" braked the bandwagon.

Three days before the election, Sunday papers carried Wilber Bickersley's nationally syndicated column, which had been expanded to article length. Its title was "Plainston Exposed."

Lydia and I were sitting before the fireplace, drinking our morning coffee and reading. Suddenly, Lydia—her face ashen—handed me the paper.

"Read this," she said.

After I finished the article, I laid down the paper and looked at her stricken face. "My God, who is this?"

"His name is Thomas Brownlee. He was a professor of theology at the University of Plainston for about ten years before he left recently. You probably met him at the Consensus meeting. He was part of that group for about a year."

"I remember him—a tall, very slender man with a shock of dark brown hair, a small chin beard, round rimless glasses. We didn't meet, but I remember that he tried to dominate the meeting with frequent Biblical references."

"That was the problem," Lydia said. "He became more and more evangelical in his approach to teaching, more and more intolerant of ideas that disagreed with his understanding of the Bible. The Consensus has never asked a member to leave, but it was being considered. His constant interruption of discussions by others wasn't in the spirit of reaching agreement by rational discussion and compromise. Luckily, he left the university in July for a job at a Bible college."

Lydia and I reread the article together, our hearts sinking deeper and deeper. Wilber's source was identified as a young professor of theology who'd agreed to break his pledge of silence to come forth and reveal to the nation the true nature of the Plainston conspiracy in order to "save us from ultimate destruction if the FINs were to gain power."

Following that was a long description of the Consensus, naming names and spelling out the ultimate global program of the conspirators. Actually, to people sick of all the ills of the world, the Plainston vision was an attractive Utopian program, but according to Wilber and his source, this Utopianism was its major defect and threat.

"Pie-in-the-sky schemes, no matter how well intentioned, always end in some kind of totalitarian control or anarchy. Human nature has not the qualities required to produce a heaven on earth. Those who propose to make such a heaven on earth are guilty of the gravest sin against the Almighty, the sin of arrogance. The FINs are co-conspirators in this threat to mankind."

The attack finally centered on the Temple and its advocacy of religious tolerance which would lead to a "smorgasbord of all faiths that produces moral indigestion and spiritual obesity."

With the election just two days away, there was no time to launch a rebuttal that would reach the numbers of people who'd no doubt read the Sunday article.

Most FIN supporters considered the source and shrugged their shoulders. Even so, some of those still trying to make up their minds were no doubt affected by the attack, especially since it came from a man of faith.

The FINs took their lumps, which were less severe than we'd feared. The FINs filled 144 House seats, only one shy of their 145 goal.

*   *   *

We didn't have time to either mourn the FINs' failure to meet their goal or to relish the fact that the election clearly indicated a mood for change in the country. Three days after the election, we made the journey to Flagstaff for the wedding. Elaine was a fourth-generation Arizonan—not a transplant wishing to escape to warmer climes. As Chris had said, her extended family was huge since her father was one of five siblings and her mother one of four. There was a whole host of first cousins and a lot of little second cousins.

The wedding was held on her parents' ranch—a beautiful, informal outdoor affair in the desert just before sunset. We all stood in a semicircle around the couple and the two attendants. Elaine wore a simple, mid-length dress with a rounded neckline and cap sleeves, adorned only with the pearl necklace her mother had worn at her own wedding. Chris had on a short-sleeved embroidered silk shirt with charcoal gray slacks. Both wore sandals. At the end of the ceremony, Chris took matching royal blue serapes, carried by the maid of honor and the best man, and placed one around his bride's shoulders and the other around his. We applauded the new couple. Then donning our jackets as the desert air cooled, we all walked behind them to a nearby cleared-out machine shed where we enjoyed a wonderful barbeque dinner and dancing to a live country band.

*   *   *

On Friday of Thanksgiving weekend, Lydia Gray paid off her bet to Wilber Bickersley. It was a beautiful Indian summer day in Washington, D.C. The FINs had properly but very quietly applied for a parade permit for 10:00 that Friday morning. The news media was on hand with television crews scattered along Pennsylvania Avenue.

At 9:55, we pulled up to the starting place in a rented U-Haul from which several bystanders and I unloaded a brand new pedicab. Lydia walked it over to the starting line. Without a word, she bowed low to Wilber and motioned him to be seated. She handed him an American flag and a large, brightly lettered placard mounted on a short stick. It read, "Bickersley Bet and Won."

Exactly at 10 a.m., she wheeled off. It was a covered cab, open only in front, so Wilber couldn't see Lydia seated behind him. A great shout and laughter came from spectators who lined the route. Wilber assumed the shouts were for him, so he vigorously waved the flag and the banner, leaning out of the cab to see the crowds. What he didn't see was the lofty banner that Lydia had unfurled above the cab. It read, "Won by One."

Everyone caught the joke. The FINs were only one short of their goal. That three-word victory was the worst defeat Wilber Bickersley had ever suffered.

And he suffered, without knowing it, for at least part of the next 1.2 miles.

At every intersection, as they headed for the Capitol, others joined the parade from side streets. From one came a sixty-piece marching band from Muskogee, dressed in full Indian ceremonial costume. Stella Rising Star Mason along with three other newly-elected FIN Congressmen from Oklahoma led them—all had won their districts handily. A bit farther, other bands joined the parade along with a large number of new FIN Congressman—all carrying banners which announced how many FINs had been elected from their states. Plainston's all-black Dixieland band joined, sitting on an old farm wagon pulled by a team of six mules—reminiscent of the poor people's march on Washington during the Civil Rights Movement. At the end came some of the FINs who'd lost their races. They carried placards which read, "Remember my name and face. I'll be here in two years."

- 251 -

As the participants poured from the side streets, Wilber realized that he'd been had. Even so, he couldn't stop the parade without facing more ridicule as a poor loser. But exactly what was he—a winner or a loser?

So the parade continued, Lydia passively pedaling away, dressed in a coolie's coat with her long gray hair in a single pigtail. At the end, Wilber disembarked and faced the television newsmen. For the first time in his life, he said, "No comment," and melted into the crowd.

News commentators that night had great fun with the story. One said it was the first defeat parade in the history of American politics. Another quipped that "Wilber Bickersley snatched defeat from the jaws of victory." Another one opined that if Plainston produced such clever, humor-loving people as those involved in the parade, she was going to take a second look at that place.

Lydia smiled all evening long, even as she soaked her tired legs in the hotel bathtub filled with hot water and scented bath oil.

Wilber soon found his voice and wrote in his column, "The ability of the FINs to conspire with the government of our capital city to permit a major parade, secretly planned to subvert its advertised purpose and to humiliate its central figure, shows the depth to which these conspirators will stoop. It starkly reveals the incredible power they can wield. What is most frightening is that this power is not lodged in the FIN party itself, but in the insidious power of that smugly walled little enclave, nestled so innocently in a lovely Midwest valley, spewing forth its gospel of godliness to cover its real purpose: to remold the world on it pseudo-Paradise model."

The FINs simply laughed at Wilber's increasingly exaggerated descriptions of Plainston—they laughed all the way to the House of Representatives, where, with 144 solid votes, they held the balance of power, joined often by some Democrats and Republicans.

When Wilber ranted at their "upsetting the balance of power," a FIN supporter wrote in response, "Have you ever tried to stand on a two-legged stool?"

Chapter 27

The New Year

After a quiet Christmas Day with just the two of us, I looked towards New Year's Eve with a sense of both wonder and hope. Just a year before, I'd been dreading Lydia's party—fearing that I was losing what I didn't even have—Lydia—to Max. In just 365 days since then, I'd married her myself, studied a remarkable school system, traveled the country, witnessed the rise of the FINs as a force to be reckoned with in Washington and the state houses, and settled into what I hoped—after my somewhat nomadic lifestyle—would be my last city of residence. Life was good.

Lydia had suggested we go to a community celebration at the university for New Year's Eve—an evening of catered food, dancing, movies for the kids, conversation, and camaraderie. I agreed.

We set out on the ten-minute walk a little before five. It was a brisk winter evening with just a skiff of snow blowing around on the ground.

When we walked into the conference center where the event was to be held, all I saw were Grays and Kornhauers—all of her kids and all of mine. Once I got over my shock, everyone, talking at once, filled me in. Lydia had arranged this, talking to each family as we'd visited during the summer. This was the wedding reception we'd never had and a New Year's Eve party. She'd been working on it for months.

Before dinner started, all the family members introduced themselves to the combined group. Then we took seats at tables for four—with all the families mixed up. We talked and talked. Every fifteen minutes, a bell rang and two of the table members picked up their plates and silverware and moved to a different table. By the time dessert was over, we felt like one big family.

Around eight, friends from Plainston began to flock in to make it the community celebration Lydia had claimed it would be. There was more talk and then some group singing and finally some dancing. Just before midnight, we broke out bottles of sparkling cider and filled many glasses. We walked out into the crisp night air, raised our glasses high to the nearby Temple, and toasted in the New Year.

Our five children and their families left one by one during the next three days—going back to their busy lives. I would bask in the warmth of their love and caring for us and each other for a long, long time.

*   *   *

Once seated in January, the FINs, true to their word, immediately began to push to accomplish what they'd promised to do. As it turned out, the Mutual Instruction educational plank was the most popular one in the FIN platform. Within months, a federal law, sponsored and guided through Congress under the leadership of Stella Rising Star Mason, who'd gained membership on the House Standing Committee on Children, Youth, and Families, provided financial aid for three years for any school starting the change to a full-scale, all-ages MI school.

The plan wasn't to get every school or district to adopt MI all at once. This wasn't to be a top-down, administration-mandated change; instead, it was to be a bottom-up development managed by teachers, parents, and students. The reason many other educational reforms have failed to make the impact hoped for is that they simply tack on something to a fundamentally flawed system.

MI's system of kids teaching kids, however, makes genuinely individualized instruction possible. MI frees teachers to be truly professional, to work largely one-on-one and with small groups. MI gives parents a meaningful involvement in planning and supervising their children's unique development. Any good instructional materials and methods can be incorporated into MI because of its flexibility.

Videos of MI in action in Plainston and in other MI schools throughout the country whipped up enthusiasm for parents, teachers, and kids to urge their school boards to set up pilot programs. The proposal to a school district was to support a single pilot school with the principal, teachers, parents, and students having been thoroughly oriented to the program.

Because Wilber and his cohorts were still attacking all that was Plainston, I was working to debunk a couple of myths. First, we had to convince people that they didn't have to wall off their cities to change their schools. Second, we needed to stress that a school didn't fully change to the MI model from one semester to the other or from one school year to the other. The change would be incremental. Third, we needed to convince administrators and school boards that beginning changes could be made without large expenditures of money. Most schools could be gradually modified over a period of years. And finally, we had to let all those interested—kids, parents, teachers, administrators, and town leaders—know that help was available.

And so Plainstans were gearing up to help. First, I, along with others, wrote articles stressing the above points. Then we wrote articles being more specific. Experienced Plainston teachers told how the program can be implemented by combining what are traditionally kindergarten, first, and second grades and training the older kids to help the younger ones. Later, more grades will be combined and more older students trained so that students will move from level to level individually when ready rather than as a whole group at the end of a semester or a year.

But more important than the how-to writing being done was the exchange programs that were set up nationwide. Almost immediately, a steady flow of students and teachers came and went from Plainston and other places where MI schools were already established. Stella Rising Star Mason was very involved in this aspect of the program since there were already so many MI schools for Native Americans.

Because the American educational system had been under attack for so many years, the climate was ripe for drastic change. And because MI is based on common sense, the idea didn't meet the usual negativity that change often brings. People's own experience tells them that kids are all different, that grouping by age doesn't work well, that one teacher—no matter how talented or dedicated—can't do enough to ensure competence in all subjects for all his or her students, that failure rarely motivates learning, that competence is the goal rather than a grade on a test, that kids like to work together and to help each other, that true motivation which leads to lifelong learning comes from within . . . . The list is long.

Even as I viewed what appeared to be a successful beginning of change, I couldn't quite overcome my doubts that, with all the thousands of little communities and hundreds of larger cities that make up the nation, grassroots change couldn't reach everyone in time to really reverse the negative trends threatening to bring down the country.

When I told Lydia about my doubts one evening, she smiled. "Maybe I can help with that."

The next morning at breakfast, she said, "We're having company for dinner this evening."

That company was a tall, dark-skinned elderly man with a bright-eyed lady, who appeared to be in her nineties, on his arm.

Lydia said, "Kiki, I'd like you to meet Grace Muenster's daughter, Amy, and her eldest son, Randolph Muenster Petrick."

At first, I just stared at two of the "characters" I'd read about in *Plainston Chronicles*.

Amy laughed. "If you've read my mother's letters, then you know what a naughty girl I was. Plainston never really tamed me."

"For which we are all deeply grateful," Lydia said, giving her a hug.

Turning to Randy, she said, "Kiki doesn't believe we can change enough schools rapidly enough to save the world. I thought that you could help him."

"Let's give him the standard readiness test first," Randy said with a smile. "You do it, Lydia."

"All right. Now, Kiki, suppose you tell me a really funny joke on the condition that I keep telling it to only one person at a time, every hour on the hour, and each person also agrees to keep telling it that way. How long would it take on that person-to-person, hour-by-hour around the clock process until 250,000 people had heard it?"

I'd heard problems of that nature before, and I knew the answer would be less than one would suppose, so I guessed low.

"A month or so," I said while thinking that it would likely be a year or more.

From at attaché, Randy produced a chart full of figures which basically explained the concept of cell division. With a bit of explanation, I could see that the doubling meant that at 20 hours 500,000 people would be laughing their heads off at my joke—and in less than a day and a half, the number would equal the population of the United States.

"The number isn't so important," said Randy. "It's the principle of organic growth by cell division that's important. That is reliable and realistic. The problem is to get a viable cell in the beginning—one able to reproduce itself—to pass its vitality and structure on."

Amy said, "It's been seventy-five years since Plainston schools were totally MI based. You know that my mother and the others in the Group you've been reading about worried that it was just their own missionary-type zeal that was making 'family style' work. They worried that it wouldn't continue to work after they were gone.

"I understand that you've spent weeks in our schools. Don't you agree that their fears were groundless? MI is working, right?"

I wholeheartedly agreed that it was.

"So the first test of viability is that 'family style' can survive—actually, has survived—after its originators handed it to the next generations. The second test is to see if it's viable in other environments. Will it transplant and live outside our notably different Plainston environment?"

I said, "We visited a transplant in California, heard about a newly growing one in Arizona, and know of many in Muskogee and on other Indian lands."

Randy said, "That's why we can ethically and confidently recommend it for nationwide acceptance. That's why we urged the FINs to include it in their platform and why they accepted it."

"Believe, Kiki, believe," urged Lydia. "Listen to the umpteen trillion cells in your body. Cell division happens."

Randy then explained that if we started with one MI school and that school helped one school each year and each new school helped a school, with the number of schools in the country, we'd need about twenty years for all to become MI schools.

My heart sank. Twenty years was too long.

"But," he continued, "we aren't starting with one school. There are about two hundred already established. In addition, there's no reason one MI school can't be involved in helping more than one other school begin the change.

Finally, once the success of MI schools becomes known, parents are going to demand change more rapidly than cell division. It won't take twenty years, Kiki."

I smiled as I looked at these two people from Plainston's early days. I certainly hoped they were right.

* * *

One popular television commentator summed up the mood of America with the following observation:

> What a contrast is this time with what was happening in the world one century ago when most of Europe was at war. Tens of thousands of soldiers were dying in battle. After a long time of peace, a saddened Englishman, Viscount Grey, lamented, 'The lamps are going out all over Europe; we shall not see them lighted again in our lifetime.'
>
> For so long, America was the light of the world. We lifted the lamp of freedom beside our golden door. Then our light dimmed. Dare we now hope that the lights are going on all over America? Dare we hope that our light will again shine brightly? Dare we hope that we are moving toward a world of peace—a world where an educational system teaches both the head and the heart to solve problems?
>
> I think we can believe in the children who are attending these new schools where they help each other learn the three C's: competence, communication, and caring. We can confidently follow children so taught. Let's give these Mutual Instruction schools our full support. They are relighting the lamps.

* * *

This is where I wanted the story to end—with the FINs making progress in Washington, with more Mutual Instruction schools being started, with me happily married to Lydia, with all being right with the world.

But that was not to be.

Chapter 28

The Meeting

As winter turned into spring, Wilber Bickersley ramped up his attacks on Plainston—demanding to know who controlled Plainston, attacking the Temple's nondenominational approach to religion, bashing it as a Utopia that would, in the end, fail—basically, covering the same ground he'd been covering for years. He wrote in one column, "I feel that it is my duty to expose that evil Eden, which is handing out its luscious-looking apples of forbidden truth to gullible Eves."

Then he wrote one particularly damaging column which reverberated with his regular readers as well as catching the attention of the national television media. The most damning part accused the Consensus of being an elite autocracy—in his words, "arrogant social engineers." He again attacked the wall with a column entitled "No Room at the Inn." He wrote,

> It's not just their eight miles of twelve-foot-high concrete walls with a ten-foot-deep moat. The most threatening and offensive walls are those of smug superiority which admit only those who meet their aristocratic criteria for purity and cleanliness. Without

recommendation from someone in their most elite clan, one finds no refuge within those walls.

Had Joseph and Mary—grimy, travel-weary, poor, and without credentials—approached their entrance, can't you just hear an offended security person say, 'No room here!'?

The Temple—the actual physical center of Plainston and the symbol of their allegedly religious life—has no room for our Savior on its huge mural. It has room for every religion and for the followers of every faith, but it has no room for their founders. If we accept such a monstrosity as a religious ideal, then America truly has eaten forbidden fruit and deserves to be cast out of God's garden forever.

The usual response of Plainstans had been to ignore Wilber Bickersley's vitriolic attacks, but with the schools and Mutual Instruction placing Plainston more and more in the public eye, the Consensus decided to offer Wilber once again the chance to come to Plainston to have a dialog with others about his views. A formal invitation, sent to both him and the media, was issued.

Wilber couldn't very well refuse, so that spring, he cast himself in the role of David facing the media Goliaths as increasing numbers of commentators sided against his views.

One commentator wrote to me personally that Wilber was going beyond the role of David. "He is taking on the martyr role, the suffering savior, the only one who is aware of the dangers besetting our society, the only one with clear vision who sees the hideous future that Mutual Instruction will lead us to. He sees a direct connection between MI's growing popularity and that Temple of yours, which is the focus of his mounting hatred."

The invitation asked Wilber to spend several days with the Consensus in quiet, private conversation before the widely advertised public meeting, but he refused—arriving, instead, only shortly before noon on the day of the meeting. He ate lunch with the four Plainstans who constituted the panel which would respond to his speech. He had no copy or outline to give to them beforehand.

*   *   *

The televised meeting was held in the university concert hall that seated 2500. Several groups came from Prairie Grove, leaving their cars at the entrance and walking through metal detectors, which had become standard procedure all across the nation. One group, however, caused some trouble. A beefy late-middle-aged man, wearing Air Force fatigues, strongly objected to surrendering his service revolver for which he had a permit. At first, he loudly proclaimed his right to bear arms, but when his companions calmly explained that no one in Plainston had guns, not even the police, he relented but said, "I'll feel plumb naked without my sidearm."

Lydia and I, who witnessed the confrontation, had an uncomfortable feeling about the man.

When all were seated and the student orchestra quit playing, Wilber gave a forty-five-minute presentation entitled "Plainston: Utopia or Dystopia?" He made it clear right away that if a Utopia were heaven, then a dystopia would be hell.

Wilber gave what he must've thought was a learned speech on the history of Utopian schemes and experimental communities, none of which endured for a century. He said, "The site of one of the most successful is within a hundred miles of your fair city, yet there were two failures there within a generation."

He gave the histories of the Rappite and Owen communities of New Harmony, Indiana—stories which all Plainstans knew by the time they were twelve. I myself had probably covered more Utopian literature in my months of contact with Nathan Kincade than Wilber had. He, of course, was looking for weaknesses. I and other Plainstans were looking for strengths while measuring Plainston against the ideals of possible success.

The head of the panel was Professor Emeritus Malcolm Harrigan, the venerable black philosopher I'd met the first time I attended a Consensus meeting. I'd learned then that he'd founded the Consensus, realizing early on that Plainston was on a Utopian path and wishing to avoid the hazards so many other Utopian societies had met. Wilber attacked the Consensus again, claiming that the group "denied citizens not only their Constitutional freedoms but their moral and intellectual freedoms—the members being wardens of this prison of mind and soul."

Since we'd expected Wilber to attack MI, especially, we'd asked Stella Rising Star to sit on the panel. She asked him point blank why MI would lead to the ultimate dystopian society he predicted. Wilber had clearly and accurately identified MI as the roots of Plainston's culture.

She said, "I suppose you agree with Proverbs 22, verse 6: 'Train up a child in the way he should go; and when he is old, he will not depart from it.' And with Alexander Pope, who said, 'Just as the twig is bent, the tree's inclined.' So, Mr. Bickersley, what specifically do you find wrong in the way Plainston's adults here depart from their upbringing? How are we bending our young twigs so they lean the wrong way?"

Wilber roared back, "You teach them to question everything and then to accept everything that has any claim of merit. Lack of discrimination, even among good things, proves disastrous. Because of this thirst for forbidden knowledge, the Lord drove our ancestors from the only Utopia He ever intended for this earth. The word of God cannot be plainer. Eden—Utopia—is closed forever to the children of our ancestral sinners. Every attempt to reenter Eden—to establish a Utopia—has failed because man has essentially a sinful nature.

"You teach your children that it is all right to rely on their own minds rather than to let faith guide their adult lives. Your children grow into adults who have pride in themselves God cannot tolerate. The Greeks called it *hubris*. Because Plainston has not yet shown the inevitable decay from this intellectual and moral pride is not testimony to your success, for your educational system is barely mature, only a generation or two old, and until recently limited to this wholly unnatural, inbred, walled hothouse. And now you arrogantly want to foist it on a naïve unsuspecting world as a model society.

"For shame! If your educational system did not lead your youth to embrace the pagan pantheism symbolized by your Temple, I would not denigrate it. But so long as that Temple stands, Plainston and its educational system stand condemned in the eyes of the one true God."

We were proud of Stella Rising Star, along with the rest of the panel and the audience, for accepting this tirade calmly. However, from the balcony, the Prairie Grove group, led by the "naked" disarmed man, cheered Wilber loud and long.

Professor Harrigan responded. "Every prophet of God, in every religion, subsequent to Adam and Eve's expulsion from that original Utopia, has called upon mankind to establish peace and justice on earth. The Christian faith asserts that justice requires love. We learn to love, or we learn to hate. We are not born loving or hating, any more than we are born knowing a certain language or the history of our country or how to add and subtract or why thunder follows lightning. Whatever we know in our heads and our hearts we must learn.

"The most important question society has to answer is how best to teach the lessons our heads need to learn to solve the problems of our material lives and what lessons our hearts must learn to live at peace with our neighbors—and to give thanks to our Creator for the privilege of living on this beautiful earth and to understand our responsibility for stewardship of it. Through almost four generations of experience, we have found that when children take more responsibility for their own learning and that of others, they learn with both their heads and their hearts.

"Now, if you, sir, can find adult Plainstans who have been twisted out of shape by this learning, adults who have departed from being responsible and helpful citizens as they were trained in childhood or who have poorly fathered their own children, please submit the evidence."

Professor Harrigan paused. The auditorium was dead quiet. Then he continued in a strong voice, louder than before. "You wear your mantle of omniscience, making this infallible diagnosis of our moral cancer and predicting national destruction, with far more hubris and arrogance than you can rightfully charge to any of us.

"We here in Plainston are only trying to build minds and souls worthy of our Creator. When you have solid evidence of our failure, present it to us and to your public. Until then, we have earned the benefit of your doubt."

The audience of mostly Plainstans rose silently in acclamation while boos rang out from the balcony. At this point, the panel realized that any attempt to have an objective discussion on additional specific issues would be futile. The moderator asked Wilber if he'd like to make a final comment before the meeting ended.

Without looking at the panel, Wilber said, "We shall see. Time will tell."

Lydia and I stayed seated as some from the audience went onto the stage to thank Wilber and the panel for participating. Suddenly, the Prairie Grove man pushed his way through the group and hugged Wilber, saying, "Bless you, Brother Bickersley. Tonight you've given me something to live for—and to die for."

He embraced Wilber again. Then, with tears streaming down his face, he left the stage.

Stella Rising Star said later with a shudder, "He glared at me as he walked by. I'm glad you'd disarmed him, or I think another Indian would've bit the dust!"

She laughed then, but it was a sad sound.

*   *   *

As Lydia and I were threading our way out, we were joined by Douglas, whom I'd first met at the airport café. He was now pursuing a master's degree in sociology and history at the University of Plainston while student teaching in a school that was in its first year of converting to MI in a predominantly black neighborhood in Prairie Grove.

When Douglas asked if he could talk to us privately, we invited him to our apartment where Stella Rising Star, who was an overnight guest, joined us. Douglas was obviously nervous and upset. It didn't take us long to figure out why. He wanted to tell us about the "naked" man from Prairie Grove.

"His name is Gus Hadley. He's part of that white supremacy group that Thelma belongs to—you remember Thelma from the café?"

I said that I did.

Douglas continued, "From what I've heard, Gus was a star athlete at Prairie Grove High, but he never got over being beaten out of county all-star status in basketball by a black player from Plainston. After over twenty years in the Air Force, he came back to Prairie Grove and set up a crop dusting business with a buddy, but Plainston area farmers have complained about the spray drifting onto their fields, especially their vegetable plots. Gus has a real hate for Plainston for several reasons—business, racial, religious—you name it."

"Is he really dangerous," Lydia asked, "or is he mostly a windbag?"

"By himself, I'm not sure, but with the racist group, he's quite a leader as you saw tonight. He's been instrumental in several vandalism attacks at our school—some religious graffiti, two broken windows, and just last week a pile of manure at the front door. I'm sure about all of this since Thelma likes to talk a lot. Gus is very upset that some white parents are petitioning to get their kids into the MI school, and there are also a number of foreign kids attending, which adds different religions into the mix."

"Would Gus and the group do anything worse than vandalize the school?" Lydia asked.

"Don't know, but I know that the police recently got someone to infiltrate the group—someone you know."

"Really?" I said. "Who?"

"It's Hank. I got to know him when I was taking MI training at Southwest. I really like him. Anyway, Hank knew some young men in Guy's group from the years when he was associating with some less than desirable types. He actually went to the police after the vandalism started at my school and volunteered. And he got accepted into the group easily—pretending to be outraged about the fines he had to work off here and those 'mongrel schools where everyone is all mixed up together.' Hank's very convincing when he plays that role."

Douglas paused, then added with a laugh, "That's a nice way of saying he's quite a liar."

Then he continued, more seriously, "This is all according to Thelma who loves to brag about new people joining her group. She particularly liked it that I knew Hank. In her mind, Hank is like another trophy on their wall and a slap in my face."

"So right now, all Hank is doing is keeping an eye on the group, right?" I said.

"I assume so."

No one spoke for a minute or so.

Then Stella Morning Star said, "As we all know, Gus, or anybody, for that matter, can't be arrested for what they say. They have to act. So now it's a matter of waiting and hoping that the group doesn't do anything."

As we thanked Douglas for talking to us, we three felt a cold chill on that otherwise beautiful spring evening.

Chapter 29

The Phoenix Rises

When sleep eluded us that night, we talked, snacked, worked two crossword puzzles together, and finally read poetry aloud. It was almost dawn before we went to bed. For days afterwards, a cloud followed Lydia and me. Then as more flowers bloomed and the days got longer, our spirits began to lift. We heard no more from Douglas, which we took to be good news.

Soon Lydia and I established a routine that suited us as a married couple. We ate an early breakfast together but usually ate a light lunch separately. We met in the late afternoon to walk or bike ride or swim. Then we prepared dinner together. It was a perfect balance of togetherness and alone time, I thought. I was busy writing and volunteering at North where I was working with Seniors who were preparing for the rigors of college writing; I was also helping in a local vegetable garden a couple of blocks from the apartment—a totally new but joyful experience for a man who'd been a city dweller all his adult life. Lydia continued to pursue her many roles in the city—ones she'd had for years. And so late spring slipped into summer.

*   *   *

On June 26th, Douglas called. He sounded worried. Thelma had been mentioning a "special big bang" for the Fourth of July. First, I talked to Douglas, and then Lydia did, but all Douglas knew was what Thelma was saying. We thanked him for the call.

"We need to talk to Hank," Lydia said.

"But we can't draw any special attention to him," I said.

We discussed the problem a while before deciding that Lydia, in her role as judge, would do a follow up visit with Hank the next day, as she'd often done while the group was working off their fines. After Hank had graduated with a high school diploma, he'd enrolled at the community college in Prairie Grove to get his associates in agriculture. Lydia called him to arrange a meeting there, sounding very official on the phone in case it was tapped.

So as not to arouse any suspicion, I wouldn't go to Prairie Grove with Lydia the next day.

*   *   *

Lydia told me about the meeting that evening. Looking official with her briefcase, she'd waited for Hank at the college's Student Center. After they were seated, she took a group of official looking papers from her briefcase and spread them out on the desk.

"I want this to look as if I am directing this meeting," she said quietly. "You shouldn't look pleased to see me. Even though I can't conceive that anyone here would be spying for Gus's group, I don't want to take the chance of blowing your cover."

Hank scowled and leaned back in his chair, arms folded.

In that manner, they talked about Gus and what Douglas had said about Thelma while Lydia shuffled papers and Hank signed a couple of them.

Hank was also worried, but so far he'd been unable to pinpoint any particular activity on Gus's part.

"What worries me the most," he said without looking up from the paper in front of him, "is that Gus has access to planes for his crop dusting business—two that are in use for spraying and a third older one that is used when one of the other ones needs maintenance. I've told the police that, but they have no cause for a warrant."

"Don't you do anything rash, Hank. You're in the group just to gather information."

"I know, but that doesn't seem like much help."

Lydia picked up the papers, put them back in her briefcase, and offered her hand to Hank, who refused it.

Back in Plainston, Lydia talked to the police and some members of the Consensus. Then it became a wait-and-see situation.

*   *   *

The Fourth of July dawned clear and cool. By noon, the temperature was 82 degrees with a soft, dry breeze from the west. All over Plainston, people were having picnics and playing in ballgames. The pools were full of happy kids. That night the fireworks display at the university lit up the sky over Plainston. With the last booms from the finale echoing in our ears, we headed back to the apartment—tired but happy. There was hope that many others beyond our walls would begin to know the joy and peace of our lives inside them.

I awakened suddenly, my eyes staring into the blackness, my heart thudding. The bright red numbers on the clock beside the bed read 12:07.

Seconds later, Lydia grabbed my hand. "Oh, my God," she said as we both recognized the sound we'd been fearing—the distant roar of a plane, coming in fast and low.

We had time only to hit the floor on the side of the bed away from the windows before Gus Hadley crashed his plane into the Temple. The explosion was deafening. The burning fuel turned the Temple into a burning inferno, changing night into day.

Fire sirens, seldom used, sounded, bringing many to the scene, most carrying first aid kits. We were there for hours as fire fighters fought the blaze. We joined other citizens who were posted around the perimeter of the Temple to report if the fire were to endanger nearby businesses and the South Towers.

Health Service personnel, with help from citizens, treated many injuries at the scene, mostly minor burns and cuts from flying glass from the many shattered windows. Some of the injured were transported to the hospital by ambulance—and within a few hours, the six most seriously burned were airlifted by helicopters, which flew in from Prairie Grove, to hospitals in Springfield and Peoria.

By mid-morning on July 5, the count was in: 187 injured, 48 of those seriously, and 21 dead. Television crews began arriving around ten a.m. The most poignant picture was of the Temple dome, sitting at a tilt in Sugar Creek, some of its glass still intact. That it had survived at all was considered a miracle. Nearby, the planets lay in the grass, still arranged in correct order from the sun. As photographs of the configuration appeared in newspapers and magazines, some in the scientific community demanded to know the secret, but that wasn't to be since the woman who'd created them and their orbits above the dome had died in the explosion.

Years before, she'd written, "I fear that the secret could be misused; therefore, I will reveal it only when the world has irrevocably given up force as an instrument of national policy—when war is as outlawed and abhorrent as slavery and child abuse. Then and only then will I reveal the secret."

Plainstans buried their dead and began to clear the debris. The reporters stuck around long enough to get the whole story—including the story of one more casualty—Hank.

When more and more people in Gus's group had talked about a "special big bang" on the Fourth, Hank decided to stay close to Gus that day in Prairie Grove. When he lost sight of Gus in the crowd during the fireworks display, he followed a hunch. Shortly after the fireworks display ended, Hank drove out to the small airfield where Gus and his partner kept their planes. As he'd feared, Gus was already there. The hangar doors were closed, but the side door was open. Gus was inside. Trying to stay in the shadows, Hank watched Gus load something onto the oldest plane. Two six packs of Miller Lite sat on a nearby work table—one partly empty and one unopened. Three empty cans littered the floor.

As Hank watched, Gus closed the plane door and took a seat in a battered canvas lawn chair near the table. He reached up for another beer and then another and another. When he stood up and staggered toward the large hangar doors, Hank stepped farther back into the shadows and ran toward a small group of trees some distance away from the edge of the airstrip.

Ducking behind the largest tree, Hank called 911. He'd only identified himself to the operator when Gus bellowed, "Hands high!"

Hank complied, his phone still in his hand. In the dark, Gus didn't see it, but the 911 operator heard the two shots when Hank tried to run. He fell to the ground with one bullet in his shoulder and one in his upper arm. He lay still, listening to Gus's harsh breathing, smelling the alcohol.

Suddenly, Gus turned and staggered back to the hangar. Hank heard the roar of the engine before he passed out.

Tracking the phone, police arrived shortly after the plane took off and stopped the bleeding that would've soon taken Hank's life. They could only guess that Gus was headed to Plainston. There was no way to stop the plane. Their call to the Plainston police came too late for the late night meditators to be evacuated from the Temple.

*   *   *

It took a grand jury hearing to get the facts about the final casualty, Gus. Immediately after the attack, Wilber Bickersley, having lost all sense of propriety, attempted to paint Gus as a sacrificial hero, "who gave his life to remove the symbol of Plainston's spiritual cancer."

He also praised Gus for choosing the early morning hour for the bombing   a time when the Temple had the fewest people there for meditation. He wrote, "If Gus Hadley had been a truly hateful, evil man rather than a fervent servant of the Lord, he would have bombed it at high noon when hundreds, maybe even thousands, of the people were there. Gus deserves our forgiveness and our gratitude for sacrificing as few lives as possible to bring light to the darkness that Plainston threatens."

That turned out to be the last volley fired at Plainston from Wilber's pen. He died from a massive stroke in mid-August, greatly diminished by the testimony of Gus's partner before a grand jury. The partner had said, "Gus was dying from an inoperable, fast-growing cancer. He had just a few months to live. He told me he wasn't going to stick around to become a stinking vegetable. He'd always said that he wanted to die in combat, so he decided to soldier for the Lord."

Wilber's "hero" was just a sick man who'd committed suicide.

The partner, who'd purchased the explosive materials on the plane, was charged with complicity to commit murder. He pled guilty.

*   *   *

By mid-October, Plainston was ablaze in every shade of yellow, gold, rust, orange, and red. The dried leaves that had already fallen crunched under our feet as we walked each evening. We breathed the crisp, clean air as the days got shorter and shorter. Plainstans were gradually healing as the year was nearing its end.

After two weeks in the hospital in Prairie Grove, Hank was moved to Plainston to continue his healing. He'd become a Plainstan, welcomed quietly as a hero by the city. He was living with a family with two teenaged sons in the Towers close to Health Services where he had therapy daily. The physical therapists there felt that he'd regain almost full use of his arm; however, it was unlikely he'd be able to do the heavy farm work he'd done before. As a result, he was planning to continue his college work at Plainston University in research—finding more ways for city dwellers to garden more months of the year.

All the others injured were also back in Plainston, most receiving continued medical treatment at Health Services. Jobs were being held for them. Financial help was available for those needing it.

The outside walls of the Temple were rising. Plainstans were cooperating once again as they had first done to build the wall over half a century earlier and later the original Temple. The mural would be recreated with the bombing added below the line. Meanwhile, there were a lot of outdoor meditation sites around the city in parks, and most of the worship services had been moved to the schools and the auditorium at the university.

In the long run, the bombing blasted away the remaining fanatical opposition to Plainston's experiment. More and more people were accepting Plainston as a model for their communities—starting with changing their schools. The steady flow of people wanting to learn about MI continued in and out of the city. No one of any stature charged Plainston with plotting to overthrow anything that didn't deserve toppling. No columnist had stepped into Wilber's shoes. The charge of conspiracy was over.

During my pre-Plainston days as a columnist, I'd often wondered if anyone paid any attention to what I wrote. In other words, was I making a difference as a writer and as a GBO employee? Now, however, I knew that what I had become a part of was making a difference. Plainston was a thriving

Utopia. Its roots were being transplanted all over the country in MI schools. More and more little kids were entering schools where no one failed to learn the 3 R's, where differences were both expected and accepted, where both giving and receiving tutoring was as natural as having teachers in charge had once been—where both their heads and their hearts were educated.

As a researcher and reporter, I'd never been much of one to use symbolism. I was interested in facts—the who, the what, the where, the how, and the why of things. I'd analyze, draw conclusions, even make predictions—but all of that was grounded in the facts.

Now, however, whenever we walked to the Temple to see the rising walls, I thought of the phoenix rising from the ashes—the phoenix which symbolized rebirth and renewal. But the rebirth and renewal wasn't just for Plainstans inside the walls. What Plainstans had had for generations was moving rapidly outside its walls—growing from the mutual instruction roots in the schools. The phoenix was rising throughout the land.

I end this report with optimism.

<u>Afterword</u>

The author regrets that all
characters, events and places
in this book are fictional.

This story <u>could</u> and <u>should</u>
have happened—but did not.

The above five lines appear at the beginning of both volumes of *The Plainston Chronicles*. It states, in my dad's words, exactly what he believed—and it belongs in this book as well. Mutual Instruction, as he envisioned it, could make a difference in the quality of education our kids receive. After forty years of teaching in traditional schools, I'm in total agreement. Schools using Mutual Instruction should be implemented.

What we're now doing defies common sense in so many ways. I speak from years of teaching experience at all levels of public schools and now in a community college where I see the results of a lot of kids graduating from high school without the skills and knowledge necessary for succeeding in college or even entering the work force. Age-based, teacher-led classes are not effective for a large percentage of students. Kids are too different for the one-size-fits-all approach currently used almost everywhere.

Nowadays, the emphasis is often on getting "better" teachers in the classroom. But improving faculty, as a solution to our educational woes, is only a band-aid. It's the ***system*** that is broken. Putting better teachers into the current system will not do much to improve the education our children are receiving. My own experience is testimony to that. I was a college honor student, earning bachelor and master's degrees at a major university. I never wanted to do anything else except teach. The fact that, after forty years, I'm still in the classroom gives testimony to that. Most of my life, I have dragged home mountains of papers to evaluate and lessons to plan. While teaching grade school and middle school language arts, I read hundreds and hundreds of young adult books on my own time so that I could recommend books to reluctant readers. I reworked units before teaching them again so that I could help more kids learn. I worked with many other teachers as hard-working as I in schools that would be judged as good ones. And yes, many of our students learned. Lots even liked school.

But—and it is a very pronounced ***but***—we failed to reach many kids. In a system where the only choice is pass or fail, many students go on to the next grade with low C's and D's and even F's in some subjects, often slipping farther and farther behind. In a system where more and more it is test results that matter the most, a lot of teaching is related primarily to testing. In a system where, at the high school level, I was out numbered 150 to 1—even 180 to 1one year after budget cuts were implemented—and, at the middle school level, often 100 to 1, I could never give the time needed to kids that just weren't getting it—or who no longer cared to even try. Dedication, hard work, and good preparation together are not enough to do the job. And that's the point Dad is trying to make.

Plainston is fiction, as are the people who live there and the critics who live in the "outside world." But what schools could be like is real—as all new ideas can be. Dad spent years trying to convince people to try Mutual Instruction—to let it build from the smallest learners to the older kids. Generally, we know that kids like to work together, that older kids like to help younger ones, that little kids look up to bigger ones. Generally, we know that kids the same year in age are dramatically different. We know that one teacher cannot be there for everyone. We know that many discipline problems stem from kids who are frustrated, on one hand, or bored, on the other. We know that what we teach we learn even better. Mutual Instruction weaves all these bits of knowledge into a workable system.

YAK Phonics is real. Dad developed it as part of his Ph.D program at UCLA. My sister Marcia and I still have some copies of the pack which include teacher materials and the wonderful whimsical colored alphabet cards and ideograph cards needed to implement the program.

Dad's concept of what schools can be deserves serious attention. *Conspiracy* may be the last chance he has of catching the attention of individuals who also believe that we need to consider a whole new approach to education, not just band-aids for the problems of the traditional lock-step system. Trying to get his last book right so that his voice can be clearly heard has been my goal. Since he was a wonderful, loving father who supported my own writing projects, I feel that he has been encouraging my efforts. His ideas are now out there . . . .

Jane Swengel Creason
January, 2013

Jane Swengel Creason at jcreason616@gmail.com.
Marcia Swengel Powell at marpo3344@gmail.com

For more information search the following:

Edwin M. Swengel
Mutual Instruction
YAK Phonics
Plainston Chronicles
Jane S. Creason

About the Authors
and
the Artist

Dr. Edwin M. Swengel was born in Neoga, Illinois, in 1917. After he graduated from high school, his parents moved to Urbana, Illinois, so that he could attend the University of Illinois while living at home. Money was tight during those Depression years. After earning his bachelor's degree, he married Elizabeth Loeffler, also an Illinois graduate, and they began a life together that included three daughters: Jane, Marcia, and Lockie, now deceased. For the next twenty-five years, Dr. Swengel, known as Mac by most, taught school, farmed, and remodeled a one-room school house to become the family home. He founded a community orchestra known as the Fithian Farmhouse Filharmonic and was active in a local church. When working on his master's degree in the early 60s, he became interested in Montessori education—believing it to be the right beginning for schools using what he would eventually name Mutual Instruction. In 1963, he went to California to pursue more Montessori training. The following year, he, Elizabeth, and their youngest daughter, Lockie, moved to Los Angeles where he earned a Ph.D. from UCLA and developed YAK Phonics. In 1969, he and his wife moved to San Diego where he became a professor at the United States International

University, both teaching classes and supervising student teachers at the high school and elementary levels. After retirement, he continued to study and read about education, which led to his writing *The Plainston Chronicles, 1919-1951* and finally *Conspiracy.*

Jane Swengel Creason was born in Urbana, Illinois, in 1942. She has lived in the same house since she was four, a remodeled one-room school house located on a small farm her mother inherited. She and her husband, Don, raised two children there, now both married. Their grandchildren, the fourth generation, know the old house well. Jane, who always wanted to be a teacher, earned bachelor and master's degrees from the University of Illinois. Then she began what became a forty-plus year teaching career at the grade school, middle school, high school, and community college levels. She began writing her two young adult novels, *When the War Came to Hannah* and *The Heron Stayed,* while teaching middle school. Having lived in the same house with the same husband and having taught English in the same county for much of her life, Jane describes herself as a contented Midwesterner who has put down serious roots.

Sarah Creason, the cover artist, became interested in painting as a relaxing hobby while working for the Department of Agriculture in Columbia City, Indiana. Within a few years, she was studying and painting during every spare minute. After retirement, she also began to teach painting. Currently, her work is displayed at the Orchard Gallery in Fort Wayne, Indiana, where she works part-time. Sarah and Jane, who are married to brothers Cliff and Don Creason, have been sisters-in-law for many years.

www.ingramcontent.com/pod-product-compliance
Lightning Source LLC
Chambersburg PA
CBHW060237290526
45789CB00001B/88